Pilgrimage
—the sacred art

Journey to the Center of the Heart

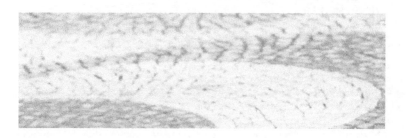

Dr. Sheryl A. Kujawa-Holbrook

Walking Together, Finding the Way®
SKYLIGHT PATHS®
PUBLISHING
Nashville, Tennessee

Pilgrimage—The Sacred Art:
Journey to the Center of the Heart

2013 Quality Paperback Edition

Library of Congress Cataloging-in-Publication Data
Kujawa-Holbrook, Sheryl A.
 Pilgrimage-the sacred art : journey to the center of the heart / Sheryl A. Kujawa-Holbrook.
   pages cm
 Includes bibliographical references.
 ISBN 978-1-59473-472-4
 1. Pilgrims and pilgrimages. I. Title.
 BL619.P5K85 2013
 203'.51-dc23
                                      2013013407

10 9 8 7 6 5 4 3 2

Manufactured in the United States of America
Cover and Interior Design: Tim Holtz
Cover Art: © Goran Bogicevic/Fotolia.com

SkyLight Paths Publishing is creating a place where people of different spiritual traditions come together for challenge and inspiration, a place where we can help each other understand the mystery that lies at the heart of our existence.

SkyLight Paths sees both believers and seekers as a community that increasingly transcends traditional boundaries of religion and denomination—people wanting to learn from each other, *walking together, finding the way.*

SkyLight Paths, "Walking Together, Finding the Way" and colophon are trademarks of LongHill Partners, Inc., registered in the U.S. Patent and Trademark Office.

Walking Together, Finding the Way®
Published by SkyLight Paths Publishing
An imprint of Turner Publishing Company
4507 Charlotte Avenue, Suite 100
Nashville, TN 37209
Tel: (615) 255-2665
www.skylightpaths.com

With all my heart—for Paul and Rachel—
companions on the pilgrimage of life

CONTENTS

CHAPTER 1

JOURNEYS ACROSS TRADITIONS AND CULTURES

A Journey of a thousand miles begins with a single step.
Lao Tzu, The Way of Lao Tzu *(ca. 500 BCE)*

The journey is essential to the dream.
—*Francis of Assisi (1182–1226)*

Follow the Yellow Brick Road.
—The Wizard of Oz *(1939)*

One of the great pilgrimage films of all time is the classic *The Wizard of Oz*, with Judy Garland in the starring role as Dorothy. I grew up in the days where one of the biggest television events of the year was the broadcast of *The Wizard of Oz*, usually on a Sunday night, the event publicized well in advance. Beginning in 1956, the telecast of this movie was considered one of *the* blockbuster television events of the year, and entire families, from small children to elders, gathered at home to watch it. It is one of the first films I remember ever watching in its entirety. To this day I wait for the transformation of the black and white images of Kansas as the landscape turns into Technicolor Oz, although I will also admit that the grumpy trees and the flying monkeys are still pretty frightening!

The film centers on the pilgrimage of Dorothy and her little dog Toto, a journey that begins in the midst of a fierce Kansas tornado. Dorothy is beginning to feel confined and unhappy on the farm in Kansas. When Toto is threatened by the nasty neighbor whom he has bitten, Dorothy sees no option but to finally leave home in an effort to save her dog from the local sheriff.

On the way out of town Dorothy encounters a traveling fortune-teller, who sends her home, but before she makes it back a fierce tornado starts brewing on the Kansas plains, and she misses her chance to enter the family shelter. Remaining inside the house, Dorothy gets hit on the head as the house is caught up in a whirlwind that transports her and Toto "over the rainbow" and into Oz.

Dorothy has never experienced as strange and beautiful a place as Oz, and she begins to wonder almost immediately what is happening to her and how she is ever going to make it home. "Toto, I've a feeling we're not in Kansas anymore," she famously says. Upon landing in Oz, Dorothy's house had fallen upon and killed the Wicked Witch of the East, much to the delight of the resident Munchkins, but incurring the wrath of her sister, the Wicked Witch of the West. Then Glinda, the good witch, points Dorothy and Toto down the Yellow Brick Road to the Emerald City, home to a great wizard who will undoubtedly answer her questions and help her to return home. Off she goes down the Yellow Brick Road to the Emerald City with her beloved Toto, wearing ruby slippers to protect her from the wicked witch.

Along the way, Dorothy meets numerous companions. She encounters a scarecrow who is looking for a brain, a tin man looking for a heart, and a cowardly lion looking for courage—all hope that this journey will transform them and bring them their heart's desire. As they travel they talk, share stories, share the dangers of the road, and become companions who would risk their lives for each other. After many stops and starts they finally reach Oz, where they have to face the reality that the Wizard cannot change their lives. What they do learn is that the answer to their deepest longings cannot be given to them by someone else—their desired meaning, heart, courage, and home has lived within them all along.

As it turns out, Scarecrow never really lacked a brain; he has all sorts of questions and ideas within him. Tin Man's kindness and dedication are surely signs of the heart that beats within him. Lion has certainly experienced fear, but it never stopped him from moving ahead or protecting those most important to him. As for Dorothy, on the journey she learns that she did not have to leave home to find her heart's desire, and the choice of returning is hers alone.

In one of the last scenes in the film, Dorothy realizes that it is time for her to go home as a changed person, but with the wrenching awareness that her new friends are not meant to return with her. They have their own homes, and the journey they shared together cannot be repeated. Chanting "There's no place like home," Dorothy returns with a newfound sense of peace and gratitude, determined that her relationships will be different because she herself is a different person. Back in Kansas, Dorothy's family and friends are overjoyed to see her again and relieved she wasn't hurt, but since they were not with her every step of the way on her journey of discovery, they are also quite amazed—and perhaps a little confused—at how much she has changed.

The sacred art of pilgrimage is deeply inscribed in the human heart. For many, going "on pilgrimage" will mean physical travel. This year alone, millions of Hindus and Buddhists will journey to the banks of the river Ganges at Varanasi, India, in the hope of healing and spiritual rebirth. In the West, five million Christians will go to the shrine dedicated to the Virgin Mary in Lourdes, France, also hoping for healing and spiritual renewal. In Europe alone, more than six thousand sacred sites will receive between seventy and one hundred million pilgrims.[1] Each year two million Muslims will make the journey to Mecca, the most holy city of the faith, to fulfill their religious obligation to visit once in their lifetime.[2] Furthermore, every year over four million people will travel to the National September 11 Memorial and Museum in New York City to remember the tragedy that occurred there in 2001.

When lived with intention, all of life can be seen as a sacred journey. "We think of a pilgrimage as a journey of great spiritual and moral significance—yet our whole life's course can be seen as a pilgrimage," writes Amy Benedict. "A simple walk from your home and back can become a ritual to enact these sacred quests."[3]

There are many ways to describe pilgrimage. The word itself derives from the Latin *peregrinus*, meaning "stranger" or "foreigner." On pilgrimage the traveler is a foreigner in several ways: a stranger to the companions she meets along the way, a stranger to places visited, and a stranger to the inward journey of meaning and transformation. On some level, pilgrimage always connotes a life-changing journey. For some, *pilgrimage* means to journey to a place where holiness is apparent or where some kind of divine and human encounter took place. Some describe the experience as a search for spiritual depth or moral significance. Others are on a search for a path toward freedom or peace. Some pilgrims are directed toward specific destinations—such as a dwelling place of a saint, or a holy place that evokes prayer and reflection, or the site of a significant life event. For others, the passage is symbolic of the journey of a soul to God and primarily an inward experience of alternative sacred geography. Still others describe pilgrimage as a threshold experience that points to a new reality or a process of inner transformation. So common is the practice to human experience, moreover, that pilgrimage has been proposed by psychologists as a Jungian archetype.

One of the most important academic sources on the study of pilgrimage was published by anthropologists Victor and Edith Turner in 1978. Titled *Image and Pilgrimage in Christian Culture*, the book frames pilgrimage through the concepts of *liminality* and *communitas*.[4] Coming from the Latin *limen,* liminality refers to the experience of being "in between" worlds. The pilgrim separates from her previous way of life but is in a transitional phase and has not yet reached a stage of integration of that experience. Within the context of ritual experience, it refers to this period of change and disorientation experienced by the pilgrim before he arrives at the new awareness he will experience when the ritual is completed. In *The Wizard of Oz*, when Dorothy exclaims, "Toto, I've a feeling we're not in Kansas anymore," she is suggesting that she too is having a liminal experience. She knows she is not in Kansas anymore, and she is aware that something important is happening, but she doesn't know the outcome. Edith Turner describes liminality as having an "out of this ordinary world" character.[5] "All journeys have secret destinations of which the traveler is unaware,"[6] wrote Martin Buber. For spiritual people, liminal experience is often interpreted as the presence of the Divine or a call from God. Others may explain liminal experience as a sense of purpose or destiny, as a feeling that they were "meant" to be in a particular time or place. According to Victor and Edith Turner's work, once pilgrims transition through the liminal phase, they then gradually reintegrate into the community and into a new social state.

When writing about the concept of communitas in regard to pilgrimage, Victor Turner is referring to the experience of oneness that is experienced by participants in shared rituals. For instance, there is the deep companionship that develops between Dorothy,

Scarecrow, Tin Man, and Lion in the course of their pilgrimage. What makes the experience of communitas different from typical friendships is that the social and cultural dynamics transcend the confines of society and the pilgrims operate as equals. For the pilgrim, the opportunity to leave behind her socially and culturally conditioned roles and relate to a wide diversity of people as equals is cathartic and transformational long after she returns home; she is a changed individual. Moreover, the experience of communitas sustains pilgrims as they traverse through the physical discomfort as well as the psychological and spiritual pain so often a part of liminal experiences.

"Communitas is a very simple thing but an enormously important part of social life," writes Edith Turner. "It does not often find its way into the social sciences because scholars do not know what to do with it. I now see it as unconditional love, outside any undifferentiated respect for rank, moral status, and social structures. It flourishes best in those precious in-between times when stress about status is low and nobody bothers about rank."[7]

Victor and Edith Turner have been referred to as the founders of "pilgrimage studies," and they actively reflect on their own pilgrimage as academic anthropologists who eventually became members of a faith community as a result of engagement in their work. In *Image and Pilgrimage*, they identify four types of pilgrimage: *archaic*, or pilgrimages related to early forms of devotion or a synthesis of traditions; *prototypical*, or pilgrimages related to the founder of a religious tradition or a saint; *medieval*, or pilgrimages arising from the traditions of the premodern period in the West; and, lastly, *modern* pilgrimages, or those concerned with the economic and social abuses of societies.[8] Although this categorization of pilgrimages relates more directly to the Western Christian tradition, it can be expanded to provide a way to think about types of pilgrimages from other religions traditions and cultures or of secular pilgrimages today.

Moreover, the Turners' contributions in respect to liminality and communitas give us a language for the important internal and external dynamics inherent in all pilgrimage experiences. We are all, at some time or another, pilgrims in this life. The sacred art of pilgrimage transcends religious, national, cultural, and linguistic boundaries.

PILGRIMAGE ACROSS CULTURES AND RELIGIONS

The practice of pilgrimage lies deep in the heart of many cultures and nearly every major religion of the world. It is likely that the practice of pilgrimage began very early in human history as people traveled to sacred nature sites, and later to local shrines, to bring offerings and to pray to the gods for protection or healing. For millennia, humans have continued to embark on pilgrimages seeking enlightenment, healing, or to fulfill an obligation. Every year faithful Muslims will undertake a pilgrimage to Mecca, as required for those in good health at least once during their lifetime. For Muslims, pilgrimage to Mecca—or the hajj— is one of the Five Pillars of Islam. Pilgrimage for members of the Bahá'í faith includes visiting holy places in Haifa and Acre, while Buddhists make pilgrimage to sites related to the life of the Buddha in modern-day India and Nepal. Hindus are encouraged to participate in pilgrimages during their lifetime, and most visit holy places in their own regions. Although adherents of the Sikh religion did not originally regard pilgrimage as a spiritual practice, over time visits to the Golden Temple, as the center of their faith, became a recognized part of religious observance. Jerusalem continues as a major pilgrimage site for members of the Abrahamic religions; Jews regard the Western Wall (also known as the Wailing Wall) in the Old City of Jerusalem as a major sacred site. The first Christians traveled to sites in the Holy Land associated with the life of Jesus and the early martyrs. Other major Christian pilgrimage sites include Rome, Canterbury, and Santiago de Compostela in Spain, among others. Island peoples, such as the Celtic tribes, envisioned their pilgrimages as voyages over the sea, with stops on neighboring islands.

Countless pilgrims around the world travel to holy destinations—local shrines, monasteries, and nature sites such as mountains, springs, and burial places. As a sacred art, pilgrimage is not limited to those with links to intentional faith communities. Millions travel to the Vietnam Memorial or the Jefferson Memorial in Washington, D.C., or to Lenin's Tomb in Moscow, to visit national secular pilgrimage sites. Thousands have made pilgrimages to Elvis Presley's home and burial site at Graceland in Memphis, and Amy Winehouse's former London home. Each year, millions of devoted *Star Trek* fans journey to conventions around the world, looking to reconnect with the shows and characters and seeking like-minded people. Since 2001 a pilgrimage tradition has also been created around the National September 11 Memorial and Museum. Businesses also participate in pilgrimage—even the Trader Joe's food chain has a regular newsletter for the "Food Pilgrimager" called the *Fearless Flyer*, for those customers interested in trying the latest foods and learning more about their origin and preparation.

Why do people become pilgrims? The answers to this question are as diverse as the numbers of pilgrims who have traveled the path before them. Like the characters in *The Wizard of Oz*, some go on pilgrimage seeking meaning; some are looking for their heart's desire; others want to heal; and still others hope to find a more authentic home. A pilgrimage is more than a standard trip or journey. While some embark on pilgrimages with a sense of adventure, it is not a journey intended for relaxation. It almost always begins with a sense of call or a deep yearning on the part of the pilgrim, sometimes with great urgency, to go forth. Often the pilgrim is called to undertake physical travel, although for some the pilgrimage is about traveling inward on a "journey of the heart," so to speak. While some do undertake their journeys in groups, the focus of most of the narratives is on the individual.

No two pilgrims have the exact same experience, even if they follow the same road. What is consistent across cultures and religions is that the path of a pilgrim is a challenging one. The adversities of displacement along with the inner struggles of the traveler combine to make the pilgrims' way a meaningful yet difficult journey. The life of the pilgrim usually involves a range of rituals, including spiritual and secular practices that serve to heighten awareness. Pilgrimage itself has been described as a spiritual practice; it always requires an internal *process* whereby individuals move from one way of seeing themselves and their world to another level of consciousness. Lastly, integral to pilgrimage is the journey home and the pilgrims' need to integrate the life they have lived with the new insights gained as they return as changed persons.

THE HINDU TRADITION

Hinduism is among the fastest-growing religious traditions in the world, with rich pilgrimage traditions that pre-date the Abrahamic traditions. From ancient times to the present day, devout Hindus have practiced the art of pilgrimage and participate in them throughout the course of their lifetimes. For Hindus, all of life is seen as a cycle with specific rites of passage. Pilgrimage is so important in the Hindu tradition that it is often included in lists of the five basic duties for every adherent, alongside daily worship, festivals, rites of passage, and a virtuous lifestyle. The traditional Hindu term for pilgrimage is *tirthayatra*, which literally means "a journey to the ford." In this case, the ford is a liminal place where the pilgrim is able to cross over the river from the profane to the divine. In the iconography of the Hindu religious imagination, the sky is a place that separates heaven and earth, and it is traversed by the gods, who descend from there into the human world. On pilgrimage, the movement is reversed, and it becomes an opportunity for humans to cross over and temporarily experience a glimpse of a higher spiritual existence. For the Hindu, therefore, pilgrimage is a passage from the patterns and routines of daily life to the world of the Divine. The reasons Hindus practice pilgrimage are as varied and as similar as those of pilgrims in other traditions. Often, local priests and gurus will offer people spiritual counsel related to their pilgrimage practices. For some, pilgrimage takes the form of a prayer to answer a personal petition; for other sacred travelers, it is an act of gratitude for blessings or favors already received. Others undertake a pilgrimage to fulfill a vow or a family obligation. Hindu spiritual geography offers a great diversity of sacred sites, including cities, rivers, lakes, mountains, and local shrines. Hindus also make pilgrimages to sites associated with the life of Krishna in India, such as his birthplace. Hindu death rituals are closely associated with pilgrimage; mourners will journey to sites where funeral offerings (*shraddha*) are considered most efficacious, and older persons will travel to holy sites in the hope that dying there will release them from the cycle of reincarnation.

Water rituals are also associated with Hindu pilgrimage, as the faithful seek to be purified from bad karma by bathing in sacred rivers, lakes, or the ocean. Thus many of the most popular Hindu pilgrimage sites are on riverbanks, including the banks of the Ganges, considered the most sacred of all rivers. The forty-two-day Maha Kumbh Mela, the largest festival in northern India, draws up to seventy million devotees seeking to purify their souls with a dip in that place where the holy Ganges and Yamuna rivers converge. In Hindu mythology, the Ganges flows from its celestial source (the Milky Way) through the hair of the god Shiva and onto the earth, where it brings forth life and purification.

Within the context of the Hindu tradition, the practice of pilgrimage involves considerable physical discomfort and discipline. On pilgrimage, the desires of the body are meant to be put aside in order to make spiritual matters the priority. Travel, particularly to locations in remote areas in India, can be slow and risky. Hindu pilgrims often temporarily adapt monastic practices such as shaving their heads and abstaining from meat, fish, alcohol, and sex. Like pilgrimage experiences in other religious traditions and cultures, Hindu pilgrimage brings with it an opportunity to relax the boundaries of caste and gender that are typically present in the broader society. All Hindus are encouraged to participate in *tirthayatra*, regardless of their social, religious, and geographical status. This sense of communitas makes pilgrimage particularly popular among lower-caste Hindus, women, and others who are normally excluded from Brahman rituals. When the Hindu pilgrim returns home, she is then reincorporated into her own community with enhanced personal status.

THE BUDDHIST TRADITION

Like Hinduism, Buddhism honors the sacred pilgrimage, shares in similar rituals, and believes in its intrinsic value as a lifelong spiritual practice. Unlike Hinduism, which has no central figure, the focus of Buddhist pilgrimage is the opportunity to draw closer to the Enlightened One. Traditionally the Buddhist monk is taught that his whole life is a pilgrimage and a search for his true home.

Historically, the tradition of pilgrimage within Buddhism is connected to the four sites most associated with Gautama Buddha. According to scripture, the Buddha was asked by his cousin, Ananda, how his followers were going to pay their respects after his death. In response, the Buddha spoke about four holy places his followers could visit "as long as they live" to remember him: the place of his birth (Lambini); the place where he attained enlightenment (Bodhgaya); the place where he turned the wheel of dharma (Sarnath); and, lastly, the place where he

attained final nirvana (Kusinara). In addition to these four traditional sites, hundreds of others have been associated in some way
with the Buddha over the past two and a half millennia.

These places associated with the Buddha are believed to be
invested with spiritual energy that supports Buddhist practice.
Buddhist pilgrims are encouraged to adopt simple lifestyles, and
many make donations to the monks who maintain the sacred
sites. Historically, pilgrims began to travel to the four sites fairly
soon after Gautama Buddha's death, and they remain in the
itineraries of Buddhist pilgrimages today. A further impetus
for widespread Buddhist pilgrimage practice came from the
emperor Ashoka, a convert to Buddhism, who set out on a journey of truth, known as *dhammayatra*, in 249 BCE. As part of his
journey, Ashoka visited the four sites, as well as others where
the Buddha worked miracles, and built monuments in each
place. Over the course of his lifetime, Ashoka visited thirty-two
Buddhist shrines and was instrumental in having relics of the
Buddha and his followers collected and distributed. He also paid
for the building of roads, water stations, and rest houses to assist
others on their pilgrimages, writing that "I have done what I
have primarily in order that the people may follow the path of
dharma with faith and devotion." Another well-known Buddhist
pilgrim, a monk from China who lived around 400 BCE named
Fa-hsien, traveled for fourteen years to the shrines in India with
his companion To-Ching and wrote that he "could scarcely contain his tears" upon arriving at a site where the Buddha lived.
Other Buddhist pilgrims travel to holy places associated with the
bodhisattvas, those saints and masters whose work was carried
out at holy places beyond India.

THE GREEK AND ROMAN TRADITIONS

Many of the themes related to pilgrimage—the solitary traveler,
the difficult journey fraught with adversity, the encounter of new
friends and the loss of companionship, the intense inner yearning

for meaning, and the return home as a changed person—can be found in the classical tradition of Greek and Roman literature. In Homer's *Odyssey*, for example, the hero spends ten years away from his home in Ithaca during the siege of Troy and then another ten journeying toward his true spiritual home: "Many the pains he suffered in his spirit on the wide sea, struggling for his own life, and the homecoming of his companions." In the ancient world there was not the same separation between the sacred and the secular that many experience today.

Participation in ancient rituals of civil religion contributed to people's identity as citizens and members of particular societies. For instance, the festival of the Great Panathenaea was held in honor of Athena's birthday and celebrated every four years, when people from throughout the region journeyed to Athens to walk in procession and to offer sacrifices. Not only did the festival bolster the individual's sense of identity, but it also bound people together with their ancestors as participants in a major pilgrimage to a holy place. Such rituals also served the political purpose of uniting people who lived in outlying territories with the city and its gods. In the same way, the ancient Olympic Games are an example of a festival that encouraged people to journey to a sacred site for the purposes of building unity and a shared identity. Also important in ancient Greece were the journeys of individuals to the oracle at Delphi and other sacred sites known for healing or prophecy.

The city of Rome has stood on sacred ground for its entire history. Since much of the wider Mediterranean world was conquered by the Romans, the empire accommodated many of the gods and rituals of the peoples who inhabited those regions. Both citizens and subjects continued to visit shrines to leave petitions, sometimes in the form of curses, or expressions of gratitude when their prayers were answered. Like the Greeks before them, the Roman landscape included many local shrines and cults. In addition, the imperial cult that worshipped the emperor and his predecessors included a network of local temples. Evidence suggests that Roman pilgrims prepared themselves spiritually for pilgrimages. "I made myself a stranger to all vice and all godlessness. Was chaste for a considerable period, and offered the due increase offering in holy piety," wrote one Roman pilgrim at a shrine in Egypt.

The Romans tolerated all religious groups, including Jews, but were deeply suspicious of former pagans who turned away from the worship of the gods of the Roman cult to become monotheists. Visiting shrines and temples in the Roman world involved complicated rituals designed to mark the significance of the pilgrim on the journey, such as shaving the head and eyebrows; animal sacrifices; abstinence from wrongdoing, particular foods, or sex; water rituals that were connected with purification and drinking; as well as maintaining an appropriate demeanor of prayer and observance. Romans also donned a garland or other marks of identification as pilgrims. "Then he sets out from his own country and makes the journey, using cold water for bathing as well as drinking, and he always sleeps on the ground, for it is sacrilege for him to touch a bed before he completes the journey and returns to his own country," writes the Roman rhetorician Lucian in the second century CE.

THE ABRAHAMIC TRADITIONS

The pilgrimage practices of the Greeks and the Romans informed the Abrahamic traditions that had their roots in the Near East—Judaism, Christianity, Islam, and the Bahá'í. Historically, the Abrahamic traditions share not only the belief in one true God, with Abraham as his prophet, but all share in a tradition of pilgrimage to the Holy Land, with Jerusalem at its center. The emphasis on ritual preparation, travel to sacred sites, and internal and external modifications to the rhythms of normal life are consistent throughout the traditions. "Thus says the Lord: 'Stand by the roads, and look, and ask for the ancient paths, where the good way is; and walk in it, and find rest for your souls,'" says the prophet Jeremiah (Jeremiah 6:16). Similarly, the motivations of the pilgrim to seek the Divine, to make a quest for healing, or to journey to gain a deeper sense of one's identity are also prevalent.

Jewish Pilgrimage

Judaism began as a nomadic religion with no fixed homeland. Four thousand years ago Abraham, a figure revered by all four traditions, left the land of Ur in Mesopotamia at the age of seventy-five with his wife Sarai in answer to God's call: "Leave your country, your family and your father's house for the land I will show you. I will make you a great nation" (Genesis 12:1–2). The story of the book of Exodus in the Hebrew Bible is focused on Moses leading the people out of bondage in the land of Egypt.

One of the injunctions given by God to Moses at Mount Sinai specifically refers to the people of God appearing before God three times a year (Exodus 24:14–19, 34:22–23). After wandering through the desert for forty years, the Hebrew people arrived at the Promised Land. Their yearning for a spiritual home focused on the city of Jerusalem, the Temple, and the Ark of the Covenant within it. In 586 BCE the people were exiled once again, to Babylon following the destruction of the Temple by Nebuchadnezzar. "By the waters of Babylon we sat down and wept, when we remembered you, O Zion," laments Psalm 137. The cataclysmic destruction of the Second Temple by the Roman emperor Titus in 70 CE marked the beginning of an exile for the Jewish people in a Diaspora that lasted nearly two millennia. Not until the creation of the state of Israel in 1948 did they gain a distinct, though contested, homeland. If a characteristic of pilgrimage is to return to one's sacred center, it is important to take note that for Jews, throughout most of history, it has been difficult to travel to the Holy Land. Central to Jewish spirituality and ritual practice are the themes of exile and return, of wandering and yearning for home. Judaism had no single founder, as did Buddhism, Christianity, and Islam; instead the heart of religious life and the focus of pilgrimage in ancient Judaism was the Temple.

Aliyah is a Hebrew word that means "ascent" or "going up." According to Jewish tradition, traveling to the Land of Israel is an ascent, both geographically and metaphysically. Anyone traveling there from Egypt, Babylonia, or the Mediterranean basin, where many Jews lived in early Rabbinic times, climbed to a higher altitude. Jerusalem itself is situated on a hill 2,700 feet above sea level, so to reach it was also an "ascent." According to the Torah, every male adult was obligated to make his way to Jerusalem three times a year: "Three times a year your males shall appear before the Lord your God at the place that He will choose at the festival of unleavened bread, at the festival of weeks, and at the festival of booths. They shall not appear before the Lord empty-handed; all shall give as they are able, according to the blessing of the Lord your God according to what He has given you" (Deuteronomy 16:16–17). The festivals referred to in the passage—Passover, Shavuot, and Sukkot—were also known as the "foot festivals" and were to be celebrated in Jerusalem.

Aliyah is an important Jewish cultural concept—when someone "makes *aliyah*" it refers to both voluntary immigration to Israel and the return of persecuted Jewish refugees who had no choice but to leave their home countries. Thus religious Jews may consider *aliyah* as a return to the Promised Land.

The Hebrew word for pilgrimage-feasts is *hag*, an ancestor to the Arabic word *hajj*, referring to the Muslim pilgrimage to Mecca. The word *hag* means "turning around and dancing"—a vivid reminder of some of the ritual practices associated with pilgrimage in the tradition, when the offerings of the people were carried through the streets of the Holy City in colorful baskets to the sounds of singing and dancing. Jewish rituals developed to help the people remember their history of exile and survival. Although scripture mentions earlier shrines at Gilgal, Shechem, and Shiloh, the city of Jerusalem became the religious center when King David established it as the capital; his son Soloman built the First Temple on Mount Zion. After the destruction of the Second Temple in 70 CE, Jews continued to journey to Jerusalem whenever possible.

In the years when Jerusalem was dominated by Christians and Muslims, Jews were technically allowed to settle there and visit from the Diaspora, but there is scant evidence that they did so in large numbers. One such visitor, Rabbi Benjamin of Tudela in Spain, was interested in visiting Jewish communities in areas dominated by Christians and Muslims and traveled to Jerusalem and Palestine in the 1160s. He describes how Jews prayed at the Western Wall: "The Western Wall, one of the walls which formed the Holy of Holies of the ancient Temple, it is called the Gate of Mercy, and all Jews resort thither to say their prayers near the wall of the courtyard."[9]

Today this remnant of the Temple, the Western Wall (or Wailing Wall), is the most sacred place in Judaism and the destination of Jewish pilgrims from Israel and around the world. While they stand in prayer at the wall, they express their sorrow at the loss of the Temple and draw strength from the fact that the stones that remain are a sign that God has not abandoned the Jewish people. Pilgrims to the wall will slip written prayers into the cracks between the stones, where they are absorbed into the prayers of those who came centuries before.

Although Jerusalem today remains a primary sacred site for Jews as well as for Christians and Muslims, Jews also visit other pilgrimage sites such as the Tombs of the Patriarchs in Hebron, Mount Carmel, Rachel's Tomb, and the Tomb of Ezekiel in present-day Iran. Modern pilgrimage sites include those around the world dedicated to the victims of the Holocaust and the synagogue at the Hadassah Medical Center with the stained-glass windows by artist Marc Chagall, to name but a few of the holy places Jews visit to be in touch with their ancient traditions.

In addition, thousands of Jewish young adults participate in "birthright tourism," that is, pilgrimage to Israel with a variety of goals, including strengthening Jewish identity, through gaining a deeper sense of the relationship between the State of Israel and Jews of the Diaspora.

Christian Pilgrimage

Like the other Abrahamic faiths, Christianity shares in a long history of pilgrimage. Among the first pilgrims associated with Christianity were the wise men (the Magi) who visited the infant Jesus, as found in the second chapter of the gospel of Matthew. The narrative of the Magi contains many of the elements of a classic pilgrim tale of a long journey undertaken in faith to a place of spiritual significance. As the story goes, the wise men in the East saw a new star in the heavens and considered it a sign that something truly wondrous had occurred. Not wanting to miss an auspicious event, the wise men began a long journey, probably from a region in present-day Iran, which eventually led them to the village of Bethlehem, where they discovered a new-born infant lying in a manger. A fifth-century Greek historian named Herodotus writes that the Magi were likely members of a Median tribe of renowned astrologers who lived in the Persian Empire. Like pilgrims from other cultures, the wise men arrived bearing offerings: gold, a symbol of royalty; incense, a symbol of holiness burned during religious rites; and myrrh, a spice used for embalming and later considered a symbol of Jesus's death. The wise men then journeyed home via another route in an effort to avoid betraying the location of the infant to King Herod, who also read the signs but was uninterested in their spiritual significance.

The story of the Magi points to a tradition of pilgrimage to sites associated with a holy person or event that was present in the Christian tradition at a very early stage. One of the earliest forms of Christian pilgrimage in the East was to visit the living saints of the desert, who were solitaries in Egypt, Syria, and the eastern

Mediterranean, in order to seek spiritual advice from them or to offer petitions and ask for their blessing.

Many major Christian pilgrimage sites, particularly in the early years of the tradition, are associated with the birth, miracles, death, burial, resurrection, and ascension of Jesus. Unlike the Buddha or the Prophet Muhammad, Jesus of Nazareth did not specifically command his followers to go on pilgrimage. Initially, some of his sayings were interpreted in a way that in fact discouraged followers from participating in traditional Jewish rituals, such as venerating the tombs of the prophets. Over time, however, stories associated with Jesus, such as his journey with two disciples traveling down the road to Emmaus (Luke 24:13–35), were interpreted in ways more favorable to the tradition of pilgrimage. While some theologians and leaders of the early church were reluctant to encourage pilgrimage—"What advantage, moreover, is reaped by him who reaches those celebrated spots themselves?"[10] asked Gregory of Nyssa—such arguments did not ultimately stop the faithful from participating in those journeys they considered powerful spiritual experiences. The impulse to walk the same paths that Jesus did and to be able to see and touch places mentioned in the Bible was a far more persuasive argument for pilgrimage than scholarly treatises. "The principal motive that draws people to Jerusalem is the desire to see and touch the places where Christ was present in the body,"[11] wrote Paulinus of Nola, a fourth-century convert to Christianity and later bishop of the church. Another fourth-century Christian pilgrim, a nun named Egeria, was amazed at the opportunities she experienced as a pilgrim to encounter places she read about in scripture. "All one had to do was think of a text, and the authentic spot could be provided. Truly this was a world which one had but to 'see and touch.'"[12]

Of course, during some of the period after Jesus's death and before the conversion of Constantine to Christianity in the early fourth century, periods of persecution made travel impractical for some Christians, particularly those closest to the watchful eyes of the Roman emperor. Here the journey to visit sacred sites was associated with visiting the remains, or relics, of those who died in the faith. The term *relic* refers to a part of the body, such as a piece of bone, or a piece of clothing or another artifact of a holy person. The relics and the graves of a martyr of the Christian faith or of an exceptionally holy person were endowed with great spiritual significance. It was believed that the holiness of the saints could be transmitted to the pilgrims who came to see them and touch them. There are hints of this belief in the New Testament, such as when the woman suffering from a hemorrhage comes up from behind Jesus to touch his clothing in the belief that the action will cure her (Matthew 9:20–22). Another example is in the Acts of the apostles, when followers of Paul attest to the healing power of handkerchiefs and aprons that had touched his skin (Acts 19:12).

Early Christians in Rome typically buried their dead in underground tombs—burial was forbidden inside the walls of the city—and these catacombs became the most frequently visited pilgrimage sites in the city. The significance of relics remained an important aspect of the Christian pilgrimage tradition from the Middle Ages to the modern era and is still strong within some religious cultures today. It is not always clear whether a particular relic is believed to be endowed with miraculous capacities itself or if it is a symbol of the power of God's work in the world inspiring the believer. Either way, within the Christian tradition relics are powerful reminders of the communion of saints who lived a life of faith, often under great adversity, and after death went to heaven, where they hear the prayers of the believers who call upon them and intercede on their behalf.

As noted above, not all church leaders of the first few centuries of the early church fathers were supportive of pilgrimage as a practice. Fourth-century historian and theologian Jerome actively discouraged pilgrimage, despite the fact that many of his followers were committed to the practice, because he felt it distracted from developing inner piety. His contemporary in North Africa, Augustine of Hippo, felt that his episcopal authority was compromised because of the numbers of unregulated spiritual wanderers. Like Augustine, other early church leaders felt that the proliferation of spiritual wanderers and begging monks were something of a problem for church order.

Within a few years of the legalization of Christianity within the Roman Empire by Constantine in 312 CE, his mother, the empress Helena, who was also the major force behind her son's conversion, visited the holy sites in Palestine associated with the life of Jesus, in part to repent for the sins of her family. Eusebius, the bishop of Caesarea in Palestine, later wrote of Helena and her pilgrimage, "Though advanced in years, yet gifted with no common degree of wisdom, she hastened with youthful alacrity to survey this venerable land." According to legend, while in Palestine Helena found the remains of the True Cross, which according to legend is the cross upon which Jesus was crucified. She also began the ambitious building of basilicas in Jerusalem and Bethlehem. Thus began the tradition of Christian pilgrimage to the Holy Land, which continues to the present day.

Soon a supportive infrastructure of churches, guesthouses, and monasteries were built to support pilgrims in their travels. The most important of these churches was the Church of the Holy Sepulchre, built on the traditional site of Jesus's crucifixion and burial. Military religious orders such as the Knights Templar were founded to protect Christian pilgrims on their journeys. Christians continued to visit the Holy Land on pilgrimage even when the region was in Muslim control, though ostensibly one of the rationales for the Crusades was to regain control of it in an effort to protect pilgrims. By the sixth century, the great basilicas and churches of the Holy Land themselves became pilgrimage sites, and the practice of visiting them became commonly accepted as an expression of personal piety and faithfulness through the rest of Christian history. For example, fifteenth-century English mystic and pilgrim Margery Kempe writes of her experience, "And when this creature saw Jerusalem, riding on an ass, she thanked God with all her heart, praying to Him for His mercy that, as He had brought her to see His earthly city of Jerusalem, He would grant her grace to see the blissful city of Jerusalem, the city of Heaven."[13]

Far away from the Mediterranean world, in Ireland and later in Britain, a vibrant Celtic Christian culture produced many noteworthy saints, monastics, scholars, missionaries, and pilgrims. The Irish were somewhat different from other Christian pilgrims in that they set off on their journeys with no set destinations. Instead, they trusted God to show them the way and to let them know when it was time to return home. Embarking on long and arduous journeys, they endured much hardship for the opportunity to pray in holy places. Some embark on pilgrimage and never returned to their homeland again. The *Anglo-Saxon Chronicle* tells of a day in 891 when three Irishmen set off from the coast of Cornwall in a boat without oars: "The men said they wanted to 'live in a state of pilgrimage, for the love of God, they cared not where.'" The famous Patrick of Ireland spent a good portion of his career traveling the countryside teaching and preaching the gospel. Characteristic of island cultures, the pilgrimage literature of Celtic Christians is voyage literature, and the journey is over water as frequently as it is over land. For such cultures, the concept of heaven or "paradise" is often pictured as an island.

One famous example of voyage literature is the story of the sixth-century Irish monk Brendan the navigator. In the narrative, Brendan sets out on a seven-year journey with seventeen fellow monks in search of the "Island Promised to the Saints." After the first forty days, they landed on the first of many islands and experienced the first of many miracles as they were led to a place with enough water, bread, and fish for all. Throughout the voyage

Brendan and his companions met many interesting characters, including Paul the Hermit, said to be 140 years old. Finally, after their last Easter on pilgrimage, they landed on the Island Promised to the Saints. After another forty days, a young man suddenly appeared, blessed them, and told them it was time to return home. According to Mary C. Earle's book which discusses Celtic Christian pilgrimage:

> Using a small boat with no oars called a *coracle* or a *curragh*, a pilgrim band would climb into the boat, cast off, and entrust themselves "to the currents of divine love." Eventually either the sea or the river would bring them to rest at a place they had not chosen, for they allowed themselves to be completely open to the movement of the water. That place would be known as 'the place of my resurrection,' for they would have been led to that place by the Holy Spirit, and would probably die there (unless prompted to make another sea pilgrimage).[14]

By the tenth century in Europe, as the violence between Christians and Muslims in the Holy Land escalated, it became prudent for Christian pilgrims to seek out other holy sites. Although Europe had been the home of pilgrimage sites for hundreds of years, the growth of additional holy places through the eleventh and twelfth centuries was rapid. Both Rome in the western Mediterranean and Santiago de Compostela in northwestern Spain emerged as two of the most important pilgrimage sites in Western Christianity. Rome offered not only the graves of the apostles Peter and Paul, but also important basilicas such as Old Saint Peter's and the catacombs of early Christian martyrs. In Spain, Santiago de Compostela, the burial site of the apostle James, became the greatest pilgrimage site in the West after Jerusalem and Rome, with an estimated half-million pilgrims annually. Medieval Christian shrines like Our Lady of Walsingham in Norfolk, England, also attracted pilgrims due to their curative powers, inspiring hope among the sick. Because sickness was at the time associated with sin, the search for healing and forgiveness was a popular motivation for pilgrims from every walk of life. The shrine at Walsingham was frequented by pilgrims for nearly five hundred years before it was suppressed by Henry VIII, although the king himself visited the shrine at an earlier time in his life. In 1997 the Anglican and Roman Catholic shrine at Walsingham marked its centenary as a restored pilgrimage site.

In England, soon after Thomas Becket's martyrdom and canonization in 1173, Canterbury became a major site in Britain as pilgrims made their way to the place where the saint was murdered and buried. "When the sweet showers of April have pierced the drought of March, and pierced it to the root ... then people long to go on pilgrimages," wrote Geoffrey Chaucer in the *Canterbury Tales*, which famously told the story of a group of pilgrims from London to Canterbury and the tales they tell each other along the way. Chaucer made the pilgrimage to Canterbury himself in 1386 and described the characteristics of the "typical" pilgrims, such as knights, monks, parsons, millers, and widows who went on pilgrimages at every available opportunity. Along with the founding of pilgrimage sites in Europe came the expansion of churches, monasteries, guesthouses, inns, food establishments, candlemakers, pilgrim badge makers, and other businesses designed to house and feed these pilgrims in their travels.

By the fourteenth century, cataclysmic events such as the Black Death—which decimated the population of Europe— along with a century of warfare, social unrest, and growing disenchantment with the church due to papal corruption, all impacted the religious lives of the people, including their attitude toward pilgrimage. As the *Canterbury Tales* suggests, by the later Middle Ages the pilgrimage was not considered a test of devotion for all Christians. For some, it became an opportunity for adventure and romance rather than purely a spiritual journey. Although there were always Christians critical of pilgrimage or its abuses, by the era of the Reformation claims that the practice was corrupt, unscriptural, and superstitious gained wider public support. The late-fifteenth-century humanist Erasmus, as well as Reformers such as Martin Luther, were highly critical of pilgrimage, including the practices associated with it—veneration of relics, belief in purgatory, and prayers for the dead. Once people no longer believed that a journey to a shrine could help them or a family member get to heaven or that prayers to a saint could bring forth a miraculous healing, the numbers of pilgrims traveling to major sites such as the Holy Land, Rome, or Santiago de Compostela grew smaller. In some Protestant regions the attacks against pilgrimage were both theological and literal, including the destruction of many shrines.

However, ingrained religious practices change slowly, and while we know that there were pressures in the Protestant regions of Europe to reject pilgrimage and other related practices altogether as outdated and superstitious, it is also true that people continued to go on pilgrimage in Roman Catholic areas throughout southern Europe. During the fifteenth and sixteenth centuries, the practice of the "Stations of the Cross" gained popularity—a slow procession around the church, stopping for prayers at each of fourteen stations representing the Passion of Jesus in visual images along the walls. This made it possible for those no longer able to go to Jerusalem or other distant shrines to make a pilgrimage following in the footsteps of Jesus in their own parish church. In Protestant regions, moreover, people began to travel to herbalists and healers and to spas in search of cures.

Although the theological rationale behind Christian pilgrimage changed for some adherents during and after the Protestant Reformation, the tradition continued. For example, John Bunyan's allegorical journey of the soul, *The Pilgrim's*

Progress, first published in 1678, became one of the classics of Christian pilgrimage literature of all time, even though as a Puritan Bunyan would have been scandalized by the medieval spiritual practices associated with pilgrimage. A very different kind of pilgrimage began in the eighteenth century, moreover, whereby affluent young men, and sometimes young women, embarked on a ritual that was known as the "Grand Tour." It involved extensive travel to the architectural and artistic masterpieces of Paris, Rome, Venice, Florence, Geneva, and other great European cities that closely resembled pilgrimage in its goal of the search for meaning, beauty, and the excitement of travel.

Travel to more local Christian pilgrimage sites and shrines such as Holywell in Wales, the location of Saint Winefride's Well, also continued in the modern era, much as it did in the Middle Ages, while pilgrimage to famous international pilgrimage sites such as Santiago de Compostela waned during times of war and conflict, but never completely ceased. Within the Christian tradition, the practice of pilgrimage experienced a renewal in the nineteenth and twentieth centuries. In the West, as Christians grew more skeptical of the traditional belief systems of the church, people's longing for spiritual experiences that directly connected them with the sacred grew more pronounced. Beyond the traditional strongholds of Western Christianity in Europe and North America, where membership in the church is currently in decline, religious commitment is growing steadily in the global south, where traditions of pilgrimage have been a part of local tradition for centuries.

A new development in Christian pilgrimage in the nineteenth century was the evolution of sites associated with miraculous apparitions, such as the appearances of Mary, the mother of Jesus, to the fourteen-year-old Bernadette Soubirous in Lourdes, France, in 1858. An annual pilgrimage to Lourdes was instituted in 1873, three years after the French suffered a humiliating defeat in the Franco-Prussian war; it provided a means for national reflection as well as a counterbalance to the influences of secularism. Known as a world center for miraculous healing, Lourdes remains one of the preeminent Christian pilgrimage shrines today. As with Lourdes, the significance of the Marian shrine at Fatima in Portugal is associated with a series of appearances made by Mary to three local shepherd children in 1917; during the last of these appearances, thousands witnessed the celestial phenomenon of the "dancing sun." Endorsed by the church in 1930, Fatima became an international pilgrimage destination after World War II, dedicated to the need to pray for the conversion of the world.

In response to the atrocities of the two World Wars, the international pilgrimage site of Taizé in France was founded in 1940 by Roger Schutz-Marsauche, known as Brother Roger. The son of a Protestant pastor, he founded the Taizé Community as an ecumenical community dedicated to bringing together pilgrims from all over the world to share in prayer, reflection, and social action. In a similar manner, the tiny island of Iona off the west coast of Scotland is the site of an ecumenical community founded in 1938 by a pastor of the Church of Scotland, George MacLeod. Like the site of Taizé, the structures on the island of Iona are fairly simple and without elaborate shrines. Rather, the pilgrim is drawn into the spirit of the holy place, the company of others on pilgrimage from all over the world, and a compelling natural landscape, which supports spiritual reflection. Overall, and despite changes in practice and the popularity of locations over time, the Christian tradition of pilgrimage has survived for more than two thousand years and is continuing to thrive in the present day.

Islamic Pilgrimage

The third of the Abrahamic faiths under consideration here, Islam, enjoys a rich tradition of pilgrimage. Indeed, of all the religious traditions discussed in this chapter, it is the followers of

Islam who have the strongest ritual obligation to go on pilgrimage. The fifth pillar in Islam states that every adult Muslim who is able-bodied and financially capable is expected to make the pilgrimage to Mecca, known as the hajj, in his or her lifetime. As the Qur'an states, "Pilgrimage to the House is incumbent upon men for the sake of Allah, upon everyone who is able to undertake the journey to it" (Qur'an, III:97). For Muslims, the hajj, which literally means "to set out on a journey" in Arabic, is an intensely individual spiritual practice, and at the same time it serves as a connection to the sacred story of the faith community, as members walk in the footsteps of Abraham, Hagar, Ishmael, and the Prophet Muhammad himself.

Although the pilgrims leave home as individuals, they come together at the center of the world as one humanity in submission to God, transformed through an experience of death and rebirth. Those returning are called *hajji* in deference to this central act of transformation in the life of a faithful Muslim. "He who leaves home in search of wisdom walks in the path of God," said the Prophet Muhammad.[15]

The rituals associated with the hajj are carefully regulated. Since the Prophet Muhammad's final visit to the city in 632, only Muslims are allowed into the sacred area of Mecca, and extensive identity checks are required by the Saudi government. (The holy city is not considered a tourist venue.) Furthermore, pilgrims must pay all debts before leaving home and are responsible for providing care for their families in their absence. No Muslim should borrow money or go into debt for the journey. Money used on the journey should be purified through a religious tax known as the *zakat*. Members of the tradition are aware that not everyone is going to be able to participate in the hajj during their lifetime, especially if they live at a distance from Saudi Arabia. At the same time, millions converge on the holy city at pilgrimage time. Although the journey was traditionally an arduous one, today pilgrims arrive in the holy city by modern transportation, many traveling in groups of family and friends from a local mosque.

The hajj begins when the pilgrim arrives at a *miquat*, or a marker, that designates the sacred boundary around Mecca. Traditionally there are six *miquats* to accommodate pilgrims that arrive from different directions. The pilgrim then enters a spiritual state, *ihram*, signified by special garments and vows. Men are required to wear a white seamless two-piece garment. Their heads must be bare, and normally sandals are worn on their feet. Women may wear a white garment or their typical clothes with a head covering. The white clothing signifies both purity and the equality of all pilgrims before God. All vow to abstain from sex, wearing jewelry and perfume, cutting their hair (including shaving), cutting their nails, eating meat, and using profane language. With the chanting of the *Talbiyah* prayer, pilgrims acknowledge that they have entered sacred time and space and affirm their relationship with God: "Here I am at Your service, O God, here I am. Here I am at Your service. You have no partners. Yours alone is all praise and all bounty. Yours alone is the sovereignty. You have no partners."

In Islam there are two types of pilgrim rituals. The first "lesser hajj," or *umrah*, is performed at any time of the year and involves two basic activities. First is the *tawaf*, or the sevenfold circumambulation of the Kaaba, a cube-shaped building draped in black and made from gray stone, approximately forty feet high. According to Islam, it is situated directly under the heavenly mosque used by the angels, and thus the spiritual axis of the world. Surrounded by a large courtyard that allows millions of pilgrims to walk around it, the Kaaba is the focus of the hajj to Mecca and a symbol of the Abrahamic covenant. Muslims pray in this direction their entire lives and finally see the Kaaba for the first time during this pilgrimage. According to tradition, the Kaaba was originally built by Adam and then rebuilt by Abraham and his firstborn son, Ishmael. As they circle the

Kaaba, pilgrims reach out to touch the Black Stone built into a corner of the building, by tradition given to Abraham and Ishmael by the angel Gabriel.

The second stage of the lesser hajj is the running, or *sa'y*, between two hills seven times in memory of Hagar and Ishmael. As the story goes, when Hagar and Ishmael were expelled from Abraham's house because of Sarah's jealousy, they were dying of thirst in the desert at Mecca until God miraculously provided them with water at the well of Zamzam. Through their running, the pilgrims reenact the running of Hagar to find water and her gratitude in God's provision through the well of Zamzam. Muslims believe that this water has miraculous healing properties, and they are allowed to drink from the spring and to take containers of the water home.

The second form of pilgrimage in the Islamic tradition, the "greater hajj," always occurs on three specific days of the twelfth month of the Islamic calendar known as Dhu'l-Hijja (Month of the Hajj). The greater hajj is, typically, the days during the year when pilgrims from all over the world converge on Mecca to fulfill the obligations of the fifth pillar. On the eighth day of the month, the whole company moves about five miles east of Mecca to the village of Mina, where they spend the rest of the day reciting *salat*, or formal prayers. On the ninth day they continue through the desert for another ten miles to the Plain of Arafat, where they participate in the "standing" ceremony, or *wuquf*, a pause that continues from noon to sunset. The standing ceremony is a form of silent meditation when pilgrims recollect the last judgment and Abraham's willingness to sacrifice his son Ishmael out of obedience to God. In Islam the belief is that participation in the standing ceremony wipes away sins and gives the pilgrim a new start in life.

Today a sermon is still preached at the nearby Mountain of Mercy, traditionally believed to be the site where Adam and Eve were reunited after their expulsion from paradise and the site where Muhammad preached his farewell sermon in 632. On the evening of the ninth day, pilgrims set out for Muzdalifa, where they collect small stones. On the tenth day of the month, the pilgrims travel back to Mina, where they throw seven stones at a *jamrah*, originally a pillar but now a wall, to symbolize the manner in which Abraham resisted the temptations of Satan to disobey God and not sacrifice his son Ishmael. Also on the tenth day, the Feast of Sacrifice, or *Eid-al-Adha*, the pilgrims in Mecca along with Muslims throughout the world sacrifice a sheep or a goat in memory of the animal God provided for the sacrifice in place of Ishmael. Typically, the food is shared in three portions: one-third for the family, one-third for neighbors, and one-third for the poor.

At the end of the greater hajj, pilgrims return to Mecca, change into their everyday attire, and cut their hair. Some will travel to Medina to visit the graves of Muhammad, Abu Bakr, and Umar, but it is not considered an official part of the greater hajj, and because of concerns about idolatry, pilgrims are urged not to kiss or touch the tombs. The rituals associated with the hajj are more focused on the traditions related to Abraham and the origins of monotheism than on Muhammad as the final prophet. Many pilgrims also return to Mecca for a final circling of the Kaaba.

It has been noted that the annual greater hajj is one of the largest gatherings of human beings in the world, similar to the Hindu Maha Kumbh Mela festival or the Roman Catholic jubilee pilgrimages to Rome.[16] Muslims also make sacred journeys to the tombs of the Shiite martyrs and Sufi mystics; the fourteenth-century Berber Muslim Moroccan explorer Ibn Battuta traveled to so many places that he came known as the "Traveler of Islam." Muslims share with other members of the Abrahamic faiths a tradition of pilgrimage to the Holy Land and consider Jerusalem to be the third holiest city on earth, after Mecca and Medina. The first followers of the Prophet Muhammad prayed facing Jerusalem before Mecca, and he is said to have paused on a hill of Jerusalem during his mystical night journey into heaven. According to some Islamic scholars, the rock was the spot where Muhammad ascended into heaven accompanied by the angel Gabriel to pray with Abraham, Moses, and Jesus. Today the Dome of the Rock and the al-Aqsa Mosque are considered the holiest sites in Jerusalem for Muslims, which is a source of considerable tension—the Dome of the Rock is built at the center of the Temple Mount, the site of the Jewish Second Temple, destroyed by the Romans in 70 CE. The holiest site for Jews is the Foundation Stone. Because Jewish prayers are forbidden on the Temple Mount, the tradition developed of praying at the Western Wall, as the point closest to the Foundation Stone.

In a similar way the town of Bethlehem on the West Bank, an important pilgrimage destination across the Abrahamic faiths, also serves as a challenge to interreligious tolerance. It is the site of Rachel's tomb, the birth of Jesus, and the place where Muhammad rested to pray on his night journey to Jerusalem from Mecca.

Bahá'í Pilgrimage

The holiest shrine of the Bahá'í faith is located at Acre in Israel, the burial site of the greatest prophet of the tradition. Bahá'u'lláh, who died in 1892, is considered to be the last in the series of great spiritual teachers, including Abraham, Moses, Zoroaster, the Buddha, and Jesus. The Bahá'í faith was founded in nineteenth-century Persia and today has over five million adherents around the world. During his time in Acre, Bahá'u'lláh visited Haifa and Mount Carmel four times. Eventually, land was purchased there to house the world headquarters and a major shrine; in 1909 the prophet's remains were buried there. Each day followers turn to face the burial site as they pray, and a pilgrimage to the site is considered to be one of the most important spiritual events of a lifetime. Bahá'ís who wish to make a pilgrimage must officially register and wait for several years until there is an opening for them to participate. The pilgrimage is formally structured to allow each pilgrim to meet other pilgrims, to participate in lectures and other presentations, and to view an extensive film on the religious tradition.

SECULAR PILGRIMAGE

The Russian author Maxim Gorky once wrote, "All of us are pilgrims on the earth."[17] In addition to the experience of religiously motivated pilgrimages we have looked at so far, it is important to note that those who consider themselves spiritual but not adherents of a particular religion, as well as agnostics, atheists, or thoroughly secular people, also participate in life passages and journeys that mirror the patterns of pilgrimage. Author James Harpur suggests that Disneyland is for many a place of "quasi-religious" pilgrimage, a journey to a different world where they can forget their daily concerns, enjoy togetherness with other pilgrims, buy souvenir "badges" of their experience, and then rejoin the outside world. Another example of secular pilgrimage offered by Harpur is the journey of California millionaire Dennis Tito as the first "space tourist" in 2001, when he spent a week aboard the International Space Station. As part of his journey, Tito underwent preparation and a demanding journey before he arrived at his sacred destination, the station over two hundred miles above the earth. Tito described the journey as the fulfillment of a lifelong dream as he "just came back from paradise" and returned to his life at home.[18]

Gideon Lewis-Kraus, in his narrative *A Sense of Direction*, writes about the importance of pilgrimage as a secular ritual for those people who do not stand in any particular tradition. Lewis-Kraus, the son of two rabbis who describes himself as a secularist, went on pilgrimage to three sites: Santiago de Compostela in northwestern Spain; the eighty-eight Buddhist temples on the island of Shikoku, Japan; and Uman, Ukraine, for

Rosh Hashanah at the site of the grave of Nachman of Bratslav, founder of the Bratslav Hasidic movement. On his journeys, Lewis-Kraus encountered both religiously motivated and secular people who were on pilgrimage for many of the same reasons. What bound them together were the experiences of "surprise and memory" on the road, as well as the need for physical endurance.

Artists of all sorts frequently refer to the power of pilgrimage in their lives and work. Singer and poet Patti Smith, in her memoir *Just Kids*, writes about her life as an aspiring artist in New York City and of how she walked through the city to visit sites associated with other great artists, such as following the spirit of Dylan Thomas to the Chelsea Hotel. Stephanie Paulsell, a professor at Harvard Divinity School, writes about how she followed in the footsteps of Virginia Woolf through Italy:

> I wanted to see that young writer more clearly and to understand how her engagement with religious art shaped her own artistic achievement.... I wanted to experience as closely as I could those moments when the shape of her vocation came into view. Woolf was genius; I am not. But when I tried to see through her eyes with the same quality of attention she brought to her pilgrimage, I felt my vision refreshed and my devotion to my work renewed.[19]

Bahkti-hop innovator MC Yogi, also known as Nicholas Giacomini, describes himself as a "working-class mystic" and composes music that combines sacred Hindu chant with urban hip-hop. He travels to India on pilgrimage with Amanda—his wife and creative partner—for spiritual and artistic inspiration, often visiting holy sites. Climbing to the mountaintop of Arunachala, considered by Hindus as one of South India's most sacred sites, was a high point of a recent pilgrimage. "It feels like you're standing on the center of a ray of light. The mountain pierced my heart and threw the doors open," Giacomini says. After climbing down the mountain, and leaving the recording studio, however, he was stuck with excruciating pain and collapsed on the floor. A voice came to him in his pain, saying that he needed to return to the mountain and that his work there was not finished. Unable to walk on his own, the singer and composer climbed the mountain again with the help of his friends. He was standing on his own by the time the group came full circle around the mountain. Giacomini refers to his experience as "a spiritual chiropractic adjustment." "That's the power of pilgrimage," he adds, "you go to a sacred place and release your pain." After spending three years in a reform school during his teens, MC Yogi took up yoga after a serious car accident. He believes that all people are on a spiritual path, whether or not they realize it. He also believes that he can best serve the world through his music:

> The miracle that we need will come when enough of us are willing to say, love is the bottom line, not only in our personal relationships but also in our political and social relationships. So if you ask me what we need to do: we need to seek in every way possible to become more loving people and then not shut up. Refuse to shut up. As I always say, God be with you—now go kick ass.[20]

Key to the nature of pilgrimage is the intention behind it, as well as the spirit of the journey. British novelist Pico Iyer believes that the dislocation experienced through physical travel is key "to being moved or taken out of yourself ... one of the easiest ways of jolting oneself out of habits and assumptions."[21] In an article titled "The Atheist Pilgrim," Stephen Bachelor, a self-avowed nonbeliever and ardent pilgrim to Buddhist holy places, explains the dynamic this way:

> "You put your body in these places. You hear the same birdsong. You breathe the same air. You are surrounded

by the same trees and foliage that the Buddha may have been surrounded by. And that, somehow, gets you as close as you ever can physically be to the source of the teachings that you are practicing in your daily life."[22]

Annie Leibovitz's extraordinary book of photographs *Pilgrimage* is not only a visual journey for the reader, but also a contemporary pilgrimage narrative for artistic renewal. The photographs are of places that Leibovitz chose to explore because they meant something to her, not because she was there on a work assignment. The journey began at Emily Dickinson's home in Amherst, Massachusetts, where Leibovitz traveled with a small digital camera. After the second stop of her journey, Niagara Falls, which she visited with her three children, the photographer began to make lists of sites, including places like Elvis Presley's home—Graceland—in Memphis, Thomas Jefferson's Monticello, Eleanor Roosevelt's Val-Kill Cottage at Hyde Park, and Marian Anderson's studio. At a site dedicated to Annie Oakley, Leibovitz found that the exhibition sharpshooter demonstrated her marksmanship by shooting through the center of a heart on a playing card. She made two trips to the Isle of Wight to pioneer photographer Julia Margaret Cameron's studio. Natural landscapes figured into the pilgrimage, too, such as Old Faithful.

Annie Leibovitz originally thought of making the pilgrimage with her partner Susan Sontag, but when Sontag died, the project was temporarily forgotten. She picked up on the pilgrimage idea once again, however, after "a pretty nasty year" and started writing down a list of places to photograph after her first visit to Niagara Falls. "And so I was off. I was off. I made a crazy list, and just sort of went down a different path," she says. "I loved, I loved doing this project. It's endless. Every single subject, you know, had mounds and mounds of history and thought. And I only touched lightly on a lot of it."[23] The stages of this pilgrimage included a yearning to explore without going on a work-related assignment, preparation through reflection and gathering a list of sites, the actual travel and exploration, and then returning home with a sense of restoration. "From the beginning when I was watching my children mesmerized over Niagara Falls, it was an exercise in renewal," said Leibovitz. "It taught me to see again."[24]

VIRTUAL PILGRIMAGE

One form of pilgrimage that has developed since the late twentieth century is the "virtual pilgrimage," or the experience of a sacred journey via the Internet. Although virtual pilgrimage has its detractors—those convinced that the effort of physical travel and bodily engagement is integral to an authentic pilgrimage experience—the fact remains that there is now at least one full generation that views spiritual experiences via the Internet as normative. Most virtual pilgrimage sites provide not only visual encounter, but also incorporate the ritual music, chant, and prayers of the community gathered there. Today it is possible to "travel" to many if not most of the major pilgrimage sites in this chapter, including Lumbini, Jerusalem, Rome, Taizé, and Iona. Hindu pilgrims unable to attend the world's largest religious festival in northern India can for the first time participate via the Internet in a computer-aided purification bath. Millions who cannot attend this forty-two-day Maha Kumbh Mela festival can participate virtually, and World Hindu Forum leader Vishnu Hari Dalmia has said that virtual pilgrimage is a reflection that India is moving on. "We don't take the bullock cart nowadays, there are ships, planes and trains. So it is fitting that in the new millennium, we are marrying the computer to religion."[25]

Even in traditions where the need for physical travel to a particular destination is stressed, virtual pilgrimage sites allow those who cannot travel or those who wish to revisit the experience to participate. For instance, there are several virtual hajj sites, some of which feature documentary video and some of which allow viewers to see portions of the hajj live.

Proponents of virtual pilgrimage argue that for those who embark on the journey with true intentionality, the experience of liminality and communitas characteristic of physical pilgrimage is present. Pilgrimage via cyberspace also allows pilgrims to experience the sense of dislocation from daily life through journey to a sacred place, and on these journeys the pilgrim encounters other virtual pilgrims with whom they form relationships via guest books and threaded discussions. Critics argue that while these aspects of virtual pilgrimage are authentic, such journeys are still by definition "mediated" experiences: "The pilgrim participates through images and material of someone else's making; and unlike 'real' physical pilgrimages, which involve time to reflect and digest, virtual pilgrimage must introduce states of transformation through the instantaneity of mouse-clicks," explains James Harpur.[26]

On the other hand, it is worth asking if our present models of pilgrimage are applicable to or even sufficient for understanding computer-mediated spiritual experiences. How are the fundamental elements of pilgrimage as put forward by Victor and Edith Turner, liminality and communitas, now changing because of the global technological expansion that has taken place since they first studied pilgrimage? Writer Mark W. MacWilliams suggests that virtual pilgrimage sites have four key characteristics as forms of religious travel. First, they create a "mythscape" or sacred geography using technology to re-create the received tradition of people, stories, shrines, temples, buildings, churches, and symbols as a real-life sacred space. Second, they act as an interactive audio and visual medium for experiencing the Divine. Third, they provide a liminal experience for the viewer. Lastly, they provide an opportunity for "pilgrims" to experience "virtual traveling communities" by connecting them to other virtual pilgrims from all over the world. These relations tend to be non-hierarchical and non-clerical, as is the case with pilgrimages taken in person.

MacWilliams further distinguishes among commercial pilgrimage websites designed to attract a broad spectrum of clientele, such as Holy Land Network (www.holylandnetwork.com); official sites, such as that of Lourdes (www.lourdes-france.com); and those that qualify as virtual pilgrimage sites by meeting his four criteria, such as the site for Croagh Patrick (www.croagh-patrick.com), which is Ireland's Holy Mountain. Interestingly, MacWilliams's analysis points to another question raised by the Turners' theory of classical pilgrimage. That is, are pilgrimages acts of communitas, or are they more often acts of individual piety that are sometimes undertaken with others? In his study, MacWilliams notes that pilgrims' postings are most often deeply personal in nature. "Perhaps," he writes, "virtual pilgrimage appeals to the person who reaches out in cyberspace in his solitariness to find some form of spiritual communion through communication."[27]

Despite the ever-changing nature of human societies and ongoing technological advances in the twenty-first century, the rituals of pilgrimage have proved to be remarkably adaptive and continue to speak to human hearts across cultures and traditions.

Questions for Your Own Exploration

1. Reflect on your own experience of pilgrimage. When have you experienced being a pilgrim? What motivated you to go on the journey? What did you discover? If you are getting ready to go on pilgrimage now, what are you seeking?

2. What images or words come to mind when you hear the word *pilgrimage*? What pilgrimage traditions most resonate with or challenge your own heritage or experience?

3. Reflect on the phrase *pilgrimage of life*. Some pilgrimages do not require physical travel. Have you ever taken such a journey? How does the phrase relate to your own experience?

CHAPTER 2

THE WAY OF
THE HEART

For where your treasure is, there your heart will be also.
                                        —*Gospel of Matthew 6:21*

There is a candle in your heart, ready to be kindled.
There is a void in your soul, ready to be filled.
You feel it, don't you?
                                        —*Rumi (1207–1273)*

The search for God
Is a very intimate enterprise
It is at the core
Of every longing in the human heart.
                                        —*Joan Chittister (b. 1936)*

The first thing all human beings hear in the womb is their
mother's heartbeat. The metaphor of a journey to the center
of the heart offers many insights into the nature of pilgrimage
in general and the inward journey of the pilgrim in particular.
One pilgrimage site that speaks to the journey to the center of
the heart is found in the small village of Chimayó, located in the

mountains of northern New Mexico. "If you are a stranger, if you are weary from the struggles in life, whether you have a handicap, whether you have a broken heart, follow the long mountain road, find a home in Chimayó."[1]

For two centuries Native American and Latino/a pilgrims have made the pilgrimage to El Santuario de Chimayó, some from hundreds of miles away, in search of healing and restoration. As the pilgrims come, some in visible pain, some on crutches, and others with photos of loved ones, votive candles, or notes of gratitude, they walk through a part of the shrine called *el pocito*, or "the little well," which contains adobe-colored clay considered to have curative powers. At the shrine, pilgrims scoop samples of the clay (known to some as "blessed earth") to take home with them. In fact, pilgrims take so many cups of clay with them to cover their heads, hearts, and knees that shrine officials have to replenish the well periodically with replacement clay that has been blessed. Along the walls of the shrine are testimonies to the healing that has occurred in this holy place. The walls are lined with images of the saints, including la Virgen de Guadalupe, patron of the Americas. "People discover that there is something special here when they come with an open heart and mind," says Jim Suntum, a priest at the shrine. "There is a kind of peace that is available here that you can't find anywhere else."[2]

Approximately 300,000 pilgrims visit the shrine at Chimayó every year, causing some to call it the "Lourdes of America." As the story goes, on Good Friday in 1810 a local friar was outside performing penances when he saw a great light streaming from a hillside near the Santa Cruz River. The friar began to dig on the spot and eventually discovered a crucifix with a black Christ. Three times the village priest attempted to install the crucifix in the town church, but three times it miraculously returned to the sacred space where it was discovered. Then a church was built on the hillside, but by 1816 it needed to be replaced by a larger shrine to accommodate the large numbers of pilgrims who came there. Next door to the Chimayó chapel is another shrine, Santo Niño de Atocha, built in 1856 and dedicated to prayers for sick children, especially infants. Here, too, pilgrims leave testimonies—photos, clothing, toys, personal notes—seeking healing and expressing gratitude for blessings received. According to Jerome Martinez y Alire of the St. Francis Cathedral in Santa Fe, the tradition of pilgrimage at Chimayó expanded greatly after World War II. Many young men from New Mexico were sent to the Philippines during the war because of their familiarity with the Spanish language, and ultimately, they were among the many troops and civilians forced on the Bataan Death March. Many prayed that if they survived to return home, they would walk from Albuquerque to Chimayó (approximately the one hundred miles of the Bataan Death March) in thanksgiving for their deliverance.

The Chimayó pilgrimage tradition remains strong today. Many of the pilgrims who travel there are not necessarily of the same religious tradition, and they are often not totally committed to the pilgrimage tradition or necessarily believe in miraculous healing. But they go on pilgrimage because they feel a longing in their hearts, and they are searching for something—perhaps divine love or inner peace, relief from a broken heart, or a more meaningful life—and they gain solace from belonging to a group of pilgrims along the way.

During the week before Easter each year, faith communities from across the state of New Mexico participate as part of a pilgrimage for peace. As one pilgrim observed, "I must tell you that I had always thought that pilgrimages were fraught with sacrifice and tribulation but instead it was absolutely one of the most uplifting experiences of my life. Picture, if you can, walking through the New Mexican countryside along narrow winding mountain roads ... silently praying for peace. And I am sure that if even for one moment only ... God heard us...."[3] Other pilgrims have been known to take the blessed earth home, hoping the miracles would extend to sacred spaces outside of Chimayó. Religion scholar Stephen Prothero writes of a visit to Chimayó when he was still in graduate school. Prothero, too, took some of the sacred earth home with him and kept it through the years and several moves. His experiences at the shrine taught him about the difference between pilgrimage and tourism, and the importance of the inward journey: "When, like the priest with the crucifix, I insisted on displacing the soil, on stuffing it away for future use in the privacy of my Cambridge apartment, I confirmed my status as tourist. Local folks, I suspect, know better."[4]

Pilgrimage, then, involves not only all five senses, but also the heart. The Talmud says, "God wants the heart." It is the heart that holds the body together. In antiquity, conventional wisdom believed that it was the heart that was the center of human intelligence and the seat of the soul. Augustine of Hippo wrote that the heart is a metaphor for our deepest and truest selves, and he frequently uses the image as a way to explain his own journey to God: "You have made us and directed us to yourself, and our heart is restless until it rests in you."[5]

"When we stop to become aware of the heart, we come to the mystery of life," writes Mary C. Earle.[6] Another writer on spirituality, Christine Valters Paintner, writes, "The heart is the place of receptivity, integration, and meaning-making. It is where thinking, feeling, intuition and wisdom come together. In this process we are called to nothing short of transformation." Painter notes that it is the "heart chakra" that is responsible for our ability to listen deeply to our inner sound in a way that leads to spiritual awakening. In yogic belief, ultimate reality emanates from this primal vibration within the heart, penetrating all matter and throughout creation. "This universal sound of the pulse of life and creation is manifested within us as the sound of our own heart beating. For thousands of years, this primal beat has been expressed by the beat of the drum."[7]

African American mystic and theologian Howard Thurman once said that "the longest journey is between the heart and the head."[8] As an educator he disparaged the modern tendency to separate the heart from the intellect. The heart is a source of nourishment for every cell of the body. In the body the heart is responsive to the needs of the whole: to pain and injury; to passion and beauty; to physical needs and to the external environment. In times of crisis, our hearts send extra support to parts of the body most affected and sometimes beat even harder in anger and in sorrow. It is also the heart that receives into itself depleted blood for replenishment. The heart is always connected and interdependent, always in relationship with other organs, and always part of a system. Ideally, the circulatory system is well organized, but at times the heart has to be adaptive and respond to unexpected events. According to Russian author Boris Vysheslavtsev, "The heart is the center not only of the consciousness but of the unconscious, not only of the soul but of the spirit, not only of the spirit but of the body, not only of the comprehensible but of the incomprehensible; in one word it is the absolute center."[9]

The sacred art of pilgrimage involves both an inward and outward journey. "We are not human beings on a spiritual journey. We are spiritual beings on a human journey," wrote French philosopher and Jesuit priest Pierre Teilhard de Chardin.[10] The pilgrim strives to hold both the inward and outward journey together, sometimes in tension, but always focused on the search for meaning, for the Divine. "Pilgrimage concerns the body as much as the mind and spirit; it bridges the concrete reality of physical life and the elusive abstraction of the holy," writes spiritual author Shirley du Boulay in *The Road to Canterbury*.[11] What most distinguishes the sacred art of pilgrimage from a tourist trip or hiking expedition, as beneficial as these are, is the characteristic inward journey, a turning of one's heart to the Divine, with the expectation of transformation on every level of being along the way. Benedict of Nursia, the founder of Western monasticism and author of the Benedictine Rule, used to advise his monks and nuns to "listen with the ear of their heart."[12] In other words, the pilgrim's first yearning is in the heart, deeply and inwardly, sometimes for years before the outward journey begins.

Pilgrims go on sacred journeys seeking nourishment and replenishment for every part of themselves. Even in relative solitude a pilgrim is always in relationship—with the self, with the Divine, with the natural environment, and with those they leave behind. Vaclav Havel, the great Czech leader and playwright, was motivated from his heart to do good for his people and the world. "The salvation of the human world lies nowhere else than in the human heart," he wrote.[13] The Latin root of the word *courage* is *cor*, which refers to the heart, also a symbol of love. In a similar way, to go on a journey as a pilgrim, to overcome the fear of the unknown, takes considerable courage. It is the heart that calls the pilgrim to go on the journey and to have the strength and courage to face what lies ahead. Dag Hammarskjold, secretary general of the United Nations, once wrote in his journal *Markings*, "The longest journey is the journey inward.... Wrestling with painful realities and injustices, and resisting the urge to be satisfied with the way our life is, or the way the world is, is at the heart of spiritual growth."[14]

PILGRIM NARRATIVES

Why do people go on pilgrimage? The answer is as varied as pilgrims themselves, although it is possible to discern patterns in the motivations. "Sacred place is 'storied place,'" writes scholar of American spirituality and sacred landscapes Belden C. Lane in *Landscapes of the Sacred*. Thus the stories of sacred travelers and the places they visit are some of the oldest stories of humankind, full of "saints and beasts that reach back into the collective memory of the people who dwell there." At a time when he was exhausted by professional commitments, Lane set out to travel throughout the United States, hoping to rediscover God through the beauty of the landscape. By his own admission, each time he set off, he hoped for some grand mystical experience in the heartland of America or on the banks of the mighty Mississippi River. Usually it took at least a day for him to adjust his expectations and to realize that all around him were simply trees, clouds, a river, and a thin line of geese flying across the sky. "Yet it is at this precise moment when I give up looking for the burning bush that my retreat usually begins."[15]

The genre of pilgrimage literature provides deep and diverse illustrations of the "journeys of the heart" of many historical, contemporary, and fictional pilgrims. "We need to renew ourselves in territories that are fresh and wild. We need to come home through the body of alien lands," writes author and pilgrim Phil Cousineau.[16] Fictional pilgrims capture our imaginations and inspire generations of pilgrims. In J.R.R. Tolkien's legendary novel *The Hobbit*, comfortable Bilbo Baggins feels that adventures are nasty and "make you late for dinner"—until he is unexpectedly visited by thirteen dwarves and a wizard. The experience changes Bilbo, he feels "something tookish" has come over him, and before he can have second thoughts ventures on a great quest.[17] The best-selling novels of Brazilian author Paulo Coelho revolve around pilgrimage-related themes. In *The Pilgrimage*, Coelho refers to pilgrimage as an experience of rebirth. "When you travel, you experience, in a very practical way, the act of rebirth," he writes. "You confront completely new situations, the day passes more slowly, and on most journeys you don't even understand the language the people speak. So you are like a child just out of the womb."[18] *The Pilgrimage* sets the stage for Coelho's subsequent work and draws on the story of his own pilgrimage walking El Camino de Santiago de Compostela. While walking this path, Coelho felt awakened not only to all the wars, hard times, and catastrophes on earth, but also to the human capacity for the miraculous when we come to claim the divine goodness that lives within. His pilgrimage guide, Petrus, taught him, Coelho writes, "without saying a word, that I would realize my dreams if I first discovered what I wanted to do with them."[19]

In another novel, *The Alchemist*, Coelho's central figure is a shepherd boy named Santiago who makes a pilgrimage from his home in Spain to the pyramids in Egypt in search of a great treasure. His encounters along the way, with a Gypsy woman, with a man who calls himself "King," and with an alchemist, turn a journey to find worldly treasure into a pilgrimage—"as a current of love rushed to his heart."[20] These stories provide vivid reminders of the motivations that encourage pilgrims to undertake inward journeys to the center of the heart, as well as the outward changes and experiences that stimulate meaning and growth.

Phil Cousineau writes, "Uncover what you long for and you will discover who you are."[21] Sometimes pilgrims are responding to a yearning to change their life or to see deeper meaning in current events. Robert C. Sibley, author of the recently published pilgrimage narrative *The Way of the Stars*, set out on his second pilgrimage on El Camino de Santiago de Compostela to honor a promise made to his son Daniel. Sibley writes that he wanted this second pilgrimage to confront his disbelief and reveal the Divine, but that was not what happened to him. Yet what was transformative about the experience was the time spent away from familiar preoccupations and the opportunity to refocus on the spiritual dimensions of his life. Although the pilgrimage did not make him a believer, he did discover what "more" there might be, and he was refreshed by the time he had to reflect on his "deepest cares and concerns."[22]

The human life cycle and the life changes brought about by family and other intimate relationships are strong motivators for pilgrimage and a popular focus of pilgrimage narratives. Elizabeth Gilbert's best-selling pilgrimage narrative, *Eat, Pray, Love*, records her pilgrimage to Italy, India, and Indonesia, which began when she was in her early thirties. After an acrimonious divorce and a crushing depression, Gilbert set out to find balance between her outward "successful" self and the anger, shame, and sorrow she felt within. Although she found human love and connection along the way, and that is certainly a significant part of her story, the narrative is also about a spiritual journey to the heart of the Divine. "I looked into my heart, at my own goodness, and I saw its capacity. I saw that my heart was not nearly full, not even after having taken in all those calamitous urchins of sorrow and anger and shame; my heart could easily have received and forgiven even more. Its love was infinite."[23]

Some pilgrims venture forth after a serious illness or when they know they have a terminal illness, as a ritual prelude to death. As the African American spiritual "Shall We Gather at the River" reminds us:

Soon we'll reach the silver river,
Soon our pilgrimage will cease;
Soon our happy hearts will quiver
With the melody of peace.

English novelist Jennifer Lash published her pilgrimage narrative *On Pilgrimage*, about her journey on El Camino de Santiago de Compostela, after cancer surgery. In chronic pain and unable to walk the rigorous pilgrim route, Lash took the train through France and into Spain, detailing her encounters and reflections along the way. A spiritual seeker who struggled with the notion of faith, she was both captivated and repelled by the religious images she encountered on her pilgrimage. Lash continued to write during her last illness, and she died two years after the book was published. Initially she had difficulty writing her pilgrim narrative, until she realized that she was letting her intellectual pride get in the way. At the end of the book Lash offers her realizations about faith: "It is something to do with leaps in the dark. Recognizing that truth is hidden."[24]

Some pilgrims undertake sacred journeys seeking healing. Some are looking for a physical cure, while others are searching for inner peace or consolation. After a health scare that landed him in the hospital, "spiritual voyeur" Eric Weiner set out on a multireligious spiritual journey that took him from California to Tibet, Turkey, China, Israel, and Las Vegas. An agnostic Jew, Weiner was motivated by an unexpected question from a nurse when he was in the hospital: "Have you found your God yet?" His pilgrimage narrative is about his far-flung search for a God he was not sure even existed. "God is not a set of missing car keys or an exit on the New Jersey Turnpike," writes Weiner. "He is not a destination. He's as close as our jugular, as the Muslims say." Eventually, he learned from his quest that the value of "good" religion is that it elevates people and makes them want to do good: "Indeed, that is the goal of all religion, all *good* religion: to transform the most repulsive parts of ourselves into something worthy not only of acceptance, but of love. 'To make our darkness conscious,' as Jung puts it.'"

Weiner emerged from his pilgrimage affirmed in his knowledge of the "primacy of the human heart." He also returned with an experience of a loving God, Jewish in foundation, supported by Buddhism, with the heart of Sufism, the simplicity of Taoism, the generosity of Franciscans, and a hedonistic streak from the Raëlians, or followers of the world's second-largest UFO religion.[25]

Historically, many pilgrimages are undertaken as an act of penance or out of the need for forgiveness. Some pilgrims undertake a sacred journey to honor a vow, in thanksgiving for blessings or miracles received, or in an effort to seek divine guidance. *The Way of the Pilgrim* is the English title of a nineteenth-century Russian pilgrimage narrative about a seeker who goes looking for someone to teach him to pray. His inner journey begins when he hears the words of Saint Paul to "pray without ceasing," and he travels widely to churches and monasteries seeking spiritual enlightenment. The pilgrim finally meets a *starets*, or holy man—in this case, an elder at a Russian monastery and a venerable teacher with the ability to look into the hearts of people he had never previously met. The *starets* tells the pilgrim to look into his heart and teaches him the Jesus Prayer, "Lord Jesus Christ, have mercy upon me, a sinner." To the pilgrim, the Jesus Prayer reveals the "inner secret of the heart" and the "knowledge of the speech of all creatures." "In no great length of time I felt that the prayer somehow was beginning to move into my heart," writes the pilgrim. "That is it seemed that as it beat normally my heart began to form the words of the prayer inside itself with every heartbeat.... I stopped saying the prayer vocally and began to listen carefully to my heart speaking."[26]

At times, pilgrims set out on pilgrimage at the invitation of another, such as a trusted friend or a spiritual guide. Puritan John Bunyan's *The Pilgrim's Progress*, first published in 1678, is a scholarly classic of English pilgrimage literature, written while the author was in prison for preaching without a license. An allegory of the believer's struggle to live the Christian life, it describes the pilgrimage of a hero named Christian as he is led from the City of Destruction via the Slough of Despond, the Hill of Difficulty, the Valley of the Shadow of Death, through Vanity Fair, over the River of the Water of Life, and eventually into the Celestial City. Almost three hundred years later, in response to *The Pilgrim's Progress*, notable Oxford don and author C. S. Lewis wrote about his own spiritual journey and titled it *The Pilgrim's Regress*. In his pilgrim narrative, Lewis reveals that he is discontented with the philosophies of his time and with institutional Christianity, yet at the same time he is drawn to a belief in God. "When you reach the thing you were desiring, if it doesn't satisfy you, it was not what you were desiring," he writes.[27]

Others believe that to set out on pilgrimage is their response to a sacred call, a sign of spiritual devotion, or religious zeal to visit a particular holy place and experience it personally. Some pilgrims find within themselves the strong desire to be close to a place recognized as holy or sacred, in response to external events. Howard Thurman, who was raised in the Deep South during the Jim Crow era, said that he did not realize the extent of the worldwide oppression against people of color like himself until he made his own pilgrimage to India. The experience taught him about what it was like to "wrestle with hate" and the "complete futility" that people feel when they are aware of the extent of imperialism. In a similar vein, Hermann Hesse, the German-Swiss author of *Siddhartha*, the story of a young Brahmin's search for enlightenment after meeting with the Buddha, was moved by the events of World War I to write about "the way within," or the road into the interior self, for an audience disoriented by the uncertainties of the political realities that surround them.

The stages of life also intersect with pilgrimage. Whether in young adulthood, middle adulthood, or retirement, some pilgrims find that they have outgrown their lives and seek the next pathway. In *Traveling with Pomegranates: A Mother-Daughter Story,* novelist Sue Monk Kidd and her daughter Ann Kidd Taylor take a pilgrimage to the sacred sites in Greece and France. Both women seek to redefine themselves and to rediscover each other. Kidd is in the midst of a creative dry spell, aware of aging, and longing to reconnect with her adult daughter. Taylor, a recent college graduate, is heartbroken, battling depression, and wondering what to do with the rest of her life. The pilgrimage experience fuels the creativity and deepens the insights of both women—Taylor returns to write a travel book and Kidd to what will become a best-selling novel, *The Mermaid Chair*. "Images well up in me more spontaneously," Kidd writes, "trailing along a stream of ideas, memories, feelings, and symbols, and I feel connected to a sourcelike place in myself."[28]

Swiss psychologist Carl G. Jung wrote about "ancestral memories," or the need for our souls to pay attention to the paths of our ancestors, who can inform our own journeys, especially during the second half of life. Thus, journeys to the cities, homes, and burial sites of our forebears are an important form of pilgrimage. Some go hoping something profound will happen to them; others go before, after, and during times when momentous personal decisions or threshold events are pressing on them to make changes in a relationship or work. The yearning on the part of some pilgrims to rediscover or reclaim lost parts of themselves is often a powerful motivation behind pilgrimage. Could another motivation for pilgrimage be about the recognition of a dream unfulfilled? For some pilgrims, the journey is an act of moral significance and the culmination of a lifetime of experiences; others are motivated by the need to alleviate their grief or lighten their depression.

Writer and actor Ted Swartz was on his way toward becoming a Mennonite pastor when he met his "comedic soul mate" Lee Eshleman, and for the next twenty years the two men created comedy shows and carved out a living in the performing arts. It was through acting classes and productions that Swartz discovered mystical and spiritual life for the first time, as well as the power of laughter as a healing art and a "sacred space." Yet after his collaborator's suicide in 2007, Swartz struggled for years with grief, anger, and guilt:

> Laughter never stopped being a sacred space; it just took awhile for me to find that space again.... Art, theater, and laughter were the barometers and light posts back from my own depression. While humor remains the launch point for all of my work, it is different now. There is a depth, a shadow, a perception only earned through grief and determination.[29]

Obviously, these motivations for pilgrimage are not exclusive. Many pilgrims set forth with a number of these motivations intertwined; others find themselves starting a sacred journey with one set of reasons in mind only to find them changing along the way.

JUNG AND IMAGES OF PILGRIMAGE

Carl Jung's theories concerning the relationship of images to the unconscious are relevant to an examination of the place of the inward journey in the experience of pilgrimage. Jung believed that the human psyche thinks, primarily, in images, or pictures that are reproduced by the environment of our imagination and represent the human psyche. Here "the psyche" refers to the whole of the human personality, both conscious and unconscious. The pilgrimage of life is made up of many such defining images, which are found in our feelings, dreams, sounds, smells, people, and places and symbolically serve as windows to our deepest selves. Only after first experiencing images can we move on to the conceptual and abstract. Jung was concerned that many people had lost touch with their images, their inner symbolic lives, and thus become too rational to fulfill their roles "as one of the actors in the divine drama of life."[30]

Images are an integral part of the inward spiritual journey, and through them we can discover much about what lies at the center of our lives. The notion of our inward spirituality as part of a "journey" is in itself symbolic of the experience of pilgrimage, because the image of journey typically connotes transitions or passages that are transformative and therefore key to our ongoing development as whole persons. One example of an important symbol related to pilgrimage and the spiritual life is the sphere or circle, commonly used to represent wholeness or completeness. Jung called the circle image *mandala*, which is the Sanskrit word for "circle." The sacred circle is a universal symbol, and circular patterns are found in art and dance in many religious traditions, including earth religions, indigenous religions, the Celtic tradition, and Asian. The mandala focuses attention and organizes patterns of meaning around the center. In this way, the image of a pilgrimage is a journey to the center of the heart and is associated with the concept of the journey inward. Mystics often refer to the journey to the center as a way of explaining union with God. In this sense, pilgrimage then creates a sacred space where the human and the Divine meet.

For Carl Jung, all of human life points to the center as both the goal and the focus of human development—it is a sacred space and the source of human meaning and orientation. Reclaiming or restoring the sacred center is therefore a means of healing and reorientation. Anthropologists Victor and Edith Turner explained pilgrimage as an outward journey that sets in motion an inward journey to the center. Although the exterior aspects of each pilgrimage are unique in terms of images, all pilgrimages have in common the inward journey to the center of the heart. Pilgrimage is an especially powerful experience: through it men and women become "dis-oriented" by leaving their typical daily lives for a time and then are symbolically brought into sacred space as they journey inward. Their gradual reorientation occurs as they begin the journey home. While many pilgrims begin a sacred journey thinking it is their own idea, they soon develop awareness that they were called to an inward journey even before they set forth.

Jung also believed that the purpose of religious symbols was to point people toward the spirit of the Divine that lives within human experience. Once organized religion gets too codified or too dogmatic, he thought, it pulls people away from their inward journey, and they lose touch with the awareness that the Holy dwells within them. This awareness is a key aspect of compassion, for out of the awareness that God dwells within us comes the ability to practice compassion for ourselves and others. If we can begin to believe that God dwells within us and have compassion for ourselves, we can then become aware of the ways God similarly dwells in others and start to practice compassion for them as well. The closer our inward journey moves to the center of the heart, the more we can see the Divine in all of creation. The more we experience the world around us as porous, the more we are open to the needs of the world.

Just as the outward journey requires an inward journey, so the inward journey makes demands on the pilgrim's outer world. For instance, when sixteenth-century Spanish mystic Teresa of Avila's inward journey was focused on the symbol of an "interior castle," she started to build castles out of wood or stone. For some pilgrims, these "mirrors" of the inward journey are symbolized through journal writing, photography, drawing, or other artistic endeavors that tell the story of their inward journey. Some pilgrims find themselves visiting sites that represent an aspect of their inward journeys, such as the homes or graves of ancestors, places of life's turning points, such as marriages or deaths, or sites of personal tragedy. Some pilgrims draw mandalas, construct home altars, or engage in other spiritual practices that reflect their inward journey.

In this way, the pilgrimage differs from tourist trips or sight-seeing expeditions. The destination of the pilgrim is not a place of relaxation or entertainment; it is not for cultural exploration per se. A pilgrim's goal is transformation that requires rigorous and intentional psychological and spiritual work, often in the context of arduous travel experiences.

In his book *Mystics and Zen Masters*, Thomas Merton, who is considered one of the great spiritual leaders of the twentieth century, interpreted the "geographical pilgrimage" as a "symbolic acting out" of the inward journey. "The inward journey," he wrote, "is the interpolation of the meanings and signs of the outer journey. One can have one without the other. It is better to have both."[31] For some pilgrims, the inward journey is integral to an outward journey during an experience of sacred travel, to a distant or local holy place. For other pilgrims, it is the desire for the outward journey to a faraway place, the hope and excitement of the trek, that is most pronounced at the onset; there can be little sense of the inward journey that will soon emerge. For others, the journey to the center of the heart is primarily an inward one, a liminal experience and contemplative practice conducted in familiar environments and occupations, yet undertaken with an underlying sense of separation, transition, and incorporation. As poet David Whyte suggests, "To set out boldly in our work is to make a pilgrimage of our labors, to understand that the consummation of our work lies not only in what we have done, but who we have become while accomplishing the task."[32]

Lastly, there are pilgrims, including many mystics and monastics, who take a broad view and consider all of life to be a pilgrimage to the heart of the Divine. African American religious and civil rights leader Martin Luther King Jr. voiced a similar belief about the process of discovering our identity: "Identity is a lifelong vocation. It is a ceaseless process. We rework our identities as we traverse the seasons of life. It is also intimately relational and communal. There is an aspect of each of us in each significant past and present relationship and experience. The tapestry of life contributes to our respective identities."[33]

Another aspect of the psyche as described by Carl Jung that is helpful to an understanding of the inward journey is his concept of the *shadow*, or the negative aspects of our personality. Our "shadow self" is made up of those qualities that we are ashamed of or prefer not to recognize. It is within our shadow, or the dysfunctional and destructive aspects of our personality, that we confront our brokenness and need for healing. Premodern pilgrimage narratives likely reveal instances where a pilgrim is confronted with evil, with the figure of the devil himself, or with some other destructive force. Like John Bunyan's "Christian," the pilgrim must then do battle, both outwardly and inwardly, with these evil forces, which may dissipate at times but are never wholly absent.

In the Middle Ages, even places of such rare physical beauty as the great cathedrals of Europe included devils and gargoyles in their design, images that looked down on the hapless pilgrims below. It is easy to dismiss these images in early pilgrimage narratives as evidence of superstition in an age that many considered less enlightened than their own. Yet at the same time, do we really know the Divine in a deeper way today? In contemporary pilgrimage narratives, it is not uncommon to read about the pilgrim's "battle" or struggles with self-destructive forces, such as addiction, fear, depression, shame, self-hatred, or dysfunctional relationships. Perhaps the shadow side of the inward journey for today's pilgrims is quite similar to that of the ancients, although today we explain our demons using more contemporary language and different visual images.

Jung characterizes our confrontation with the shadow as the descent into the unconscious, those aspects of the personality of which we are not fully aware. One of the recurring themes of pilgrimage narratives is the unexpected event that occurs along the way. A pilgrim often sets out with feelings of control and a predetermined course, yet invariably the unexpected happens; either the inward journey, the outward journey, or both change, often in profound ways. Unexpected or traumatic outward events steer the pilgrim in another direction, or the inward journey reveals feelings or issues that were initially unknown.

Key to the pilgrim's inward journey is a growing sensitivity to the inconsistencies and destructive aspects of the shadow. Significantly, the unconscious is the place at the center where, according to Jung, we are the most open to experience the Divine. "There is no birth of consciousness without pain," Jung writes.[34] During the first stages of pilgrimage, the pilgrim is often relieved by a break with the ordinary, relishing the freedom of the road. But this enthusiasm wanes as the pilgrim confronts these inner forces. Our shadow side, our inner demons, can have a great deal of control over us and, when confronted, do not always quietly go. The pilgrim's paradox is that going forward means moving inward, which brings with it a painful confrontation with what is unfamiliar and threatening, yet trying to stand still will also cause pain. Both paths bring stress and strain, yet only one of them leads to the center. "Knowing others is wisdom. Knowing oneself is enlightenment,"[35] wrote the ancient philosopher and father of Taoism, Lao Tzu.

Sadly, Jung notes, for some people the journey never begins, and rather than confront their shadow, they choose never to delve into the deeper questions of life. For others, these inner demons obscure their own giftedness, and they refuse to take responsibility for their own journey. Healing and transformation occur, however, with deep reflection on these inner images, despite the strain, and emerge with a new state of consciousness. As French existentialist Gabriel Marcel once wrote, "All life holds within itself a promise of resurrection."[36] Through the confrontation and struggle with the shadow, the pilgrim emerges transformed and renewed.

THE STAGES OF PILGRIMAGE

As we look back on the history of pilgrimage as a human phenomenon, it is possible to discern patterns in the experiences of sacred travelers. There are several stages to any pilgrimage, and the chief advantage in knowing about them is to assist other pilgrims on the road ahead. French anthropologist Arnold van Gennep studied the rituals of the rites of passage from childhood to adulthood along with the personal, social, and psychological changes that occur during the journey. These three phases mirror the progress of the pilgrim's journey, although in addition to the three factors he names, many pilgrims are also motivated by a spiritual force that is interwoven with the other forces that inspire their journey.

The first stage is one of *separation*, in which the pilgrim discerns the motivations encouraging—for some, driving—her to make the journey. Ancient and medieval pilgrims realized that their journeys were filled with physical danger, as well as intense internal anxiety and questioning. They knew people died along the way. Traditionally, commitment to a pilgrimage was not something entered into lightly. Moreover, in the West, the decision to go on pilgrimage was not only an individual commitment, but also a community event. An individual's family and religious community were part of the discernment process and provided financial support, encouragement, and prayer. In Christian pilgrimage, the church also had a role, through endorsing the pilgrims and providing blessings, as they were sent off from their home communities.

The second stage, called *transition*, begins when the pilgrim has separated from life as she used to know it and begins the reflective practice of making meaning from these new experiences. This is the point in the journey where the pilgrim enters a liminal state, experienced by many as feelings of disorientation or ambiguity. Although pilgrimage puts the sacred traveler in touch with the Divine, many pilgrimages are also journeys into the unknown. At this middle stage of transition, the pilgrim finds himself on a threshold: he no longer connects with his previous way of being but has not yet incorporated a new way of being into his identity.

The third stage is one of *incorporation*, where the pilgrim integrates new learning and new ways of being into her life and journey home. Sometimes this experience of incorporation brings joy for all concerned, but more often than not, returning pilgrims, along with those closest to them, are challenged to make adjustments and build relationships anew. When a pilgrim returns a dramatically changed person, it is not easy for those close to her who did not have the same experience to relate to the "new normal." For some pilgrims, it takes a long time to fully realize the implications of their inward journey.

Shirley du Boulay writes about her experiences as a pilgrim on the road from Winchester to Canterbury in England. In *The Road to Canterbury*, she explains how her incorporation after the pilgrimage focused on her journey experience and her daily life back home:

I had been changed by this pilgrimage, but I do not expect to know how for a long time. Though on this Sunday morning I knew the pilgrimage had reached some sort of completion, it has not ended. This symbolic microcosm of the inner journey has to find its resonances with the longer day-to-day pilgrimage.... This pilgrimage from Winchester to Canterbury had not ended on arrival any more than life ends with death. But I did feel that I understood a little bit better where the sacred place is to be found.[37]

The three categories that van Gennep developed in his work on rites of passage and the study of liminal experiences became the basis of Victor and Edith Turner's work on pilgrimage. Although scholars who study pilgrimage today have published variations on Van Gennep's stages of pilgrimage, the basic structure of *separation, transition, incorporation* remains fairly consistent. Joseph Campbell, a scholar of mythology, describes the pilgrimage as a hero's journey, characterized by a rupture with the past, the experience of an ordeal, and then a return to daily life. Campbell frames the pilgrimage sequence in the three steps of *separation, invitation, return.*[38]

Psychotherapist Jean Dalby Clift and theologian Wallace B. Clift concur. After studying pilgrimage, they concluded that it should be considered as archetypal in the Jungian sense—that is, a pattern of universal human experience:

The person who is gripped by an archetypal symbol feels as though in contact with some mysterious and irresistible power or overwhelming compulsion, highly charged, luminous, life changing. The pilgrimage experience is one of those human experiences that continue to be manifested. Varying very likely with each individual, it is still found, in some sense, *meaningful* and often has overtones of a "religious" experience.[39]

Their work describes the universal human experience of pilgrimage in stages similar to those we saw earlier and explains why many people feel an overwhelming compulsion to set out as pilgrims. At the outset, during the separation phase, some pilgrims are disoriented or unclear about the path they are taking, yet also feel a compulsion to pursue it. Words from Rainer Maria Rilke's *Letters to a Young Poet* ring true: "Be patient toward all that is unsolved in your heart. And try to love the questions themselves."[40] Other pilgrims feel an inward certainty about the journey they are about to undertake, but this sense of clarity at the same time confuses or angers those around them. The middle phase, or the liminal stage, is experienced by some as freedom from the confines of "normal" life and home as a new sense of identity emerges.

This newfound freedom encourages camaraderie among pilgrims who have had the same experience, but the potential misuse of this stage—as Jung would say, the shadow side of pilgrimage—has contributed to the condemnation of the practice throughout history. The last phase, the return home, as the Clifts point out, also has universal repercussions. "Pilgrims all over the world attest to the profundity of their experience, which often surpasses the power of words."[41] For example, integral to the inward journey is the sense of deep yearning, or longing, characterized by some as "the call" to a search for greater meaning or purpose in life. There are times in many adult lives when we feel that what we are doing is fine, we might even be considered successful, but is it really doing what is right for us? Some experience a vacuum all their lives until the call is in some way made manifest. Pilgrimage is about the search to recognize that call or to find ways to integrate it into adult life. Theologian Frederick Buechner writes about call as "the place where your deep gladness meets the world's deep need."[42] In this way a sense of call evokes our passions; it is not simply about talents or a job but evokes a sense of purpose. For some, following a sense of call is about religious or spiritual experience—the belief that God is calling at a particular time and place and that it is a good idea to take notice.

For others, the sense of call is about living toward a higher purpose, moving nearer to an ideal, and contributing to a higher good. In both cases, I would argue, a sense of call emerges from within us. It is not about an external life force dictating what we should be or do with our lives. Rather, it is about a gradual turning from within and an emerging understanding about our authentic selves and what we are called to do with our lives. As Quaker educator and activist Parker Palmer writes, "What a long time it can take to become the person one has always been. How often in the process we mask ourselves in faces that are not our own."[43] The Divine Light shines from within our hearts when we find the answer to this call. Even more important, if we are genuinely called to do something, we also will have the means and skills to answer that call. We are never asked to be someone else or take on a call that is not our own.

Other key characteristics of the inward journey are pain and struggle. Pilgrims are known to suffer fear, disorientation, and discomfort in both their inward and outward journeys. "Fear is not a bad place to start a spiritual journey," writes spiritual author Kathleen Norris in *Dakota*. "If we know what makes us afraid, we can see more clearly that the way out is through the fear."[44] While there may be times that a pilgrim on the road is comfortable, the goal of the journey is more about meaning than it is about taking a respite from life's challenges. Throughout history, pilgrimages have been about navigating rough terrain in both the outward and inward journeys. The need for physical endurance brings a heightened awareness to the pilgrim that assists her in the process of self-discovery and reinforces the importance of the journey. Rather than a glorification of needless suffering, the emphasis on suffering in the pilgrimage tradition is more about the recognition that we all suffer, and because of those experiences, we can become more compassionate toward the suffering of others, as well as the suffering of the world.

In his book *The Alchemist*, Paul Coelho tells a tale about an Andalusian shepherd boy named Santiago who yearns to travel away from his home in search of wealth but who learns to listen to his heart instead. "'My heart is afraid that it will have to suffer,' the boy told the alchemist one night as they looked up at the moonless sky. 'Tell your heart that the fear of suffering is worse than the suffering itself. And that no heart has ever suffered when it goes in search of its dreams.'"[45]

In a similar vein, Jean and Wallace Clift, in their study of pilgrimage, note that "difficulty of access" is a common motif in pilgrimage narratives. Sometimes this difficulty of access is because of a remote pilgrimage location. Sometimes it is the physical difficulties pilgrims encounter on the road, such as aching feet, strained backs, unfamiliar food, and rough accommodations. Sometimes pilgrims even approach holy places on their knees. On another level, "the difficulty of access" is a symbol of the fact that change is painful and that all human growth requires effort and movement away from the more comfortable status quo. Jung called the inward journey of pilgrimage the "path of individuation" in which we discover our unique selves. It is the journey of a lifetime, with difficult challenges along the way. In this way, the pilgrimage to remote and faraway regions is symbolic of the inner journey.

Other common motifs that occur across pilgrimage narratives include the wearing of special dress that symbolizes the distinct nature of the journey, such as ritual head coverings and prayer shawls for Jewish pilgrims, the simplicity and purity of dress suggested for Buddhist pilgrims, and the pilgrim scarves and badges worn by Christian pilgrims. Water rituals, as symbols of transformation, refreshment, or cleansing, are characteristic of many pilgrimage journeys. Water, a symbol of the unconscious in Jungian thought, is also symbolic of the beginning of all life, as each of us came out of the waters of the womb to be born. Another motif discerned by Jean and Wallace Clift throughout pilgrimage accounts echoes the thoughts of other writers— namely the spirit of community among pilgrims as a source of transformation. Similarly, the Clifts found that pilgrims tend both to leave something behind at pilgrimage sites and to take something home that is symbolic of the journey.

A final motif common to many pilgrimage stories is the sense that sacred sites exude a sense of "presence," where God, the gods, or the beauty of nature dwells. These motifs constitute the shape of the archetype of pilgrimage and point to its meaning and value to the human community.

SPIRITUALITY OF THE HEART

Many living religious traditions today reflect on the spirituality of the heart and stress its importance for the inward journey. There is an old Hasidic saying: "Carefully observe the way your heart draws you, and then choose that way with all your strength." In spiritual terms, when we speak of the "heart" of a person, we are referring to the inner self, the interior life, the deepest longings, and the fondest hopes, though we all find ourselves at dis-*heartened* times by suffering and struggle. It is through our hearts that we experience divine love and renewal. Thus people who are said to be "heartless" have lost touch with their inner core and shared humanity. It is through heart-to-heart talks that we communicate to our depths; it is with open hearts that we are able to love others and to feel greater compassion for the whole world. Joan Chittister, a Benedictine sister and the author of many books on the spiritual life, believes that what is most central to the pilgrim's inner journey is the desire to grow spiritually and to come to know the Divine in a deeper way, through pain and struggle, as well as through peace and joy. The journey to the center of the heart takes the desire and commitment on the part of a pilgrim to move to another level of insight, rather than contentment with less demanding practices. "It depends on the willingness to let God lead us through the deserts of a lifetime, along routes we would not go, into the Promised Land of our own lives," writes Chittister.[46]

Joan Chittister's spirituality is Benedictine in character, based on the idea of the *monastery of the heart*. Two fundamental insights of Benedictine spirituality claim that the presence of God, or the Divine, is everywhere, and that we meet the Divine (or, for Christians, we meet Christ) through other people. The Divine is active in our daily lives, in relationships, in family life, in work, in community, and in prayer and meditation. Prayer in the Benedictine tradition concentrates on the inner movements of the heart as the person grows in self-knowledge and in deeper awareness of God. Spiritual maturity, then, is a process of continuing growth and conversion of the heart. The Benedictine tradition also stresses that genuine spirituality is anchored in community and encourages all pilgrims to share their spiritual lives together and to learn from one another.

As an experienced spiritual guide, Chittister is aware that in terms of the inward journey, no one size fits all. Instead it will vary depending on the temperament, character, and life experiences of the pilgrim. For some pilgrims, the sacred is most easily experienced in nature, far away from the noise and busyness of cities and towns, while others gravitate to the holiness of temples, shrines, churches, and other holy places. Still others see the Divine in the faces of people and in the experience of community. For some pilgrims, the inward journey is replenished through solitude and time apart, while others gain courage for the journey through close association with fellow pilgrims. Throughout the history of spirituality, pilgrims are often reminded of the need for *balance*, meaning a combination of solitude and community as part of the pilgrimage journey.

This Benedictine spirituality of the heart is an ancient tradition that has nourished pilgrims for over fifteen hundred years.

The Benedictine Rule of Life assumes that the journey is a life-long evolutionary process; in this sense, the inward journey to the heart never ceases but is intrinsic to the whole of life. Part of Benedictine spirituality's durability as a wisdom tradition is due to its adaptability across times and cultures, its sense of moderate asceticism, its understanding of the need for human beings to do useful work, and its desire to welcome seekers from everywhere. Chittister refers to this spirituality as a potential monastery "without walls," or a monastery of the heart, an ancient pathway to the Divine. "We are all seekers of the God who is here but invisible to the blind eye; who calls to us but is unheard by those who do not listen; who touches our lives wherever we are, but is unfelt by those whose hearts are closed to the presence of God—who is everywhere, in everyone, at all time." she writes.[47] Asking hard questions in the company of fellow pilgrims is at the heart of the deepening quest, the broadening of understanding, and the journey beyond our limited understanding.

Chittister writes that *a conversion of heart* occurs when we integrate all the parts of our lives toward seeking the Divine, just as the pilgrim focuses her heart—all she is—on the quest for the sacred. For Chittister, conversion of the heart means that nothing, ultimately, is secular, or left out of divine consideration. "The will of God in life does not come in straight lines, or clear signs, or certain choices," she writes.[48]

Chittister warns that there are many obstacles along the inward journey, but for the sake of growth we must be willing to persevere in order to be transformed, to reach our potential. She views the inward journey as a lifelong pilgrimage, the search for a God that is already alive in every human person, but which we need to learn to experience more deeply as a constant presence. The spirituality of the heart is ultimately about abundance; it is a call to learn to love more deeply and fully and to embrace the love of the Divine as freely given. One of the most difficult spiritual tasks for many people is to believe that, far from being judged unworthy, their hope lies in a God that loves them infinitely, just as they are. "To those seekers who find their souls a Monastery of the Heart," Chittister writes, "the possibility of happiness is unbounded, the promise of fulfillment eternal."[49]

We live in a world today where there is a deep hunger for the journey to the center of the heart. For most of our lives, we are pressured to turn our focus outward to meet the demands of the world, and that is what most of us do, at least until persistent dissatisfaction or some traumatic event challenges us to take stock of our inward journey and find our authentic selves. It is often when the outside world fails us that we realize that the source of real resilience lives within. It is through the resources of the inward journey that we survive change, cataclysmic events, and even death itself.

One of the key differences between Western and Asian perspectives on spirituality is based on where the source of the Divine is to be found. While Westerners believe that God (or the Divine) is located above us or around us, from an Asian perspective the Divine lives within the heart. That is why much of Western religious practice is focused on outward observance, on *doing*, while the spiritual practice of Asian religions tends to focus instead on the inward journey, on *being*. I am not suggesting in any way that Westerners should do without outward spiritual practices, especially since our strong prophetic tradition emphasizes involvement with the world outside and justly challenges us to respond to the suffering in our midst. Indeed, without this prophetic tradition, many would train themselves to ignore the suffering around them, choosing comfortable "unknowing" instead. It is through our outward focus in the West that we practice social engagement in order to feed the hungry, respond to natural disasters, and support the most vulnerable in our societies.

The world's suffering will not disappear any time soon. However, it is through the inward-focused mystical traditions found in both Eastern and Western religions that we are encouraged to develop our hearts and, in doing so, enrich our outward practice of compassion as well. From the perspective of spiritual growth, the outward journey of action in the world and the inward journey of the heart are not binary opposites; they are meant to work together and to bring balance to the self. Through the process of pilgrimage, many seek to achieve greater balance by realigning the outer world with the inward journey, and vice versa. Carl Jung believed that it is the task of spirituality to "reconcile and reunite the opposites in the individual through a special development of the human soul."[50] His insights are relevant today to the many people who wish to embrace spirituality yet do not find their hearts enriched by organized religion. Some do turn to Eastern practices, such as meditation and yoga; others gravitate toward psychotherapy or philosophy. The point here is that human wholeness is achieved only when we take seriously the inward journey and bring it into better balance with our responsibility to engage the world.

Camaldolese monk Cyprian Consiglio writes about what he calls "the universal call to contemplation," or "prayer in the cave of the heart." Consiglio believes that people all over the world are longing for something more, looking for new ways to explore ancient truths, and searching for the means to grow in their inner lives. All people are called to contemplation, not only monks, nuns, or the professionally religious: "It is the reason why zendas and ashrams and yoga centers are full."[51] He also believes that an outgrowth of this universal call to contemplation is the fact that people with deeper inner lives tend to be more adept at experiencing their commonality with other human beings and with the planet, influenced by yoga, Zen Buddhism, and Eastern Christianities.

Consiglio advocates for a spirituality that recognizes the entirety of the human person—body, mind, and spirit—with the goal of total transformation of our whole selves. Each part of the body contributes to the way we know the Divine. The body learns by gathering information through the senses; the soul through our use of the intellect; and the spirit through mystical intuition that transcends consciousness and rational processes. Consiglio writes about the resurrection of Jesus as "matter transformed," whereby the Divine lives within and our bodies are no longer limited by space or time. "This is the transformation that is taking place in our own bodies. This is the real goal of all our meditative techniques and methods: the transformation of the body and the soul by the power of the indwelling Spirit of God."[52] In this way pilgrimage, too, can be seen as a practice of the body, mind, and spirit, with a goal of the transformation of the whole human person.

One of the limitations of using the image of the "heart" for the inward journey, as we do in the West, is that we often associate the word with romantic love and the emotions, tending to see "matters of the heart" in sentimental ways fairly far removed from the real grit of human relationships. From the perspective of Eastern religions, the meaning of *heart* is much broader. For example, in the Eastern Orthodox tradition, the heart not only is the center of the physical body, but is the heart of the soul and the heart of the spirit as well. For example, in the fourth century, Gregory of Nyssa, one of the Cappadocian Fathers, believed that what really matters in spiritual terms is the quality of our heart and not the places we visit while on pilgrimage. Gregory saw the heart as the central organ of the physical body as well as of the psyche and spirit. Orthodox Bishop Kallistos Ware reminds us that in this mystical tradition the heart is referred to as the "ground" of the soul, or the place where we come face-to-face with the Divine.[53] In this context, the idea of love, too, expands in a way that includes our affections but points far beyond them to a divine love capable of touching our innermost being. Our intellect is a helpful tool for spiritual growth, yet it is limited if our desire is to journey into the center of the heart, or, as the Upanishads say, "the cave of the heart." Various special practices—including meditation, breathing exercises, chanting, yoga, walking, and running—begin by focusing on the physical heartbeat, which then becomes internalized in a way that returns our focus to the center of our being, where we encounter the Divine and experience the love of God.

Spiritual writer David Steindl-Rast, a Benedictine monk who studied with Zen masters, also writes on the connections between the inward journey, spiritual growth, and the heart in his book *A Listening Heart: The Art of Contemplative Living*. Steindl-Rast believes that the human quest for a full life, a life of happiness, is more than a question of good luck. Rather, it is based in a peaceful heart and the ability to "listen" with the heart in the midst of pain and struggle. Citing the example of the biblical tradition, Steindl-Rast writes that God speaks to us in the midst of great sorrows, working through them and making them an opportunity for deepening the inward journey. By listening deeply to the messages of the heart, he explains, "I shall be able to tap the very Source of Meaning and to realize the unfolding meaning of my life."[54] For Steindl-Rast, the heart is located at the center of our being and is a symbol for the place where we are truly "together," not divided into body, mind, emotions, intellect, and spirit.

Within the Buddhist tradition, the spiritual path is about developing the mind to grow in wisdom and developing the heart to grow in compassion. The Buddha taught that anyone who died during a pilgrimage to a holy shrine with a "devout heart" would be reborn in the heavenly world. At the same time, he also emphasized the importance of the inward journey as integral to pilgrimage: "You cannot travel the path until you have become the path," he taught. In the same vein, Vietnamese Buddhist Thich Nhat Hanh teaches that while many consider Buddhism to be a religion, it is more accurately portrayed as a way of life. "Please do not think because there is pain in your heart that you cannot go to the Buddha," he writes. "Your suffering and my suffering are the basic conditions for us to enter the Buddha's heart, and for the Buddha to enter our hearts." While the outward aspects of pilgrimage contribute to the path of enlightenment, it is the inward journey, the journey of the heart, that can bring the pilgrim closer to nirvana. The heart is the center of our inner goodness and most compassionate self. It is at the center of our connection with all living creatures—with ourselves, with other people, with the world, as well as that which is beyond us and dwelling within us. "We do not have a stem linking us to our mother anymore, but when we were in her womb we had a very long stem, an umbilical cord," writes Thich Nhat Hanh. "There are hundreds of thousands of stems linking us to everything in the cosmos.... If you do not see it, then look more deeply and I am sure you will see. This is not philosophy. You really need to see."[55]

The Buddhist tradition teaches that our relationships are an important source for our journey to the Divine, for the heart in each of us is awakened through meaningful connections that are both inward and outward. A sense of compassion that helps us become more sensitive in our relationships, more giving to others, and more loving is one of the fruits of the awakened heart. In the Buddhist tradition, rather than seeing suffering or life's obstacles as a disruption to our spiritual growth, they are the raw material necessary for awakening genuine compassion. American Buddhist nun Pema Chōdrōn writes:

> The first step is to develop compassion for our own wounds. It is unconditional compassion for ourselves that leads naturally to unconditional compassion for others. If we are willing to stand fully in our own shoes and not give up on ourselves, then we will be able to put ourselves fully in the shoes of others and not give up on them. True compassion does not come from wanting to help out those less fortunate than ourselves but from realizing our kinship with all beings.[56]

In recent years the Dalai Lama, one of the world's most renowned spiritual leaders, has been speaking to packed auditoriums the world over. "All beings are equal to you in their wish to find happiness and their desire to overcome suffering. Recognizing this, you make a pledge to develop a good heart"—this is one of his frequent teachings. In his book on basic Buddhist teachings, *An Open Heart*, the Dalai Lama discusses the importance of opening one's heart and finding compassion through meditation and Buddhist teachings. At the same time he cautions against the misuse of meditation, explaining that it is not a cure-all, because genuine spiritual growth depends on motivation and accountability for oneself. It is possible to awaken your heart and find it empty, or to open your heart and feel exposed. Realistically, it is also difficult to open one's heart to the world and not experience sadness, given the pain and suffering that abounds. As American Buddhist Jack Kornfield writes, "It is the pure raw heart that has the power to heal the world."[57]

Other spiritual traditions also address the importance of the inward journey to the center of the heart. "I do not go to see sacred shrines of pilgrimage, or bathe in the sacred waters; I do not bother any being or creatures. The Guru has shown me the sixty-eight places of pilgrimage within my own heart, where I now take my cleansing bath," reads the Sikh holy text *The Guru Granth Sahib*. Despite the teaching that pilgrimage is primarily an inward journey, the followers of Guru Nanak completed the magnificent Golden Temple at Amritsar, Punjab, in 1604, on the site of an ancient pool used as a focus for meditation by wandering monks, including the Buddha himself. Guru Nanak believed in equality for all people, regardless of caste, religion, gender, or any other form of difference, and from there Sikhism was born. The Golden Temple is now a world-renowned pilgrimage site. Resembling a fusion of Hindu and Islamic architecture, it welcomes pilgrims from all over the world for ritual music and chanting, the reading of holy texts, and hospitality, including forty thousand meals a day.

Sufism, a mystical tradition within Islam, is considered a "spirituality of the heart." It recognizes the value of pilgrimage as a spiritual quest, the primary focus of which is the inward journey of the heart. The Arabic word for heart is *qalb*, whose root means "always changing, turning." Sufism recalls the words of the Prophet Muhammad, "The heart of the believer is the sanctuary of God, and nothing but God is allowed access there." For Sufis, the heart is the center of perception, or "seeing with the heart's eye," as the expression goes. Pilgrims must first look inside their hearts before going forward. Neither a separate religion nor a sect, its adherents desire to keep an open door to the truth. Thus Sufism, which means "wisdom," respects all beliefs, at the same time carefully avoiding (as they see it) the fanaticism of the followers of other religions who have altered ancient truths beyond recognition. As one commentator noted, "One might say that Sufism is a process leading to the widening of the horizon of the heart, so that Truth might shine within as a brilliant sun, illuminating all that is receptive of its rays of light."[58]

Jalāl al-Dīn Rūmī, popularly known as Rumi, the greatest Sufi mystic and poet in the Persian language, wrote, "Surely there is a window from heart to heart: they are not separate and far from each other.... When the lightning of love for the beloved has shot into this heart, know that there is love in that heart. When love for God has been doubled in your heart, there is no doubt that God has love for you."[59] In 1204 he was born in present-day Afghanistan to a Sufi family, but his father later moved the family to Turkey to escape the invading Mongols. As a Muslim and as a mystic, he wrote about the strength of his conviction that humanity meets in the heart, despite all conflicts and divisions. "Not Christian or Jew or Muslim, not Hindu, Buddhist, Sufi, or Zen. Not any religion or cultural system. I am not from the East or the West...." Rumi profoundly believed that the Divine lives in everyone and everything, that all space is sacred space, and that the most important sacred text is life itself.

With great spiritual authority and gentleness, this remarkable poet and teacher spoke directly about the need for people to open their hearts and unite in an age that saw the bloodshed of the Crusades. The rebirth of his popularity after seven centuries is a testament to the power of the spirituality of the heart today. To be a pilgrim is to travel with an open heart and a willingness to risk transformation along the way, for, as he wrote, "Only from the heart can you touch the sky."[60]

Questions for Your Own Exploration

1. Search for as many images of the heart as you can find until you find one (or more) that truly resonate with your own heart. In your own words, how would you describe your own *journey to the center of the heart*? Refer to your chosen image if it helps you articulate how you envision your own heart.

2. Listen to your own heartbeat. Where does the experience lead you in the present moment?

3. What is your heart's desire? Your deepest yearning? Your most profound aspiration? As the poet Mary Oliver asks, "What are you doing with your one wild and precious life?"

CHAPTER 3

HOLY PLACES, SACRED SPACES

*Take off your shoes, for the place on which you
stand is holy ground.*
—*Exodus 3:5*

Find your path, enter the forest, seek the Grail.
—*King Arthur*
(twelfth- to thirteenth-century legend)

*In a mysterious way, tangible things have the capacity
to stir the inner eye, as though there exists a kind of
inner harmony between things of the spirit and objects
of sense.*
—*Cynthia Ozick (b. 1928)*

The search for the Holy Grail is one of the most enduring stories
of the court of King Arthur and his Knights of the Round Table.
According to legend, the Holy Grail was the cup that Jesus used
at the Last Supper before his crucifixion. The most commonly
accepted origin of the word *grail* comes from an old French
word, *grail*, meaning a cup or bowl of earth, wood, or metal.

Legend says that the Holy Grail was brought to Britain by its first protector, Joseph of Arimathea. Mentioned in the gospels as a member of the Sanhedrin who obtained the body of Jesus after his death, Joseph provided a proper burial place, possibly a tomb he had prepared for himself. He also has an important mythological role in the story of the bringing of Christianity to Britain. As one version of the story goes, it was Joseph who obtained the cup after the Last Supper and used it to catch the blood of Jesus during the crucifixion; another suggests that Joseph of Arimathea obtained the cup from Jesus personally in a vision. Several years after the crucifixion, Joseph decided to go on a journey and to take the cup with him. Perhaps he was imprisoned by the Roman authorities for hiding the body of Jesus after the resurrection, and so he decided to depart on a journey to Britain after he was released. Another legend suggests that Joseph was a trader who took the cup with him on his travels; still another version claims that Jesus himself directed Joseph to take the cup (and any of his followers who wanted to go along) to Britain.

Either way, legend has it that Joseph of Arimathea brought the Holy Grail to Britain, where he buried the cup for safekeeping at the foot of Glastonbury Tor (a teardrop-shaped hill formed through slow erosion) and where water immediately sprang forth, bringing healing to all who came in contact with it. The spring is now called the Chalice Well, said to be the place where heaven and earth meet. Other legends suggest that Joseph of Arimathea was not only the first protector of the Holy Grail, but also an early ancestor of King Arthur himself.

"There is on the confines of western Britain a certain royal island, called in ancient speech Glastonia, marked by broad boundaries, girt round with waters rich in fish and with still-flowing rivers, fitted for many uses of human indulgence, and dedicated to the most sacred deities," wrote Augustine of Canterbury, a Christian missionary to Britain in the sixth century. Glastonbury Tor, also known as Avalon to spiritual seekers, was considered a holy place as early as the third century BCE, when it was a Celtic village. The unusual shape of the tor suggested to the inhabitants of the area that something supernatural was at work, and it was also sacred space for the Druids. The sides of the tor have been terraced, causing some to speculate that it was an ancient processional route, or labyrinth, while others suggest that worship focused on the earth goddess may have occurred at the site.

In 1930 the artist Katherine Maltwood discovered the signs of the zodiac etched into the landscape at the site. At the summit of the tor stands a tower, the remains of the fourteenth-century Church of St. Michael. From Christian times it is said that Jesus visited the site beyond the tor when he was a boy and built a church there with Joseph of Arimathea. When Joseph returned after the crucifixion, he took his staff (possibly made by Jesus with wood from the cross) and drove it into the ground on Wearyall Hill, where it took root and became the sacred Glastonbury Thorn. This thorn tree was kept alive for centuries through careful tending and cuttings, and its descendants live in the abbey gardens nearby. Pilgrims visited the thorn tree for centuries, leaving prayers and offerings in its branches. In the Middle Ages, the number of pilgrims going to Glastonbury rivaled the number visiting the Becket shrine at Canterbury. It remains a sacred site for Christians, pagans, and New Age pilgrims today. Unfortunately, the Glastonbury Thorn was attacked by vandals in 2010 and cut to a stump, reducing many townsfolk and pilgrims to tears.

The publication of recent thrillers like *The Da Vinci Code* and *The Holy Blood and the Holy Grail* have added new pilgrims to the quest for the Holy Grail. This tradition also suggests that Jesus did not, in fact, die at the crucifixion but somehow escaped and went on to marry Mary Magdalene and have children. As the story goes, the Holy Blood is the living bloodline of Jesus Christ, and the Holy Grail is the womb of Mary. The small hamlet of

Rennes-le-Château on top of a hill in the Languedoc region of France is believed to be the final resting place of the descendants of Jesus. Considered a place of mystery to many pilgrims, an average of one hundred thousand Christian, pagan, and New Age pilgrims now visit the village each year.

The legends surrounding the Holy Grail have captured the human imagination for eight hundred years and provide timeless insights into the nature of pilgrimage and the quest for that which is holy. For those called on the quest for the Holy Grail, the search was all-consuming; the journey was begun only after deep prayer and, once started, it became foundational to a searcher's sense of purpose and identity. If you hope to find the Holy Grail, the tradition says, look first within. Why do you search, and what is the quality of your heart? Courage is a helpful characteristic if you strive for the Holy Grail, though not in the traditional sense—while it may be handy to be skilled with a sword, it is ultimately more important to be brave when it comes to the search for truth. Seek out spiritual or moral guidance, as the road to the Holy Grail will most certainly challenge who you are as a person, and the way ahead may not always be clear.

In addition, the quest for the Holy Grail may also be fraught with danger of a more physical nature—monsters, inclement weather, and natural disasters—so it is best to be prepared. Lastly, in order to search for the Holy Grail, the pilgrim needs to know what she or he is really seeking. What is your heart's desire?

SACRED LANDSCAPES

Although much of the morality in the Holy Grail legends is of the medieval Christian variety, the sacred landscape of the stories is Celtic—related to the ancient peoples of Ireland, Scotland, and Wales—and therefore it is important to be aware of the ways holy places and sacred spaces interrelate with humankind's quest for meaning. Celtic Christians described sacred spaces as "thin places" in the veil between heaven and earth, where the two are transparent to one another. Thin spaces are those that reveal the interrelationship between heaven and earth, the invisible and the visible worlds; for the Celts, holy places are those that "touch heaven." They never doubted that the invisible and visible worlds are interconnected. What separates us from the invisible world is a permeable membrane of consciousness—what author Margaret Silf refers to as a "kind of spiritual ozone layer."[1]

Sometimes the distance between the worlds may seem as solid as a brick wall, yet at other times it appears to be a porous veil. Sometimes the intensity of our feelings for a holy place may break through; sometimes, in ways we cannot always predict, the Divine seems to break through the veil to reach us. "Heaven joins earth at sacred places and the Divine brushes against the human in sacred shrines," writes Australian author Val Webb.[2] In those sacred spaces the feeling of the presence of the spiritual is so strong that it is palpable. It is said that those people who enter "thin spaces" are greeted by angels.

One of the characteristics of the Celtic tradition is its connectedness to the elements—earth, stone, fire, and water. There is a respect for the natural cycles of day and night and of the seasons of the year. The Celts believed that God's creation is good and that God is both immanent and transcendent. Moreover, if God's creation is good, the human body is a sacred space, as are the earth and the cosmos. Within the broad span of Celtic spirituality, the elements and their power are always present. "The world itself is a stunning miracle," writes Mary C. Earle in *Celtic Christian Spirituality*. "The diversity of creatures, plants, and habitats on the earth, and the stunning array of the heavens, all lead us to be caught up in wonder."[3]

Within the Celtic sacred landscape, all of humankind is knit together through bonds of kinship. The ancient Celts were always aware of the need to welcome the poor, the foreigner, the weary traveler, and the penitent. From their perspective, it was not appropriate for human beings to dominate or exploit the natural world, because we are all from the same Source. Wind, rain, rock, the sun, the moon, fire, thunder, birds, animals—all are evidence of the Divine Presence at work in creation and thus deserve our reverence and respect. In our day, those people who are interested in eco-spirituality, or the spirituality of the earth, often embrace these values of the Celtic tradition. As with ecological theology, it supports the belief that "the whole creation is sustained by God at every single instant, and because of that immediate presence in and through the elements of matter, we may discover the means of healing in the natural world that surrounds us."[4]

"A site becomes sacred through the accumulation of universal forces and the quality of veneration over time," writes Freddy Silva in *Legacy of the Gods*.[5] Holy places and sacred spaces— whether they are geographical sites, internal destinations, intentionally religious, decidedly secular, or deeply personal—all have special power and, Silva argues, are living organisms. "Pyramids, stone circles, menhirs, dolmens, sanctuaries and mounds. Regardless of their shape and size, they all were built by faceless experts from forgotten ages to the same end: to be mirrors of the heavens so that ordinary men and women may be transformed into gods."[6] Holy places and sacred spaces speak to our spirits and to our hearts. They evoke feelings of the immanence or the transcendence of the Divine. They resonate with the call of our deepest yearnings.

Each pilgrim on the road, has what are called "archetypal landscapes" that speak to our hearts and, for those who are spiritual, that evoke the Holy or Sacred. Obviously, pilgrimage sites that have received visitors for centuries evoke the Sacred, yet at the same time, not all people respond to all holy places in the same way. Some holy places and sacred spaces speak to us more clearly than others; what some find sacred may evoke a similar visceral reaction in me or not much of a reaction at all.

For the Celts, the archetypal landscape was naturally lush with springs, wells, rivers, hills, and groves. For them, paradise was an island to be reached by boat. For other spiritual traditions, archetypal landscapes that have evoked the sacred for centuries are also part of natural landscapes—mountains, caves, deserts, or rivers. Some traditions have found their archetypal landscapes in buildings that evoke holiness, such as monasteries, temples, churches, or shrines. Sometimes a place becomes holy gradually, as when a church becomes "soaked" with the prayers said by pilgrims over long periods of time.

Spiritual author Christine Valters Paintner writes, "When we go on pilgrimage it is through the heart of the outer and inner landscape."[7] What she means by this is that all pilgrims possess their own inner and outer archetypal landscapes, the power of which helps move them along the way to deeper meaning and spiritual growth. Holy places and sacred spaces encourage pilgrims to use all the senses—what we can see, hear, feel, touch, and taste—on the journey. They call us to appreciate the interconnectedness of the inner and the outer worlds and awaken in us a sense of awe and connection with the other human beings who walk the road alongside us.

Holy places and sacred spaces are particular and local, yet they share characteristics with all the religions of the world. Wherever human beings have lived on the earth, there have evolved sacred landscapes, those places that are considered pathways to the Divine. According to Roger W. Stump, professor of geography and religious studies, sacred space "encompasses imagined, superhuman regions that exist beyond the realm of sensory experience, heaven, nirvana, or the spirit world. At the same time, it comprises crucial points of contact between human and superhuman domains, such as places of revelation or worship."[8] For instance, Africa hosts a broad range of holy places that African traditional religions, along with Christianity, Islam, and other faith groups, have made into sites of pilgrimage for generations. The traditions of Judaism, Christianity, and Islam evolved in a region known as the Middle East, which includes parts of North Africa and southwest Asia. The sacred landscape of Asia is marked with an array of *stupas*—Buddhist shrines, temples, and pagodas. Hinduism has its origins in northern India, while Buddhism evolved from Hinduism and spread to Myanmar, Cambodia, Indonesia, China, Korea, and Japan. Indigenous traditions that also thrived in Asia include Taoism, Confucianism, and Shintoism.

Within Europe, pilgrimage has been practiced since the fourth century and is now on the increase, as are the numbers of people who consider themselves agnostic, atheist, or spiritual but not religious. The earliest sacred sites in Europe were located around the Mediterranean and associated with the religions of ancient Greece and Rome, Judaism, Christianity, and Islam. Since the fall of Communism in Eastern Europe, pilgrimage as a spiritual practice has revived in the Orthodox Christian world as well, and each year an estimated 15 percent of Poles make a pilgrimage to some sacred site.[9] For example, each year Jasna Góra in Częstochowa, Poland, attracts nearly five million pilgrims drawn by the icon of the Black Madonna. By now the sacred landscape of Europe spans the whole continent and represents a rich religious pluralism. In the Americas, the oldest sacred spaces are associated with thousands of tribes of indigenous peoples whose ancestors, according to legend, were there from the beginning of time. Eventually, holy places associated with the religions of Europe, Africa, and Asia also contributed to the sacred landscape. Aboriginal sacred sites have been located in Australia, New Zealand, and the Pacific islands, where the sacred landscape bore a close relationship to the natural world long before Europeans arrived there.

Today, opportunities for pilgrimage across traditions and cultures to holy places for prayer and meditation enable sacred travelers to build community across religious, national, and cultural divides. The significance of sacred space extends beyond the physical reality of a natural site or a building, as Bernard of Clairvaux wrote in the twelfth century: "More things are learnt from the woods than from books; trees and rocks will teach you things not to be heard elsewhere—you will see for yourselves that honey may be gathered from stones and oil from the hardest rock." Sacred spaces are metaphors for the spiritual experience of those who inhabit them; those who pray, sing, grieve, and experience joy there. Through light, color, stone, fabric, wood, and art, sacred spaces support the spiritual lives of individuals and communities. Holy places are artifacts integral to the sacred art of pilgrimage and to building international communities as they educate and inspire generations of pilgrims, offering hospitality to those along the way. In doing so, sacred spaces become transcendent in that they embody human hope.

Within sacred spaces, pilgrims come together to walk, pray, read, cry, sing, and live in ways that for many are a source of sustenance and healing. Sharing sacred spaces, bringing people together to understand their different perspectives and build a better world, is a form of interreligious dialogue. Holy places link spiritual consciousness with the deepest yearnings of the human heart. Events of great spiritual significance happen in sacred spaces on a daily basis; they are the intersection of all humanity. As Michael J. Crosbie, the author of *Architecture for the Gods*, suggests, sacred spaces recount "a life that is, in some way, holy and wholly other than what is experienced now. This is the tremendous burden placed on religious architecture—to serve as a firm foundation of faith and a platform for courage and creativity."[10]

Finding holy places and sacred spaces is critical to deepening spiritual practice, and it better enables pilgrims to be open to more than their limited experience of the Divine and of the world. Throughout history and across religious traditions, the definition of those places that touch heaven is expansive and contextual, including sites found in the natural world as well as the shrines, temples, and churches built by human hands. Historically, there are basic types of holy places across traditions that offer a useful way of looking at humankind's relationship with sacred spaces.

First, there is what are known as *memory places*, those sacred sites where pilgrims gather to commemorate an event or person that has special significance. *Quiet places*, both external and those within the human psyche and spirit, are considered sacred as they free us from distractions and invite meditation, prayer, and healing. Lastly, *divine activity places* are places where it is evident that the Divine is in touch with humankind. Just as holy places are found in stillness and solitude, so too they are found where the Divine is experienced as active and alive amid humankind in celebration, dance, or song. Of course, there are also many pilgrimage sites across traditions that contain elements of all three types.

MEMORY PLACES

The United States Holocaust Memorial Museum in Washington, D.C., and other memorials to this tragic event in human history worldwide are powerful examples of places devoted to sacred memory. The expressed purpose of the museum is "to inspire citizens and leaders worldwide to confront hatred, prevent genocide, and promote human dignity." Dedicated in 1993, it has welcomed over thirty million visitors, including nine million schoolchildren and ninety-one heads of state. Many visitors experience a journey to the Holocaust Memorial Museum as a deeply tragic spiritual experience. Given the reality that soon survivors of the Holocaust will no longer be alive and that the rise of genocide and anti-Semitism still continues around the world, the museum stands as a means of remembering these atrocities and as a challenge to the human community never to tolerate such acts of violence again.

Today the majority of those who visit the Holocaust Memorial Museum are not Jewish, nor do they claim a specific religious tradition. The site's website, translated into twenty languages, receives hundreds of thousands of visits from persons around the world. James Ingo Freed, the museum's designer, has said that he conceived of the museum as a "resonator," or a space to recall the horrible reality of those events. "In many ways, that is the purpose of religious architecture. On one hand worship spaces are crucibles of memories. On the other hand, they can help the worshiper imagine how things might be. This combination of memory and imagination can help some people survive."[11]

A place of sacred memory similar to the Holocaust Memorial Museum is the Hiroshima Peace Memorial Park in Japan, commemorating the dropping of the world's first atomic bomb on that city on August 6, 1945, and three days later on nearby Nagasaki. The survivors of those events—the *hibakushas*, a term for people affected by the explosion—number over two hundred thousand. The death of eleven-year-old Sadako Sasaki in 1955, from leukemia induced by radiation exposure, became a catalyst for a memorial dedicated to peace in memory of all the children killed in war. As the story goes, before her death Sadako set out to make one thousand origami paper cranes, for an ancient Japanese story says that anyone who folds one thousand cranes will be granted a special favor from the gods. Sadako was unable to complete the task before her death, but the cranes were eventually completed by her classmates and buried with her.

Today ten million cranes are received by the Hiroshima Peace Memorial Park annually from all over the world. Each year on August 6, the park hosts an annual ceremony, visited by pilgrims, that is a ritual form of rededication to peace and reconciliation, respect, and contemplation, with the tolling of a bell and the release of white doves—a universal sign of peace. The Memorial Cenotaph—the official tomb, or designated site of memory, for all those who lost their lives in the catastrophe—symbolically shelters the souls of the victims, whose names are inscribed here.

Another type of holy place of memory, the river Ganges of India, is often cited as one of the most visited pilgrimage destinations in the world. Known in India as "Mother Ganga," personified as the goddess Ganga Devi, the daughter of Meru, the god of the Himalayas, the river flows for 1,557 miles from its source in the mountains to the Bay of Bengal in Bangladesh. "The Ganga, especially, is the river of India, beloved of her people, round which are intertwined her memories, her hopes and fears, her songs of triumph, her victories and her defeats. She has been a symbol of India's age-long culture and civilization, ever changing, ever flowing, and yet ever the same Ganga,"[12] wrote Jawaharlal Nehru, first prime minister of India. The Ganges is an archetypal landscape for the half-million people in India whom she nourishes, conveys, irrigates, cleanses, and heals.

At auspicious times, it is believed, bathing in the Ganges can cleanse the souls of the living from their sins. "O Mother Ganga, cleanse us of our sins and bring peace to our souls. Help our dreams come true and give us long lives. We salute you, O Mother Ganga, and bestow upon you this gift of flowers," goes the Hindu prayer. As a holy place of memory, the river Ganges is the site of many important festivals held on its banks. The great Kumbh Mela festival, celebrated every twelve years, is a mass pilgrimage celebrated at four locations, two of which are on the Ganges. The major event of the festival is the ritual bathing in the river. At the first festival of the new millennium in 2001, an estimated crowd of seventy million pilgrims attended, making it the largest recorded pilgrimage gathering in history. As many as ten million devotees at a time bathed in the river. The holy city of Varanasi (Banares) on the Ganges is sacred to Hindus, Buddhists, and Jains alike; the shallow steps (*ghats*) leading down to the river are used for cremation. The ashes are then immersed for forgiveness, and the dead are, symbolically, carried home by the river.

It is believed that the waters of the Ganges have healing properties. It is considered auspicious to drink the water of the

Ganges at the time of death and/or to die on the riverbank. Many of India's greatest leaders were cremated on the banks of the Ganges.

Another holy place of memory found in the natural world is Mount Kilimanjaro, Africa's highest mountain, known as the "Roof of Africa" and the "House of God." "Sacred mountains can be seen as landscape temples made by nature and later identified as such by human beings."[13] Legend has it that King Menelik of Abyssinia, the son of King Solomon and the Queen of Sheba, haunts the sacred mountain. Local peoples, the Chagga and Massai, believe the mountain to be holy and bury their dead facing it. "Wide as all the world, great, high, and unbelievably white in the sun," wrote Ernest Hemingway in 1936, describing Kilimanjaro. His short story "The Snows of Kilimanjaro" contributed to the numbers of people from outside of Africa who come to view the mountain each year. Up to twenty thousand people attempt to climb Mount Kilimanjaro each year, many of them as spiritual pilgrims, but fewer than half actually reach the summit.

Another natural site of sacred memory, the Grand Canyon in North America, has been the home of indigenous tribes for at least four thousand years. According to the tradition of the Hopi people, guardians of the canyon, their ancestors were born in an underground cave in the canyon and still live there. The Navajo people, also known as the Diné, likewise consider themselves guardians of "Grandmother Canyon." It must be protected as a place where the spirit of the ancestors, the Kachinas, dwell and therefore must be respected. Although tourists are welcome to visit the Grand Canyon, and do so in droves, the site has for much longer been an ancestral holy place and a pilgrimage site.

On the other side of the world lies another holy place of memory, the legendary Isle of Iona. Located in the Scottish Hebrides, off the coast of western Scotland, Iona is believed to be one of the most sacred places on earth and has a long history of

welcoming pilgrims. Having journeyed as a pilgrim to the sacred
island several times myself, I can personally attest to the remote
beauty of this "thin place" between heaven and earth. From
many places in North America, it can take two airplanes, three
trains, and two ferries to reach the island.

The island itself is made from some of the oldest rocks on
earth. Thought to have been an ancient sacred site for the Druids,
Iona was originally known as Isla na Druidhneach, the Isle of the
Druids. At one time the island was reputedly filled with stone circles, and Roman mapmakers suggested that Iona was considered
a retreat for holy men and a holy place for the local people. In the
Christian era, the island became the site of an abbey, founded by
Saint Columba in 563, and the base from which his evangelizing
efforts spread. Columba was not only a deeply spiritual man who
is credited with many miracles, he was a pragmatic and energetic
leader who made Christian Iona a center of Celtic Christianity
and a place of great learning—legend has it that the *Book of Kells*
was created there long after the saint's death. Attracting pilgrims
from the seventh century onward, Iona served as the final resting
place for saints as well as for sixty kings of Scotland, Ireland, and
Norway, supposedly including the legendary Macbeth.

Another sacred site in Britain, Lindisfarne in Northumbria,
was founded by monks from Iona. One legend suggests that Mary,
the mother of Jesus, had visited Iona, while another holds that
when Christ returns to earth, he will appear on the island. In the
eighth and ninth centuries, the original abbey was pillaged three
times by seafarers from the north, prompting one commentator to
say that monasteries filled with riches were like automatic teller
machines to the Vikings. Saint Margaret, who was also queen of
Scotland, rebuilt the ruined abbey in the eleventh century. Around
the year 1200, a Benedictine community rebuilt the abbey again
and reinstituted the island as a place of pilgrimage.

As it did for hundreds of other monastic sites in Britain,
the English Reformation brought the dissolution of the abbey

on Iona. In the 1870s, the site was once again partially restored by the island's owner, the Duke of Argyll, who believed in the island's "atmosphere of miracles" and sought to preserve the sacred history of the island. The present-day Iona Community was founded on the island in 1938, and the abbey was once again restored, as were some of the ancient sites associated with Columba. The ecumenical Iona community was founded by a Church of Scotland pastor, George MacLeod, at a time in history when the devastation of war challenged people of faith to look for new ways of promoting peace and building human community. MacLeod came from an aristocratic family and served in World War I; the trauma of that experience led him to join the church and work with the poor in Glasgow.

Over the course of the twentieth century and into the twenty-first, the Iona Community has continued this legacy and, within a faith context, addressed questions of peacekeeping, ecology, economic injustice, the arms trade, and racism. Today Iona is a vibrant pilgrimage site for Christians of all types, pagans, Druids, New Age religionists, artists, and social activists. More people visit Iona today than at any other time in its history; an estimated one hundred thousand pilgrims visit the island annually. Some live in the community fulltime, and others for a brief period; still other pilgrims come for a retreat or a day trip. The Iona Community considers itself a "dispersed" community, linking those who live and work on the island with hundreds of members throughout the world. Members of the Iona Community commit themselves to lives of prayer, Bible study, meeting together, accounting for the use of time and money, and working for peace and justice. "None can understand it who does not see [Iona] through its pagan light, its Christian light, its singular blending of paganism and romance and spiritual beauty," writes Celtic visionary Fiona MacLeod.[14]

Today, there are no famous shrines on the island to attract visitors; rather, the emphasis is on the beauty of Iona's unique physical landscape and the memories it preserves of centuries of pilgrimage, healing, and miracle working. Once a week on Iona there is the opportunity for visitors to make a pilgrimage on the island to the holy places and sacred spaces there, from St. Martin's Cross to the ruins of the Augustinian nunnery and from there to St. Columba's Bay. "Norsemen should have known," goes the pilgrim's poem, "people who carve their Christ in stone are rooted as rock, intend to stay no matter what."[15]

QUIET PLACES

There are holy places and sacred spaces across the world that evoke solitude, meditation, and prayer and are visited annually by pilgrims seeking tranquility from across many cultures and traditions. One such "quiet place" is Walden Pond, the site just outside Concord, Massachusetts, where Henry David Thoreau wrote his classic *Walden, or Life in the Woods*. "I went to the woods because I wanted to live deliberatively," wrote Thoreau, "to front only the essential facts of life, and to see if I could not learn what it has to teach, and not, when I came to die, discover that I had not lived." Observing that "the mass of men lead lives of quiet desperation and go to the grave with the song still in them," Thoreau chose instead what he believed to be a life of intentional simplicity, more in tune with the natural world and resistant to the temptations of consumerism. "I wanted to live deep and suck out all the marrow of life," he wrote. Thoreau's literary journal has since inspired generations of spiritual seekers, as has the pond and surrounding woodlands that were his inspiration. Thoreau's reflections on the natural environment, civil disobedience, and the evils of slavery attracted the interest of philosophers and activists alike, including Mahatma Gandhi and Martin Luther King Jr., to name a few. Thoreau's journey was about trying to live a life that was close to the natural world and that adhered to his moral principles and personal spirituality.

Thoreau built his cabin at Walden Pond on land on loan from his friend Ralph Waldo Emerson, and he furnished it sparsely: a bed, a desk, two chairs, a table, and a copy of Hindu scripture, the Bhagavad Gita. Like Emerson and other transcendentalists, Thoreau was not interested in religious doctrines as much as he believed in developing the spiritual and moral attributes of the individual.

Walden Pond is actually a lake covering sixty-one acres that reaches depths of over a hundred feet and attracts over a million visitors a year. "A lake is the landscape's most beautiful and expressive feature," Thoreau wrote. "It is earth's eye: looking into which the beholder measures the depth of his own nature." After leaving his cabin in the woods, Thoreau worked on multiple drafts of his journal before its publication. Some suggest that *Walden*, due to its personal and reflective prose, is an early example of a writer's blog.[16] Thoreau devoted the rest of his life—he died in his forties of tuberculosis—to the study of the natural world. At the site of his cabin in the woods, Thoreau's friend Bronson Alcott, father of the writer Louisa May Alcott, built a memorial cairn of stones. Stones are still added by pilgrims who come to the site.

The most famous quiet place and perhaps the most famous natural landmark in Japan, Mount Fuji, is also known as the Mountain of Immortality. Considered sacred from the earliest times, the name *Fuji* was given to the mountain by aboriginal people, the Ainu, and means "fiery goddess." Like other indigenous peoples, the Ainu believed that Spirit lived in everything and believed therefore in the importance of giving honor and respect to all of creation. "This mountain is born from between heaven and earth. It is the origin of yin and yang," reads the *Book of the Great Practice*.

Mount Fuji is a source of inspiration to several religious traditions found in Japan and throughout the world. Shintos see the Sacred in mountains as the sources of water that gives nourishment to all creation. Many of the shrines on the mountain are dedicated to the Shinto goddess Konohana Sakuya Hime, a deity known to offer protection from fire and the dangers of childbirth.

Japanese Buddhists call Mount Fuji "the Home of the Cosmic Buddha," believing that because it is a peak that rises high above everyday life to reach another state of being, it inspires meditation. Followers of the Shugendo tradition are mountain ascetics who believe that their founder, En no Gyoja, was the first person to climb Mount Fuji in the seventh century.

Thousands of people climb Mount Fuji as a spiritual exercise every year. The official climbing season is in July and August to avoid bad weather, and shrines and teahouses along the way to the summit host the pilgrims. But many attempt the climb during other times of year to meditate and pray in greater quiet, or at night in order to experience the breathtaking views of the holy mountain at sunrise.

On Apparition Hill in Medjugorje, Bosnia-Herzegovina, pilgrims travel in silence up the rocky path and through the Stations of the Cross to the peak of Mount Sipovac. The summit has been renamed Krizevac, "the Mountain of the Cross." As the third most-visited Christian pilgrimage site in Europe today, the path to the top is not nearly as silent as it was when the stations were first erected in 1934. Beginning in 1981, on a hill nearby, the Virgin Mary first appeared to six young people between the ages of ten and seventeen, bringing messages of peace and reconciliation. By the third day, news of the miraculous encounters began to spread, much to the dismay of the local authorities, who brought the children in for questioning, threatening arrest, and pressured the local priest to denounce the visions. Having received his own divine instruction to protect the children, Father Jozo Zovko hid them and evaded the authorities with the help of the local townspeople, who also became pilgrims to the site. The apparitions still continue today, as one of the original children receives messages of love and peace on the twenty-fifth day of every month. Now a busy shrine is located in the parish.

Several religious communities, as well as people from abroad, also work in an orphanage, a home for single mothers, and a home for disabled children in Medjugorje. Prayerful pilgrims leave crosses at the top of the mountain, often tied with prayer cloths. The climb to the top of the rocky mountain remains a time for quiet reflection, away from the comings and goings below.

Monasteries, ashrams, and retreat centers throughout the world are quiet places that evoke meditation and prayer from many pilgrims, as well as for the permanent communities established in their orbit. The Monastery of the Transfiguration on the Island of Valaam in Russia has been known as a place of solitude and refreshment in the Russian Orthodox tradition for centuries. Founded by Saints Sergius and Herman in the tenth century (their relics are still venerated there), the monastery is situated on the largest island of an archipelago—a place of intense natural beauty on Lake Ladoga, the largest lake in Europe. It became a center of music and art in the nineteenth century under the leadership of Abbot Damascene—reportedly Tchaikovsky was inspired to write his first symphony, *Winter Dreams*, while visiting there. Although abandoned during the Soviet era, the monastery resumed its regular monastic routine in 1989. Its choir is well known for singing the ancient Znamenny chant during services, and many pilgrims visit in the summer months for the feast days of its founding saints.

Also founded in the Orthodox Christian tradition, Mount Athos in Halkidiki, Greece, is equally isolated on its long peninsula and has been a holy place for over two thousand years. The landscape is wild and unspoiled, with many valleys, gorges, and streams. The first people who came to Mount Athos worshipped the gods of antiquity; later, legend has it, Mary the mother of Jesus also landed there with Saint John the apostle, blown off course in a storm. They both recognized the holiness of the site, and Mary prayed to her son, asking to have it consecrated as her garden. There have been Christian monastic communities on Mount Athos from the fifth century, and a large foundation was well established in Byzantine times; by the fifteenth century an estimated twenty thousand monks lived there. Today, Mount Athos is accessible only by sea, and about three hundred monks live there in monasteries and hermitages.

For the last half century, an annual pilgrimage has been made to a cluster of Armenian Christian monasteries and chapels in the province of West Azerbaijan in the Republic of Iran. The site is considered to be the burial place of the apostle Thaddeus, who was martyred preaching Christianity there. Saint Thaddeus, also called Saint Jude, is believed to have brought Christianity to Armenia and has since become known as the patron of lost causes and desperate situations. The tradition holds that Thaddeus himself built the first monastery there in 68 CE. Known as Tadeh Monastery, it is the oldest Christian landmark in the country, with just one service held there annually. Nonetheless, the site has been an important pilgrimage destination for Armenian Christians not only from Iran, but also from Lebanon, Syria, and beyond since 1954. The pilgrimage to Tadeh involves arduous travel into the mountains, where it not only provides an opportunity for quiet prayer, but allows the Armenian diaspora of the region an opportunity to continue to honor the sacredness of the location.

Other quiet sacred spaces include ancient ruins and burial sites where centuries of meditation and prayer connect with the quests for meaning of contemporary pilgrims. One such world-renowned site, located in a field on Salisbury Plain in Wiltshire, England, is the megalithic structure known as Stonehenge. The function of this prehistoric circle of standing stones has never been completely explained, although scientists reckon that the "henge"—meaning "to hang"—was constructed in three stages. The first stage of the site's construction dates to 3100 BCE, when a ditch and bank were made with timbers. About six hundred years later, huge rocks, known as "bluestones," were brought over two hundred miles from Wales. Two hundred years after the five-ton bluestones arrived, they were rearranged into a horseshoe shape and surrounded by a ring of sarsen stones that were hoisted on top of the bluestones as lintels. Across peoples and cultures, circles have a variety of meanings, most commonly associated with infinity, harmony, and warding off evil.

Stonehenge is not the largest stone circle in the world, but it is the only site with stones at the top. Given the weight of the stones, how exactly they arrived in Wiltshire, and how the people managed to lift them into place, is still a mystery. It is known that the area was used for burials. Furthermore, the positions of the markers indicate the movement of heavenly bodies, so it is likely that the winter and summer solstices were celebrated on the site. Today, modern followers of the ancient Druid religion journey to Stonehenge to celebrate the summer solstice just as they have done for eight hundred years. As a sacred space, Stonehenge elicits a great deal of emotion from the pilgrims who venture there, as well as from those who are interested in its preservation. Despite the many visitors to the site and the traffic from the road nearby, Stonehenge remains a quiet place of mystery and awe filled with divine power.

DIVINE ACTIVITY PLACES

"There is no better way to fix an event or a person in the mind than to visit the actual place where the event occurred or the person lived," writes novelist Cynthia Ozick.[17] Divine activity places are those holy places where the relationship between sacred and humankind is evident. Also known in some traditions as *incarnational* places, they evoke heaven on earth and harmony among humankind. The word *incarnation* comes from a Latin root that literally means "enfleshment." At incarnational holy places we experience the Divine through humanity as we come together in the spirit of connection and timelessness. In a similar manner, the Hindu gesture and greeting *Namaste* represents the belief that there is a divine spark within each of us that is located in the heart chakra. The gesture is an acknowledgment of the soul in one by the soul in another. *Nama* means "bow," *as* means "I," and *te* means "you." Therefore, *Namaste* literally means, "I bow to you."

Such places of divine activity are often sacred spaces filled with ritual celebration and community engagement. For a brief moment in time, human divisions are suspended or cease, and we are brought together as one humanity. For example, the Bodhi Tree in Bodhgaya, India, marks the spot where the Buddha reached the state of enlightenment. Although there are many holy places in Buddhism, Bodhgaya is the most sacred, and it has welcomed pilgrims for centuries. While the exact dates are not recorded, historians believe that the Buddha lived sometime during the fifth or sixth century BCE. At the time of his birth, it was predicted that Prince Siddhartha would become either a great king or a great spiritual leader. Although his parents raised him to become a great king, Siddhartha was transformed as he watched the human suffering that existed outside the palace walls. Instead he became an itinerant monk, took the name Gautama, and left the world of the palace. After six years of the ascetic life, he arrived at Bodhgaya and sat under a fig tree for forty-nine days until he achieved enlightenment, or nirvana. Having reached this state, the monk became known as the Buddha, or the Awakened One, and people began to travel many miles in the hope that they, too, could benefit spiritually from the divine activity of this place.

The Mahabodhi Temple on the site draws many sacred travelers, who come to pray there every day as well as for the great festivals and organized events. At Bodhgaya, not only is the divine activity in the life of the Buddha as a single human being celebrated, but also the belief that each one of us has the potential to awaken our essential Buddha nature. The actual tree has been replanted many times at Bodhgaya, and the sacred ground from which it springs is considered the world's center and the source of all enlightenment. Centuries of pilgrims took seeds from the tree away with them, and thus the ancestors of the original tree line the pilgrimage route to this day.

Another holy place of divine activity is the ecumenical Christian community found in the village of Taizé in France, which has welcomed pilgrims since its founding by the French-Swiss monk Brother Roger in 1940. It is now one of the most active international pilgrimage sites in the world, especially among young people. Located in Burgundy, just outside the ruins of the third Benedictine abbey at Cluny, the area was dev-astated by World War II. Roger Schutz-Marsauche, born the son of a Protestant pastor in 1915, sought ways to alleviate the suffer-ing of the defeated French people and decided to open a house of prayer that would offer assistance to those in need.

Brother Roger left Geneva on his bicycle in search of a suit-able house and ended up in Taizé, a nearly deserted town with no running water or telephones. While viewing a house, he was so deeply moved by the words of an elderly woman—"Stay here with us, we are so poor, and isolated"—that he bought the house, cleared some land, and established a small chapel. Refugees began to come to the house almost immediately, many of them Jews. The Nazis eventually closed the house while Brother Roger was in Switzerland on a fund-raising trip, forcing him to live abroad until 1944. He then returned to Taizé with a small group of friends, intent on founding a monastic community dedicated to serving those displaced by war, a tradition the community continues today. Taizé grew ecumenically—by the 1960s there were brothers from the Reformed, Lutheran, and Anglican tra-ditions. In 1969, the first Roman Catholic member entered the community.

"One passes through Taizé as one passes close to a spring of water," said Pope John Paul II in 1986. "The traveler stops, quenches his thirst, and continues on his way."[18] A similar sen-timent was echoed by the former archbishop of Canterbury,

George Carey, as he made his own pilgrimage to Taizé with one thousand young Anglicans in 1992: "Taizé is a place for the seeker after truth, the searcher after God, and in this life our Christian pilgrimage is never complete."[19]

Brother Roger's vision for Taizé as a pilgrimage site and as a place of divine activity is influenced both by his belief in the need to provide people with spiritual refreshment and by the challenge to go forth and do good for others in their local communities. For Brother Roger, the inner pilgrimage of the heart is inextricably linked with external action or, as he calls it, "a pilgrimage of trust on earth." Although there are no formal guidelines on how to live out the pilgrimage of trust, the Taizé community provides a number of methods to support pilgrims along the way. The community distributes open letters, often addressing key issues in the poorest human communities in Asia, Africa, the Americas, and Europe. The community also sponsors "European meetings" where young adults from all over the world gather to pray, chant, share conversations, and participate in workshops.

At a time in history when church attendance is in decline among many Christian denominations in Europe and North America, particularly among young adults, it is especially striking to see the thousands who go on pilgrimage to Taizé every year. The pilgrimage site itself is simple, with concrete buildings, dormitory accommodations, basic food, and shared household chores. Some pilgrims arrive with tents for their accommodations. Worship is in a large hall, known as the Church of the Reconciliation, or in an outdoor tent for major feasts, and is simple in structure, with candlelight and periods of silence. All those who are able to sit on the floor. What was perhaps the most striking element of Taizé worship for me during my visits was the use of chants sung in many languages, which filled the sacred space as the candles danced. The experience is electric. Here is a place where heaven meets the earth, and pilgrims not only receive refreshment in their everyday lives, but get a glimpse of a reconciled humanity. Over one hundred thousand young people visit Taizé during the summer months alone, many of them making the pilgrimage in groups. In addition to the personal spiritual growth gained during a pilgrimage to Taizé, these pilgrimages provide young people with a community of solidarity and commitment while encouraging them to form friendships with others at the sacred site from different countries and cultures. The Taizé pilgrimage encourages young people to learn and struggle alongside other pilgrims, developing empathy with each other and making connections to their home.

COMMERCIALIZATION
AND ENVIRONMENTAL IMPACT

International pilgrimage, known in some quarters as "pilgrimage tourism," yields at least $8 billion a year in income and provides employment for thousands in local economies throughout the world.[20] To some extent, pilgrimage has been a commercial enterprise for centuries, ever since the first hostels, food vendors, and other businesses designed to support pilgrims were established adjacent to holy places. In some locations, entire towns were built as pilgrimage centers, including souvenir stalls, restaurants, hostels, and, in the modern era, tour operators. In addition to the advantages of pilgrimage for local economies, it has also been noted that large crowds of pilgrims attract crime—pickpockets, thieves, and merchants that prey on the vulnerable. Beyond the economic factors, the increasing popularity of travel to holy places around the world has raised questions about the environmental impact of pilgrimage on ancient sites.

If one of the characteristics of pilgrimage to holy places and sacred spaces is to bring the experience home in some way, it is important to look at that reality in terms of its impact on the sites. Across the major religions of the world, objects are made for pilgrims and brought home with them as reminders of their experiences. Like the relics of holy people in the Middle Ages, these objects are not only personal treasures for pilgrims, but also serve as vehicles to let others know about the pilgrimage site. Although today's "relics" from holy places and sacred sites are not as likely to be a bone fragment or vial of blood from the body of a holy person—although that still *does* happen—the memorabilia are usually either of the natural or commercial variety. For some sacred sites, the memorabilia of pilgrimage are of the natural world: water from the Jordan River, the Ganges, or Niagara Falls; seeds or cuttings from the Bodhi Tree or the Glastonbury Thorn; earth from Chimayó; or stones from Jerusalem or the Great Pyramids.

These natural memorabilia evoke strong associations with the power of the experience for many returned pilgrims. At the same time, it is important to assess the impact on the natural environment before obtaining memorabilia from the natural world. English pilgrim Jennifer Lash, on her journey through France, writes that she learned to overcome the need to take things from each site, just as she learned to enjoy rather than pick the wildflowers. "Place has a mighty tongue of its own," Lash writes. "You can become an aspect of it, simply by being there, if you lose the sense of yourself as a passing outsider. You can gather up the mystery of yourself, and confront all the other mysteries and wonders."[21]

At a time when pilgrimage to holy places and sacred places around the world is growing, the sheer numbers of people, along with environmental factors in general, are taking a huge toll on sacred sites. For example, the growing numbers of pilgrims arriving to bathe in the Ganges has resulted in environmental damage as forests are cut down to accommodate them. Moreover, the World Wildlife Fund issued a warning that the Ganges could start to dry up as early as 2030, due to the global warning that is causing the glacier at its source to recede. The drying up of the river will have disastrous implications for the five hundred million people who depend on Mother Ganga for water.[22]

Another great river system, the Nile, is under stress. In northern Ethiopia, the sacred source of the Blue Nile is facing drought and desertification at an alarming rate.[23] Global warming has also affected the glaciers and snow cover of Mount Kilimanjaro; scientists estimate that the plateau ice cap will be gone by 2040.[24] Refuse left behind by pilgrims and the erosion of the paths to the summit of Mount Fuji, especially pronounced during the summer months, have had a negative impact on that holy site.[25] These are but a few of the reminders of the environmental challenges facing holy places and sacred spaces today.

The overall commercialization of pilgrimage memorabilia and sacred travel has contributed to the growth of a profitable industry. On the positive side, the explosion of souvenir shops and inexpensive memorabilia at some sites provides income and contributes to the local economy, though it is often unclear if the local vendors receive their just portions of the profits of such items. On the negative side, critics of the souvenir industry suggest that such items cheapen the pilgrimage experience by overexposing a holy image or artifact. Another criticism is that the commercialization of holy places and sacred spaces such as the Old City of Jerusalem and other spiritual centers not only disillusions pilgrims, but detracts from the pilgrimage experience itself and makes the site seem like "just another tourist trap." Seminarian Kathryn Glover writes of her discomfort with her own ability to feel anything at the holy places in Bethlehem and the Old City, which seemed to stand in sharp contrast with the realities of Israel today. "I have already said that I would like to go back, but the next time I will go prepared ... prepared for the political and human reality that is Israel in its entirety and prepared to have the story of our Lord brought to life by merely being where he was and walking where he and so many others have walked in faith."[26]

Faster and more convenient means of travel, along with the greater availability of support services for pilgrims around the world, together combine to make sacred sites accessible to more people than ever before in human history. Not too many years ago many holy places and sacred spaces around the world were accessible only on foot to devout pilgrims but are now major international tourist sites. For instance, the sacred mountains of China now have cable cars to carry visitors to the summit.

Michael Stausberg, a professor of religion at the University of Bergen in Norway, points out that the boundaries that used to exist between "tourism" and "pilgrimage" no longer hold true. These days, he argues, with the availability of "spiritual tourism" and "socially responsible vacations," travel for some may replace traditional religious observance. For example, Finca Esperanza Verde is an organic coffee farm and ecotourism lodge founded in Nicaragua by an American Unitarian Universalist couple with dreams of helping local people find profitable and sustainable ways to share their country with tourists. The staff teach tourists about Nicaraguan culture, arts, foods, history, nature, and wildlife. Profits from the venture have built six local schools, a maternity center, a home for seniors, and a guide club for local teens. What shapes the experience for tourists is the site's commitment to the environment and the whole human family. "Not your typical Mai Tai vacation," said one recent visitor.[27]

Both tourism and pilgrimage, moreover, are social processes where the sacred traveler is engaged in a search or quest. Stausberg notes that holy places and sacred sites are frequented not only by pilgrims, but also by "ordinary" tourists who happen to visit those sites for a range of reasons not linked to spiritual enlightenment or connection with the Divine. For example, Notre Dame Cathedral in Paris is considered the largest tourist attraction in Europe, surpassing Disneyland Paris in the number of annual visitors. At times, the desire to make holy places and sacred spaces into wider attractions has involved making modifications in the environment that may limit the access and use of the site for local people. As an Aboriginal woman once said,

"If you came here to help me, please go home, but if you came because you know that somehow your destiny is tied up with mine, please stay and we can work together." In some cases, local people are even displaced from sacred sites to make way for tourism. For example, villagers near the Buddhist Borobudur and Hindu Prambanan temples on the island of Java in Indonesia were forcibly removed to make way for tourism.[28]

Theologian Miroslav Volf, in an article titled "Reluctant Pilgrim," writes about his pilgrimage to the site of Jesus's baptism on the Jordan River. Volf had always been skeptical about going on a pilgrimage; he had been disappointed with what he viewed as the scriptural, archeological, and documentary inaccuracies behind the sites of the Holy Land, as well as the signs of religious intolerance. But the pilgrimage to the baptism site was qualitatively different for Volf, not only because of its historical authenticity, but because of the sensitive preservation of the holiness of the site itself. The new pilgrimage house, churches, and monastery built on the grounds, courtesy of the Jordanian government, are at a distance from the holy site; they are designed to support pilgrims, yet do not get in the way of a spiritual or religious agenda. Although memorabilia may be purchased at the visitors center, there are no shops at the sites themselves. According to Volf, the site of Jesus's baptism turned him and his son "into pilgrims because it presented itself to us as a sacred space—a space free from the mercantile culture in which we are drenched and a space inscribed with sacred narratives that point a person to the spring of living water and the tree of new life."[29]

The answers to these problems lie not so much in limiting access to the most sacred sites in the world, but in looking at the relationship between pilgrimage and the ethical obligation to care for the earth and the people who live near sacred sites. If pilgrimage is a sacred art and a spiritual practice, then how do we as pilgrims honor holy places and sacred spaces? How might our offerings contribute to the longevity and preservation of the people and places where we travel? How can we travel more "lightly" on the earth to ensure that holy places and sacred spaces are open to future generations of pilgrims? Kathy Galloway of the Iona Community writes:

> Pilgrimage is ... a sign of contradiction and of resistance to our prevailing value system, that of the market. Pilgrimage, after all, has no value other than itself; its means is as important as its end, its process as its product. Its utility value is small, and its benefits cannot be quantified or costed. Its value is intrinsic. It is something that is good to do because it is good to do. It states clearly that the extravagant gesture (because it is extravagant in terms of time and commitment) is an irrepressible part of what it means to be human and to walk the earth.[30]

For the last sixteen years, Bernie Glassman and the Zen Peacemakers have sponsored a pilgrimage to the Auschwitz and Birkenau Nazi concentration camps in Poland, in an effort to bear witness to the vast suffering that occurred in those places. As one participant described the experience, "In order to be with someone else's suffering I had to recognize that there was no inside and no outside ... that what another person, a so-called different person is experiencing, outside of me is really being experienced within me...."[31]

One of the temptations some pilgrims encounter is that because of their greater wealth and education, they can hold the real world at a distance and only seek out those experiences that support a vision of the world as they would like to see it. The fact remains that many holy places and sacred spaces are located in some of the poorest regions of the world, where the general population live lives marked by hunger and deprivation. How might the contradictions that confront us as we visit holy places and sacred spaces contribute to the growth we seek through pilgrimage? If the spiritual journey of the pilgrim is the pathway of the heart, how might we also open our hearts to the human suffering in our midst? How might we better practice "sustainable pilgrimage"? These are pressing questions that shape the reality of pilgrimage to holy places and sacred spaces today.

Questions for Your Own Exploration

1. Put aside a table, mantelpiece, or windowsill in your home, office, or some other significant place and begin to assemble a personal "altar." Bring together your "sacred objects" to display in this holy place. For some people, these sacred objects may be intentionally religious or spiritual in nature. For others, the sacred objects may be from the natural world—stones, water, earth. Still others might want to include photographs or other visual images. What makes these objects and this space holy or sacred for you?

2. Reflect on your own sacred geography. What are the holy places and sacred spaces in your own spiritual landscape? What do they look like? Why are they holy or sacred?

3. How do you honor your body? If the body is a sacred space, what practices shape this understanding for you?

CHAPTER 4

WALKING THE
LABYRINTH

The Labyrinth is a riddle
It is the cosmos and the world
The life of human kind, the womb of the earth
The journey, the way to the center
The way to ourselves
                    —*Ursa Krattinger Tinga (twentieth century)*

To take the first step in faith, you don't need the
whole staircase;
Just take the first step.
                    —*Martin Luther King Jr. (1929–1968)*

Life is not a particular place or destination.
Life is a path.
                    —*Thich Nhat Hanh (b. 1926)*

The symbol of the labyrinth has been part of human consciousness since prehistoric times. A labyrinth walk is a journey to the
center, to the heart. "God help us to live slowly, to move simply,
to look softly, to allow emptiness, to let the heart create for us,"

writes Australian poet Michael Leunig.[1] Many different images and metaphors are used to describe the network of winding paths that lead into the center called the labyrinth. Writer Virginia Westbury uses the term "gateway to the heart" to describe the labyrinth and its healing and spiritual properties.[2] Novelist Umberto Eco calls labyrinths "doorways to mystery."[3]

For some, walking the labyrinth is an experience of rebirth and, as such, mystic Ursa Krattinger Tinga refers to it as "the womb of the earth."[4] For others, the labyrinth is known as a path, a way through the wilderness, or a journey inward to deeper levels of consciousness. Today many are walking the labyrinth who claim no particular religious or spiritual connection but who are aware of the need to nourish their souls, minds, and bodies. In this way, the labyrinth is a form of pilgrimage where people of diverse beliefs and philosophies walk a common path. Jill Purce in *The Mystic Spiral* writes:

> There are two approaches to the Divine, both spiral. One is an inward process of regeneration and integration achieved with the aid of a mandala, and is a concentration into and through the center; the other is the outward pilgrimage of Parsifal, Gilgamesh or Jason. The essential unity of the two is illustrated by the inward spiral of Bunyan's Pilgrim's Progress to the Celestial City, of Dante's climb to the summit of Mount Purgatory, and of Sudama's journey to the Golden City of Krishna.[5]

The labyrinth is more than a series of concentric circles; the way through it to the center is fraught with twists and turns, just as life does in bringing us its struggles and its joys. Inherent in the labyrinth path are the contradictions and questions of human existence—hope and fear; beauty and destruction; good and evil; sorrow and contentment; love and isolation; peace and conflict. It is a pathway to transformation, and the growth and challenge characteristic of the journey. "It is a symbolic pilgrimage to still the mind so that the heart can open up and you can return to the world with a deeper and clearer understanding of who you are. Like with all journeys it begins with a single step."[6]

History has taught us that increased interest in walking the labyrinth recurs, especially at times of rapid change when interest in more traditional religious structures wanes, as evidenced by the rise of the global Labyrinth Movement of the late twentieth century. In our age, when many favor more intellectual and scientific forms of intelligence over forms of knowledge grounded in experience and spirit, walking the labyrinth is a response to the need to return to wholeness where all forms of knowing are valued.

The labyrinth is related to the maze, though with an important difference. (At times the terms are used interchangeably, which is inaccurate.) The maze is designed with dead ends, while the more ancient symbol of the labyrinth, despite the twists and turns, always leads to the center. "Mazes are designed to get you lost, labyrinths are designed to get you found," observed peace activist Wavy Gravy.[7] As a pathway for spiritual growth and healing, the design of the labyrinth supports the belief that the center is reachable and that the pilgrim is always guided along the way. The design of a maze values the outer world, making choices about which direction to take and responding to those choices, while the labyrinth is designed to support both an inward and outward journey to instill trust through reflection. Its proven ability to enhance spiritual growth, bringing healing and a sense of peace to individuals, has contributed to its use as a tool for building tolerance and promoting healing and peacekeeping in local communities and globally.

"Every one of us gasped when we first entered the labyrinth, which led to the various sacred rooms: the Hall of Water, of the Earth, of the Spheres, of the Metals. What makes these more than just museum pieces, though, is the sacred science upon which Damanhur is founded," writes musician Steve Halpern about Damanhur and the Temple of Humankind, a contemporary sacred site that lies in the Valchiusella Valley, in the Piedmont region of northern Italy.[8] The founder of the Damanhur Federation and the Temple Project is Italian philosopher and healer Oberto Airaudi, also known as Falco.

The name *Damanhur* comes from a city named after the god Horus, northwest of present-day Cairo. In 1978, Falco was inspired by a rare shooting star that left behind a trail of stardust and convinced his small community to start building a temple into the local hillside, since there were no regulations about building underground. "It was a positive sign, a good moment to begin to dig a tunnel into the mountain, toward the heart of Earth, to create a synchronic contact, to build a temple the likes of which had not existed for a thousand years or more."[9] This pattern of building into hillsides and mountains has been characteristic of human communities for millennia: the Ellora Caves in central India, the rock temples in Petra, and the Kinver Edge rock houses in Staffordshire, England, which inspired J.R.R. Tolkien's *The Hobbit*, are but a few examples of ventures involving tunnel building.[10]

As the fifteen Damanhur community members, none with previous building experience, began digging tunnels into the hillside with hand tools, they became aware of changes within themselves and of the strengthened bonds the work created among them. As a result they began to integrate their digging with their spiritual practice, including meditation and ritual. Like pilgrims on the road, community members felt they were "digging into themselves" and were encouraged on their journey by a sense of mystery and the spirit of companionship. Knowing that they were unlikely to get building approvals for such an unrealistic project, the community worked in secrecy. After several months, the first niche was built to make contact with the earth in meditation practice. Eventually, a circular cavern was formed that allowed groups of people to gather. The circular space became the Blue Temple, the oldest part of the complex.

The Temple Project expanded from there into a series of underground temples. Built by an alliance of alternative communities, the temples are dedicated not to a god or to particular gods, but to the Divine that lives within all humankind. The vast Hall of the Labyrinth leads into other sacred rooms and is designed to take the walker through the history of humanity, awaken the Sacred that lives within them, and encourage meditation and reflection. It reminds walkers both of their inward spiritual journey as well as their place within the larger human community. At crossing points are statues of men and women, representing the guardians of the labyrinth. The walls of the area are completely painted with reminders of major events of documented human stories—the creation of civilizations, the waging of wars, the making of inventions, and the unfolding of events in the human story. "These images serve as a memory, a warning, and a propitiation for future choices that lead us into respect for cultures and diversity, harmony, peace, and the evolution of humankind."[11]

In 1992, a former community member divulged the site of the project to the police. Although the police threatened to destroy the place with explosives, their investigations resulted in a change of heart. Awed and inspired by the beauty of the project, the Italian authorities emerged from underground with a commitment to protect the site and now consider it the "Eighth Wonder of the World." Future plans include an underground "Temple of the Peoples" where men and women can meet together in a "spiritual parliament" to exchange wisdom on current issues and the world environmental crisis. The temple itself will also be an environmental restoration, created out of two abandoned pits of a former lime quarry. "Instead of delving into one's painful past to heal one's inner being, the idea at Damanhur is that by nurturing that which is of beauty in each person, all will flourish," writes author Randy Peyser.[12] The Temples of Humankind at Damanhur are one example of emerging sacred sites today and the prominence of the labyrinth as both an ancient and contemporary symbol of the spiritual path.

A SINGLE PATH

As an archetypal symbol of healing, wholeness, unity, and divine center, the labyrinth is found in many cultures, stretching from prehistory to the present. Some of the designs of labyrinths are adapted to their environments. Today, labyrinths are found in nature, churches, schools, retreat centers, nursing homes, hospitals, and other built and natural environments. The most common characteristic of labyrinth patterns is that they are *unicursal*—meaning they incorporate "a single course or path." If you follow the path, you will eventually arrive at the center. "There is no such thing as an incorrect path—for on this journey you cannot 'not get' where you are going," writes Neale Donald Walsh in *Conversations with God*. "It is simply a matter of speed—merely a question of when you will get there."[13]

In her work on the healing aspects of the labyrinth, Helen Raphael Sands observes that walkers do not have to make any decisions about whether to turn right or left. Consequently, the left side of a walker's brain, which governs the right side of the body—controlling verbal, rational, logical, linear, and abstract faculties—is allowed to rest. It is the right side of the brain, controlling the intuitive, synthetic, nonverbal, nonrational, and concrete, that is dominant for the labyrinth walker. Sands observes that the twists and turns of the labyrinth mirror the interior of the human body: the coils of the brain, the surface of the inner ear, and the shape of the small intestine. Similarly, the life-giving umbilical cord that attaches us to the womb is a coil. Labyrinth patterns are also reproduced in the outer natural world through fingerprints, spiderwebs, fern patterns, the spiral of pinecones, ripples on water, and snail shells.[14] Over time, those committed to walking the labyrinth as a spiritual practice begin to recognize the patterns as they walk through their daily lives. As we walk the labyrinth we are, in a sense, returning to the source of life itself. "We are perfectly made to see and hear God," says poet Paul Holbrook.[15]

Labyrinths are described by the numbers of circuits they have. A *circuit* refers to the number of circles, rings, or pathways that comprise the labyrinth, excluding the center. Many of the most ancient labyrinths are three-circuit; also common are the *classical* seven-circuit and *medieval* eleven-circuit labyrinths, though numbers of circuits vary for modern labyrinths. The place where walkers enter is known as the *mouth* of the labyrinth. The *threshold* is the area outside the mouth of the labyrinth where walkers pause to enter and remove their shoes. The walkway of a labyrinth is referred to as the *path*, and the sides are known as the *walls* or the *fields*, depending on whether the space between the paths is made of solid materials or is a flat border. Ancient three-circuit labyrinths tended to be the simplest in design and were constructed with two crossed lines at the central axis. The so-called *classical* labyrinths are an extension of the three-circuit design, with seven circuits and eight walls around the central two crossed lines.

During the Middle Ages, throughout Europe, as the labyrinth developed Christian significance, they were installed on the floors of several major cathedrals. Expanding from seven to eleven circuits, with the north, south, east, and west axes broken at different places, the effect was to increase the number of twists and turns a walker experiences on the path to the center. The centers themselves were left open, without symbols, as spaces of reflection and new possibilities for the walker. Different styles of labyrinths have different centers; classical seven-circuit labyrinths usually have smaller centers that accommodate one person at a time, taking a single step, while medieval eleven-circuit labyrinths have larger centers that allow for more people at one time and for more movement.

Over time and across cultures, the meaning and symbolism of the center has varied, as has the role of the labyrinth itself. The circle is a universal symbol of wholeness and unity that translates across cultures and traditions. A circle has no beginning and no end; it reflects the cosmos and the flow of human existence from birth to death. Traditionally, sacred circles have been symbols of power, wisdom, rebirth, balance, and spiritual energy. "There is nothing so wise as a circle," wrote the poet Rainer Maria Rilke.[16] In ancient Egypt, the sacred circle was considered a cosmic creative force, with the Absolute at its center. A variety of other spiritual traditions—among them nature religions, the ritual dances of the Celtic peoples, and Sufi whirling dervishes— include sacred circle dances. Joan Chittister writes, "Now, in a century with eyes wide open to the evils of domination, the sin of exclusiveness, the other humanity of the feminine, a God of infinitely gentle heart waits for all of us outside of old systems and old rules at someplace new."[17]

For some today, the center of the labyrinth is as simple and as complex as the Truth you find there. In the spirituality of the Divine Feminine, the sacred circle is likened to the cycles of the moon that guide the seasons as well as the internal biological cycle of all women. Thus to step into the labyrinth is to align one-self with the movement of the moon, the stars, and the sun. For some who walk the labyrinth, the center is a symbol of the Divine within them. Others experience God, Jesus Christ, or the Buddha at the center. The center of the labyrinth is described as the source of the goddess, the Divine Feminine, encircled by the phases of the moon. For those who do not relate to religious or spiritual tradi-tions, the center of the labyrinth often symbolizes the realm of the unconscious, or the ultimate Truth, or an energy source.

The symbolism of the circle relates to cyclical time and the phases of the moon. In the Northern Hemisphere, our annual calendar and the season of winter coincides with the longest nights of the year; the winter solstice (December 21) is the shortest day and the longest night of the year. Gradually the days and nights are of equal time, and the spring equinox (March 20 or 21) marks this occurrence. The sun is at its highest point in the sky for the summer solstice (between June 20 and 22) and days grow longer. With the autumn equinox (September 22 or 23) days and nights are equal once more. The seasons are reversed in the Southern Hemisphere. Not surprisingly, many traditional and religious holidays occur around these key points in the year. Individuals sometimes note that they feel their internal calendar is set differently than the seasonal calendar, and this awareness is important to experiencing the journey of the labyrinth.

"The fundamental action of a human being is walking upright," writes spiritual author and retreat leader Benedicta Ward.[18] Ideally, by reaching the center of the labyrinth, the walker has not only traversed the path, but has also had the opportunity to go on an inward journey. The walker who reaches the center of the labyrinth may discover new knowledge or insights, or she may learn that she had the wisdom within herself all along. The motive for walking the labyrinth is left up to the individual. Labyrinth facilitators tend to agree that the experience of arrival at the center of a labyrinth is deeply moving for many walkers and a transformational event for some, who may feel they have reached the center of the universe or the center of the circle of life. In this way, labyrinths are designed to help us get in touch with the Sacred in everyday life. Others feel connected to the centuries of walkers who followed the same path before them. Some feel a sense of enlightenment, of inner healing or of coming home, while others experience the fear or anxiety that emerges because of issues in the past they have never been resolved.

For example, labyrinth facilitator and author Helen Raphael Sands writes of her "fear of the center" after experiencing a mugging: "It was time to look inside at patterns of abuse I carried since childhood.... I felt I was being led to the heart of the labyrinth, and to my heart within, where I had to meet my worst fears: inactivity; silence; the void."[19] Sometimes tears are shed, or a walker who is overcome by awe will drop to his knees in the center. Reaching the center of the labyrinth is often a time for silent contemplation, prayer, or reflection. "In my best moments I see the entire center as a place of the Holy of Holies, including all of the realms of creation. I can see the Divine in everything and everyone, including myself," writes labyrinth facilitator Helen Curry.[20]

ORIGINS OF THE LABYRINTH

The exact place and date of origin of the labyrinth are a mystery, yet labyrinths emerge and reemerge across regions, cultures, and traditions from the earliest peoples. The symbol of the Tree of Life, found in the Jewish mystical tradition of Kabbalah, is a labyrinth symbol described as the Path to God. Tibetan sand paintings in the shape of a mandala also reflect the design of the labyrinth; though they are not walked, they are designed to quiet the mind. Similarly, early Celtic peoples used the figure of the labyrinth in art and manuscripts; its patterns are found in the tattoos of Pacific Islanders, for example. The indigenous peoples of the Americas used the symbol of the labyrinth in their art and rituals, such as the Hopi medicine wheel and the man-in-the-maze traditions of people from the Southwest—Tohono O'odham, Papago, and Pima-Maricopa, to name a few.

The Tohono O'odham, an indigenous people from the Sonoran Desert in southeast Arizona and northwest Mexico, began to use the labyrinth pattern in their basketry by 1900. For them, the pathways describe the difficult journey to finding a deeper meaning in life. The twists and turns are life's struggles and lessons learned, while the center is a symbol of death and union with the Creator. Long before Carl Jung tapped into the power of mandalas, they had a spiritual and ritual significance in the Hindu and Buddhist traditions for thousands of years. The sacred circle represents the womb of creation, or the cosmos, and the designs within are symbols representative of the inner workings of the universe.

Mandalas serve as interdimensional gateways that transcend language and the rational mind, moving human consciousness to the realms of infinite wisdom. What these diverse cultures have in common is that they consider the labyrinth to be a symbol of transformation.

Both intact labyrinths and remains can be found all over the world; some have been neglected or buried over time, while others are in the midst of restoration. There are hundreds of seven-circuit spiral designs found in stone across Scandinavia and in Russia, some dating from the Bronze Age or earlier. In Siberia, there is a spiral pattern dating from 20,000 BCE, leading some scholars to suggest that Siberia may indeed be the place where the labyrinth was born. We have physical evidence of a labyrinth carved into a mammoth ivory tusk found in a Siberian tomb dating from before 5000 BCE, while classical labyrinths on rock carvings, paintings, coins, and tiles have been found in southern Europe and North Africa from roughly 2000 BCE. These same patterns were duplicated in rock carvings, paintings, sculptures, and baskets in Asia, southern Africa, and the Americas. In ancient Taoist texts, sacred caves were considered labyrinths, often with a special spiritual treasure at the center. Labyrinth designs were later incorporated into animal totems in the Americas, which were intended to give the walker the power of the particular animal represented.

Many archeologists believe that the labyrinth pattern comes from the Greek key pattern based on the twisting path of the Meander River of Phrygia, in present-day Turkey. The word *labrys*, referring to the "double-head axe," comes from the same region and is believed to be the root of the word *labyrinth*. This

kind of ax was the symbol of the bull in ancient Greek civilization, an important aspect of worship and associated with the
Cult of the Dead. A related interpretation is that the axe symbol
came from Amazon women, and the coil pattern is related to
the cycles of fertility and reproduction. Either way, the symbolism of the labyrinth seems associated with the cycles of fertility,
life, and death.

Although we do not know the exact origins of the labyrinth,
evidence suggests that people from ancient societies walked them
for many of the reasons we do today—for spiritual insight, prayer,
protection, healing, and pilgrimage to the center. In the Hebrew
Bible, the prophet Jeremiah advised, "Stand at the crossroads
and look and ask for ancient paths, where the road lies; and walk
in it, and find rest to your souls" (6:16). Archeological evidence
of the longevity of the labyrinth includes a clay tablet found in
Pylos, Greece, that is said to be over three thousand years old,
and a Syrian pot showing a labyrinth from the same period. A
wine jar from the seventh century BCE found at Tragliatella,
a town near Rome, features the image of a soldier riding out of
a labyrinth with the word *Troy* inscribed in the outer circuit.
Prehistoric labyrinths can also be found at Pontevedra, Spain,
and Naquane, in Val Camonica, Italy.

The Romans preserved the symbol of the labyrinth on
mosaic floors dating from 165 BCE to 400 CE, found in vil-
las, bathhouses, and tombs throughout the empire. Considered
symbols of protection and guardianship of the sacred, labyrinths
were located near important sites in cities and places of worship. Evidence suggests that the labyrinth was also associated
with early Christianity. For example, a Roman-style labyrinth
was found in the floor of a small Christian church in Algeria,
dating from the fourth century. In the center, letters spell out
the words *Sancta Ecclesia*, or "Holy Church." From the Middle
Ages to the present day, walking the labyrinth has been considered a source of protection from inclement weather and bad

omens in fishing villages along the Baltic. "Furthermore, we have not even to risk the adventure alone, for the heroes of all time have gone before us," adds mythologist Joseph Campbell in writing about the labyrinth. "The labyrinth is thoroughly known. We only have to follow the thread of the hero's path and where we thought to find an abomination, we shall find a god.... And where we had thought to be alone, we shall be with all the world."[21]

The most famous story in Greek mythology about the labyrinth is the legend of Theseus and the Minotaur. It takes place in Knossos, on the Greek island of Crete, the legendary site where the architect Daedalus built a labyrinth for King Minos after his son died in Athens. At its center, the underground labyrinth housed the Minotaur, a fierce creature who was half-man and half-bull. Every nine years the Athenians were required to send tribute victims to King Minos, eventually to be sacrificed to the Minotaur in the labyrinth. One tribute year, Theseus, the son of the king of Athens, was determined to slay the Minotaur and volunteered to be one of those sent to Knossos.

To assist him in his plan, Theseus enlisted the help of King Minos's daughter Ariadne. She gave him a ball of golden thread, with instructions to unwind it behind him so he could find his way out of the labyrinth after he had killed the Minotaur. The hero Theseus was victorious at the center of the labyrinth, killed the Minotaur, and escaped with Ariadne (whom he later deserted) to the island of Delos. There they had a great party and performed the Crane Dance, which is said to simulate not only the mating of the crane, but also the walking of a seven-circuit labyrinth! This myth of Theseus, Ariadne, and the Minotaur had great cultural significance and became the central story associated with the labyrinth in Europe.

"In the symbology of the labyrinth, Ariadne's thread is the guiding force that leads Theseus to safety," writes Lauren Artress.[22] Some scholars suggest that the labyrinth originated in goddess-worshipping cultures. It has been suggested that Bronze-Age Crete, the setting for the Minotaur myth, was one of the last civilizations to worship the goddess. As Helen Raphael Sands notes about Theseus, Ariadne, and the Minotaur, the story represents a departure from other myths in that the woman, Ariadne, considered by some to be a goddess, is a hero in her own right and not simply a woman awaiting rescue. Ariadne is the compassionate figure in the myth. She holds the cord of life that allows the hero to find the center of the labyrinth and return after his ordeal. "Honey to all the gods, but the most to the Mistress of the Labyrinth," reads a thirteenth-century prayer found at Knossos. In a similar way, the ancient Greek city of Troy, also a goddess-worshipping center, is featured in labyrinth artifacts found across Europe.

The themes of birth and rebirth associated with walking the labyrinth place women at the center. It has been suggested that the Chartres Cathedral labyrinth is, in fact, a birthing instrument because of the 272 stones that comprise the path, which is the same number of days in a human pregnancy. The center of the mother and child labyrinth of the Hopi people—also referred to as the "journey symbol"—symbolizes the amniotic sack, the center of life. The lines represent the stages of life, the umbilical cord, and the path of moving, always under the watchful gaze of the Mother.

THE LABYRINTH OF CHARTRES CATHEDRAL

The Middle Ages in Europe marked the beginning of another wave of labyrinth practice and design. Toward the end of the ninth century, a monk named Otfrid of Weissenburg designed a labyrinth that added four circuits to the classical seven, thus creating the eleven-circuit labyrinth first seen in the margins of manuscripts and on maps of the era. Although the "Otfrid Labyrinth" was short-lived, the design provided the impetus for the development of later variations adapted to Christian contexts.

Perhaps most significantly, during the Middle Ages the spiritual practice of walking the labyrinth became enmeshed with the pilgrimage tradition. A vow to make a pilgrimage to Jerusalem to walk in the steps of Jesus was common for devout Christians of that era, but as the impulse to go on pilgrimage grew in popularity, so did the hazards of the journey, particularly during periods of warfare. Accordingly, great cathedrals were built throughout Europe as pilgrimage centers containing important relics of the faith. Labyrinths within the stone floors of the cathedrals marked the dramatic end of the pilgrim's journey. These medieval floor labyrinths in great cathedrals were meant to be walked, as were the turf labyrinths constructed in northern Europe from the twelfth to the fifteenth centuries.

The accessibility of labyrinths in Europe gave a new option to those who desired to go on pilgrimage to the Holy City but were unable to do so for a variety of reasons, including the danger, family hardship, financing, and sickness. Another practice that developed at the time was the placing of small labyrinths at the entrance to churches, possibly to encourage spiritual seekers to trace the path with their fingers before entering. Although the origins of the labyrinth are pre-Christian, during the Middle Ages both the symbolism of the design and the spiritual practices surrounding it were reinterpreted for Christians within a framework that was generally supported by the church, though more conservative religious leaders were wary of encouraging lay people to have direct spiritual experiences.

When Christians began to reinterpret this tradition for themselves, the purpose of the labyrinth became a symbol of the soul on a journey toward God. Walking the labyrinth was thus a pilgrimage along the one true path to eternal salvation. For medieval Christian pilgrims, arrival at the center of the labyrinth, facing east and the altar, symbolized their arrival in Jerusalem. For this reason, the pathway of the labyrinth is sometimes referred to as the *Jerusalem Road.*

Probably the most well-known labyrinth in the world was laid sometime between 1194 and 1220 in the floor of Notre Dame de Chartres, also known as Chartres Cathedral, about fifty miles southwest of Paris. Technically known as a *pavement labyrinth*, it is one of the few remaining labyrinths of its time. Chartres Cathedral is considered one of the most magnificent examples of Gothic architecture in the world and was built on the site of a pre-Christian holy well and grotto that may have been a worship site for the Druids and, during Roman times, for the indigenous Gallic tribes. The first Christian church was built on the site in 64 CE, about thirty years after the death of Jesus. Various churches on the site and the first cathedral itself burned down; the current structure was begun in the late twelfth century. Eventually, a statue of a mother and child was added near the grotto, which some scholars believe served as the model for the Black Madonna now resident in the cathedral crypt. The cathedral spires stand twice as high as any previously built; the church also contains some of the finest stained glass in the world. The majestic columns within the cathedral are said to represent the great forests of the ancestors who stood on the site.

The Chartres labyrinth has survived intact for over eight hundred years, and adaptations of the design are used throughout the world. For example, a granite copy of the Chartres labyrinth can be found in New Harmony, Indiana, which was settled in the nineteenth century by a German sect and became a prosperous utopian community, while the Dominican Sisters in Saugerties, New York have an eighty-foot turf labyrinth also based on the Chartres design. The labyrinth found at Grace Cathedral in San Francisco has played a major role in the revival of the practice of walking the labyrinth in North America and throughout the world.

The Chartres labyrinth is composed of eleven circuits, or concentric circles, plus a twelfth at the center. It is approximately forty-two feet in diameter, filling the entire width of the nave, and divided into four quadrants—north, south, east, and west—intersected at different places along the path. The pathway is made of gray stone, with walls made of blue-black marble. Walkers who travel the entire pathway to the center walk approximately one-third of a mile. There are a total of thirty-four turns as the pilgrim journeys inward, twenty-eight of which are full U-turns. This medieval design is considered an innovation because the repetitive twists and turns on the way to the center more closely resemble the many challenges inherent in the journey of life.

The walker's heart gradually opens as she gets closer and closer to the center of an experience that invites meditation. Interestingly, the Latin root for the word *meditation* is *meditere*, or "to find the center." As the Chartres labyrinth walker follows the path, he gets close to the center, only to have to pull back and begin again from the periphery. Unique to the Chartres labyrinth is a pattern of small circles around the outside called *lunations*. The term comes from the word *luna*, or "the moon," which both illuminates and sheds light and is related to the cycles of life. It is believed that the lunations had a role in following the lunar cycles.

Helen Curry reports that researchers using a Bovis biometer measured the energy frequencies in Chartres Cathedral and found the highest vibrations at the sites of the high altar and the center of the labyrinth. The Chartres labyrinth and others styled after it have large open centers surrounded by a circle of six petals, often referred to as "the rose." Depending on the tradition, the symbol of the rose has a variety of meanings. Across religious traditions the rose is a symbol of love. Within the Christian tradition, the rose became the symbol of the Virgin Mary, the "Mystic Rose," as well as the inspiration for cathedral "rose windows." The rose is also known as a symbol of the human heart and as the center of the labyrinth, where we connect most deeply with ourselves and with others.

For medieval Christians, red roses were also identified with the blood of the martyrs, and five red petals symbolized the wounds of Christ. In Sufi poetry, the rose is associated with the quest for divine love and spiritual enlightenment. Some labyrinth facilitators write that the six petals of the Chartres labyrinth stand for the six days of creation, each corresponding to a different realm—beginning with the minerals of the earth and moving through the plant realm, the animal realm, the human realm, the angelic realm, and, lastly, the realm of the Divine. Helen Raphael Sands interprets the center of the Chartres labyrinth slightly differently. She views the petals as "the flowering of energy," and the images of flower and path as uniting the masculine and feminine spiritual traditions. In Christian terms, the pilgrim walks the path in Christ, yet is also sustained by his mother, Mary. The flower symbolism is also replicated in the Rose Window, thereby uniting the window with the labyrinth below. "In this crucible, where masculine and feminine are in balance and where love moves, transformation and healing can take place."[23]

Chartres Cathedral has been a pilgrimage site for more than a thousand years. Many pilgrims stop there on the way to Santiago de Compostela; others come specifically to reverence the cathedral's famous relic, the *santa camisa*, "sacred shirt," which is said to have been worn by the Virgin Mary either at the Annunciation, when the angel Gabriel prophesied the birth of Jesus or else when she gave birth to him. The relic was given to Chartres in the ninth century and has contributed to the cathedral's reputation as a center for the Divine Feminine; it became one of the first cathedrals in the world dedicated to the Virgin Mary. Mythologist Joseph Campbell referred to Chartres Cathedral as "the womb of the world."[24]

Today Chartres remains a major pilgrimage site not only for Christians, but also for labyrinth walkers and those drawn to the goddess. The Black Madonna in the cathedral crypt was joined in the thirteenth century by a second image installed in the main body of the church. There are many statues of "black virgins" in France alone, in addition to others found throughout the world.

Many miracles are attributed to these figures, though their origins are disputed. Some scholars interpret the black virgins as descendants of the earth goddess or the Egyptian goddess Isis, while others attribute the black coloring to the materials used in creating the statues. But what is probably most important is the way these images have touched the hearts of pilgrims for centuries to the present day.

Walking the labyrinth as a spiritual practice reached its peak in the late fifteenth century, but by the Age of Enlightenment this practice began to fall out of favor within the Christian churches. Instead, as desire to walk the labyrinth waned, garden mazes grew in number and became even more popular than a single path. The reasons given for this shift vary. Some authors suggest that the motivation of the church was to root out those practices with obvious pre-Christian origins and thus superstitious, if not theologically suspect, origins. Others argue that the labyrinth fell out of favor with clergy and churchgoers because the practices associated with it included boisterous dances and games; still others attribute it to the rise of the new science and logical, linear thinking. The anticlericalism and fervid iconoclasm of the French Revolution also led to the destruction of labyrinths across France. Fortunately, at Chartres the remedy was to cover the labyrinth with chairs rather than rip it out of the floor, which is what occurred in other cathedrals.

By the end of the nineteenth century, however, interest in the labyrinth began to resurface as new trends in Christian spirituality grew more tolerant of practices with pre-Christian origins. Another hypothesis is that scientific discoveries, such as the spirals found in DNA, have reintroduced the archetype of the circle into the collective consciousness. An increased ecological consciousness and concern for the earth have also contributed to a spirit that seeks harmony and balance with all of creation. Although all of the historical mysteries of the labyrinth have not been solved, there has been a new wave of research by archeologists, theologians, anthologists, and historians interested in this remarkably resilient tradition. The tradition of walking the labyrinth is flourishing once again in many parts of the world. In the United States alone there are over a thousand labyrinths; more than a million people have walked one, and the numbers are growing. As a pathway for transformation and a journey to the center of the heart, the labyrinth continues to speak to new generations today.

WALKING AS SPIRITUAL PRACTICE

A few years ago, one day in June, Mingyur Rinpoche, a Buddhist monk and best-selling author at the Tergar Monastery in Bodhgaya, India, left his monastery behind to begin life as a wandering yogi. He took nothing with him but the clothes on his back. His absence from the monastery was discovered when an old monk carrying lunch knocked on his door and, upon hearing no response, opened it to find a white ceremonial scarf on the bed along with a letter. Mingyur Rinpoche wrote that from a young age he had wanted to practice by walking alone from place to place in the style of a wandering yogi and realized that it was time to do it. "Though I do not claim to be like the great masters of times past," he wrote, "I am now embarking on this journey as a mere reflection of these teachers, as a faithful imitation of the example they set."[25] No one knows the exact location of Mingyur Rinpoche today, though there have been possible sightings; those close to him believe that he will stay for at least part of his journey in the mountains he loves, because the environment there is so conducive to meditation. His monastic community expects that he will be away for three to five years, perhaps longer, and most likely will return as suddenly as he departed.

The life of a wandering yogi is not an easy one, and it is not a popular practice today. Many find the relative safety of more settled monastic life, with its regular hours and consistent food supply, a great support to meditation and to continuing the monastic tradition. These wanderers relinquish possessions, comfort, as well as more subtle attachments, such as controlling their schedule and their sense of personal identity, to be able to respond to where the path leads. Perhaps the most famous wandering saint of the Tibetan Buddhist tradition, Milarepa, walked through the mountains for half of his lifetime, often living in caves and eating little else but nettle soup. He taught along the way, and wrote many songs and poems. When the crowds clamoring for his teaching became too large, he would move on.

Walking is an important form of Buddhist meditation and spiritual practice. It is said in the *Lotus Sutra* that the Buddha was the most beloved creature who walked on two feet. For the Buddha, walking was effortless. He walked in a state of mindfulness and thus stayed in touch with all of life within him and around him—his mind and body were two aspects of the same thing. Contemporary Vietnamese Buddhist monk and teacher Thich Nhat Hanh says that walking is difficult for us because although we are physically moving our feet, our minds are elsewhere, and therefore our body is walking one way while our consciousness is moving in a different direction. "When we understand the interconnections of our bodies and our minds, the simple act of walking like the Buddha can feel supremely easy and pleasurable," he writes.[26]

Thich Nhat Hanh teaches that we can walk to get somewhere, but we can also walk as a form of meditation. "People say that walking on water is a miracle, but to me, walking peacefully on the earth is the real miracle," he writes. "Each step is a miracle."[27] To begin this practice, breathe in and take one step, focusing your attention on all of your foot. Wait to take the next step until you are fully present in the here and now. When you are absolutely sure that you are in the here and now, touching reality deeply, then smile, and take the next step. As you walk, be fully aware of your foot, the ground underneath it, and the connection between them—your conscious breathing. In walking meditation, the foot is like a seal: each step makes an impression. "When you walk like this you print your stability, your solidity, your freedom, your joy on the ground.... Looking in your footstep, to see the mark of freedom, the mark of solidity, the mark of happiness, the mark of life. You can take a step like that because there is a buddha in you—buddhanature, the capacity of being aware of what is going on. There is a Buddha in everyone of us and we should allow the Buddha to walk."[28]

Augustine of Hippo famously said, "*Solvitur ambulando*," "It is solved by walking." *Circumambulation*, or the ritual of moving around a sacred center, is found in many of the world's religions. Aboriginal peoples in Australia use the term *walkabout* to describe this sacred journey. The walkabout follows the threads that connect the human, physical, and divine worlds in a sacred circle.

In many Hindu temples there are pathways for worshippers to practice circumambulation as a symbol of the journey from daily life to spiritual perfection. In Islam, the Kaaba, the holiest spot on earth, is also considered the most circumambulated shrine in the world. The Kaaba in Mecca is circumambulated by pilgrims at all times—except during prayers, when it is believed that the ritual is being fulfilled by small birds and angels. In Judaism, circumambulation is practiced at the end of the Festival of Sukkot. In Christianity, it is traditional to circumambulate a holy place or object, such as the movement of a pilgrim around a sacred center. Fourteenth-century mystic Catherine of Siena wrote about "walking on the two feet of love," as the balance between the love of God and the love of neighbor in spiritual practice.

The act of walking is in itself a spiral pattern that benefits the whole person. Scientific research has shown that walking labyrinths has a positive effect on overall health and is an effective method of stress reduction. Like yoga, walking can be used as a way to clear your mind and as preparation for meditation. Mindful walking is a way to increase awareness of the presence of the Divine and to meditate on that relationship. William Tenny-Brittian writes in *Prayer for People Who Can't Sit Still* that walking meditation is a way to exercise our hearts and free our souls. It also serves as a spiritual tool because the integration of body and mind opens the heart to the Divine, to God, and to the beauty of the environment. Carolyn Scott Kortge writes in *The Spirited Walker*, "Movement in the body brings movement in the mind. It is natural alchemy. So many of us seek this kind of movement in our lives, a fusion of being and doing. We long to restore wholeness within ourselves and to connect with one another and with the spiritual values that sustain and guide us."[29]

Members of the medical community have also come to appreciate the labyrinth as a place where patients and caregivers alike can process their innermost feelings during times of illness, grief, and death, and labyrinths have been installed in hospitals and hospices around the world. The Johns Hopkins Bayview Medical Center has a labyrinth next to the geriatric center, with paths wide enough for wheelchairs. The Jersey City Alliance to Combat Drug and Alcohol Abuse has several portable labyrinths that rehabilitation centers, schools, and treatment centers may borrow. Similarly, the spiritual and therapeutic benefits of walking the labyrinth have contributed to installing them at retreat and counseling centers. Prison chaplains have integrated the use of labyrinths into jails, prisons, and other correctional institutions. Helen Curry and the Labyrinth Project of Connecticut regularly take the labyrinth to the Federal Correctional Institution at Danbury as a means of support for the women there. Schools, colleges, and universities in the United States, Canada, and Australia are installing labyrinths as a means of developing the inner lives of students and unleashing creativity and imagination, and as resources for stress reduction and conflict resolution.

Labyrinth facilitators suggest that there are several "movements" involved in walking of a labyrinth. Most labyrinth facilitators stress that walkers should approach the labyrinth with an open heart and without any assumptions about the outcome. Each person's experience of walking the labyrinth will be different, and individual experiences will vary from time to time. What is important is openness to the experience and the willingness of participants to place their hearts, minds, and souls in the labyrinth. Chinese philosopher Chuang Tzu, who lived in the fourth century BCE said, "Cease seeing with the mind and see with the vital spirit." Each encounter with the labyrinth is an opportunity for insight and transforming experience. "When you get into that state of mind—you know the one, where you see everything in slow motion and you can hear the blood in your ears—you know there is something more to all of this," says one labyrinth walker at the Greenbelt Festival.[30]

Di Williams, the first labyrinth master in the United Kingdom, writes that walking the labyrinth entails a three-part process of *releasing*, *receiving*, and *returning*. Unless a walker has the opportunity to access a labyrinth when no one else is around, it is helpful to maintain an inward focus on the path, with peripheral awareness of other walkers. Williams suggests that upon entering the path of the labyrinth, walkers should let go of their daily preoccupations, quiet their mind, and, as much as possible, feel a sense of spaciousness. If nagging concerns attempt to creep back, Williams's advice is to try to release them with each physical step. Williams finds that releasing anxieties and preoccupations makes space for gaining new insights.

Upon entering the center of the labyrinth, Williams advises walkers to place themselves in a receptive mode, taking note of thoughts and feelings that resulted from the walk and receiving what is to be learned in the moment. Lastly, the returning process is where the walker reflects on the experience of the labyrinth and what was experienced along the path. Williams also urges walkers upon leaving the labyrinth to take the time to reflect on learning from the whole experience.

Helen Raphael Sands suggests another way to look at walking the labyrinth, this time through a four-step reflection process. "Open your heart and mind on the labyrinth and let the energy of its coiling pathways flow through your body," she writes.[31] Sands suggests that those who do not have access to a labyrinth designed for walkers or who are unable to walk a labyrinth due to physical challenges are still able to mirror the process through the use of finger labyrinths (using the nonwriting hand) or by drawing or tracing the design. For Sands, the four steps include *on the threshold*, *journeying in*, *the resting place*, and *journeying out*. Each movement adds another layer, and further opens the heart, to the experience. The threshold is a movement of focus and taking stock of where you are in the moment. As you begin walking, you are journeying to the center; the energy released opens your heart and mind as you move to the center. The center is a place of rest and reflection.

Some labyrinths are large enough to allow several walkers in the center at the same time, yet each of them has their own unique experience. Some walkers will say that they met themselves at the center, waiting. This experience is not unlike the story of *The Wizard of Oz* when Dorothy, having finally reached Oz, discovers that she had the power inside herself to return home all along. Poet T. S. Eliot referred to the experience of returning to the center when he wrote,

> We shall not ease from exploration
> And the end of all our exploring
> Will be to arrive where we started
> And know the place for the first time."[32]

The journey out is an opportunity to begin to integrate the new possibilities, new awareness, and new questions that have been revealed at the center into one's daily life.

Lauren Artress is the founder and creative director of Veriditas, an organization devoted to connecting people with the labyrinth. An Episcopal priest, psychotherapist, and spiritual director, Artress is the author of *Walking a Sacred Path: Rediscovering the Labyrinth as a Spiritual Practice*, as well as other works that have renewed and sustained interest in the labyrinth throughout the world. "The labyrinth is a spiritual tool that has many applications in various settings," she writes. "It reduces stress, quiets the mind and opens the heart. It is a walking meditation, a path of prayer, and a blue-print where psyche meets Spirit." The labyrinth teaches how to quiet the mind and to practice meditation methods. It is a pathway that for many cultivates self-reflection, a greater sense of self-acceptance, and more fluid responses to life's choices. Walking the labyrinth makes us more aware of the condition of our bodies, of our life force, and the need for integration of body, mind, and spirit. "In the labyrinth, a whole, integrated world presents itself. You can have a heart-to-heart talk with your body. You can have a heart-to-heart talk with Spirit. They all work together in the labyrinth," writes Artress.[33]

This practice also instills a sense of community; though everyone's journey is unique, we are all on a path, and in a sense, we are all sharing the same space. Lastly, the labyrinth allows us to practice living with an open mind and a compassionate heart, two concepts found throughout the world's religious traditions. One way to view the labyrinth, as "the dance between Soul and Spirit,"[34] suggests that walking it evokes new capacities and opens the imagination to new ways of experiencing the world.

Artress believes that spiritual hunger is a dominant characteristic of our time, and her work on the healing effects of the labyrinth has a great deal to offer those with searching hearts. She finds that spiritual hunger has three major dimensions: the need for healing, the longing to be co-creators with the Divine, and the search for self-knowledge. Walking the labyrinth is a means of shedding the painful burdens of our past and achieve psychological healing, as well as providing a source of strength and courage for those coping with physical illnesses. The longing to be a co-creator with the Divine comes from the deep need of all people to discover their true vocation and best contribute their gifts and talents in a meaningful way. Thus it can help pilgrims discover the source of their contribution to humankind and unlock the ways they can use it creatively. In the realm of self-knowledge, the labyrinth is instrumental in assisting people through life's major transitions by revealing the shadow sides we wish to ignore and by helping us to meet ourselves at the center. Lastly, the path of the labyrinth is forgiving—not the "straight and narrow" path, where a mistake means we might lose our way, but a "wide and gracious" route. As soon as we discover that we are lost, we can find our way again.

Since this practice is a form of body prayer, dancing, skipping, and crawling as well as walking are all welcome in the labyrinth. The labyrinth can be walked both as a form of meditation and as part of a ceremony, exercise, or ritual. Artress offers a "fourfold path" that is drawn from the wisdom tradition in the Hebrew scriptures, which stresses that all we are is a blessing from the Divine. This path is intended to be a map for walkers to better understand what can happen while walking the labyrinth. It is not a fixed process, nor does it determine what will happen; rather, it serves as a framework for interpreting the experience. These four stages include *remembering* (the *via positiva*), *releasing* (the *via negativa*), *receiving* (the *via creativa*), and *resolving* (the *via transformativa*). It takes a labyrinth walker from initial preparations for the journey to letting go and opening the heart at the entrance of the labyrinth until the center is reached. At that point the walker receives from the Spirit guidance, love, peace, insights—all depending on the individual journey. The fourth stage begins as the walker leaves the center and, on the path out of the labyrinth, resolves to take the next steps. Again, these steps are as diverse as the walkers themselves.

The return path is distinctive to meditative walking and to pilgrimage in general—you take back into the world what you have received on your journey. Some experience a feeling of rebirth or rejuvenation; others find a creative solution to a nagging problem. Artress sees the labyrinth as a form of the Holy Grail in that it meets you where you are, gives you what you need, and connects you to your destiny in service of others and the earth. Like the Grail castle, the labyrinth is a physical portal into an unseen world of the spirit and a source of transformation. "It is a crucible of change, a watering hole for the Spirit, a tool for manifestation, a mirror of the soul, a path of prayer, a beacon of light, and a crucible for community. It is a place where we who are walking the Path can recognize one another."[35]

Walking the labyrinth is a pilgrim's path and an inward journey to the center of the heart. The rapid growth of the labyrinth movement all over the world suggests it opens the path of healing and spiritual transformation and brings solace, renewal, hope, and wisdom to many people. As Psalm 16:11 reads, "You will show me the path of life; You will fill me with joy in your presence." Labyrinth walkers align themselves with walkers throughout time, tapping into ancient symbols that have the capacity to transform human consciousness.

"The labyrinth addresses the spiritual hunger of our time," writes Lauren Artress. "We are starved for meaningful symbols that are free from sin and guilt. We long for ways to quiet our minds and open our hearts to embrace the differences between ourselves and others. We long to break through our isolation and create community. We want to step beyond cultural barriers and join others different than ourselves."[36] The path of the labyrinth is an expression of the pilgrim's journey to the center of the heart.

Questions for Your Own Exploration

1. Take a walk and try to identify the spiral "circuit" pattern found in a labyrinth in your surroundings. Where are the patterns visible in your natural world?

2. Draw an image of your own spiritual journey, marking significant people, places, events along the way, and projecting into the future. What are spirals and other significant patterns in this experience? If you're reflecting within a group, share your images with one another. Sometimes others are more adept at discerning patterns in our experience than we are.

3. Locate and walk a labyrinth in your own community. How did you experience it? What is the relationship for you between walking a labyrinth and pilgrimage?

CHAPTER 5

THE JOURNEY HOME

The ache for home is in all of us,
the safe place where we can go as we are and not be
questioned.

—Maya Angelou (b. 1928)

To be rooted is perhaps the most important and least
recognized need of the human soul.

—Simone Weil (1909–1943)

We are all visitors to this time, this place.
We are just passing through.
Our purpose here is to observe, to learn, to grow to
love ... and then
we return home.

—Aboriginal proverb

El Camino de Santiago (The Way of St. James), also known simply as "El Camino," has been a major pilgrimage route for over a thousand years. Millions of pilgrims throughout the ages, including travelers as disparate as Francis of Assisi and Shirley MacLaine, have walked El Camino. "Baby, you are almost there. Each step, each day brings you closer to yourself," wrote MacLaine in one of the pilgrim hostel registration books.

The route begins in Saint-Jean-Pied-de-Port in France and leads to the cathedral in Santiago de Compostela, Spain, the legendary tomb of the apostle James. Centuries of pilgrims have walked this route for varied reasons: for miracles, forgiveness, enlightenment, relief, adventure, thanksgiving, and often for reasons and desires that could not be fully articulated when the pilgrims first set off on the five-hundred-mile pathway. Like other pilgrimage sites around the world, the destination is the same, but the nature of the inward journey makes each pilgrim's experience different. "There is a great moment, when you see, however distant, the goal of your wandering," wrote British explorer Freya Stark. "The thing which had been living in your imagination suddenly becomes part of the tangible world."[1]

Twenty-five years ago a few thousand pilgrims made the trek along El Camino annually. Today between one hundred thousand and two hundred thousand pilgrims each year make their way to Santiago de Compostela by foot, bicycle, train, bus, horseback, car, and even by donkey. There is a rich tradition of hospitality to pilgrims in the region. For example, eighty-two-year-old Paca Luna Towar is the fourth generation of her family to welcome pilgrims. Every day she goes to the hermitage of the Virgen del Puente to arrange flowers and light the candles on the altar. "I come to be with the pilgrims. No matter what language they speak, I understand them all, although I am not sure how this happens," she says.[2]

Pilgrims on the road to Santiago de Compostela are the focus of a 2012 film, *The Way*, produced by Emilio Estevez and starring his father, actor Martin Sheen. Estevez based the screenplay on *The Wizard of Oz*—it is a story of four searching characters coming together on the road and being forever changed through the walk and the relationships formed during the journey. Martin Sheen plays Tom, the lead character, an ophthalmologist whose life on the surface seems privileged and full of interest, yet a bit hollow underneath. Ironically, Tom believes that the eyes are the most important organs in the human body and, as one of his physician friends chides him, "the windows of the soul." But Tom is not really interested in his inward journey—he is only going through the motions of life. Although functional in his profession, Tom is in denial about his grief at his wife's death, estranged from his only son, and alienated spiritually. When his parish priest, a family friend, asks to pray with him, Tom's response is, "What for?" In one of the early scenes in the film, Tom takes his son, Daniel, to the airport. Daniel is on his way to walk El Camino de Santiago, and Tom is definitely unimpressed. It is beyond him why a forty-year-old man like his son would have nothing better to do than go on a pilgrimage, especially when he has a dissertation to finish. Daniel invites his father along, but Tom scorns him. The two men can hardly talk to each other without getting angry, because both are feeling an absence, the missing person in both their lives—Tom's wife and Daniel's mother. But they are unable to come together in their grief. Daniel's last words to his father as he leaves the car are, "You don't choose a life, Dad, you live one."

Soon afterward, Tom receives a phone call while on the golf course informing him that his son Daniel has been killed on El Camino, on the first day of his pilgrimage. Travel on El Camino can be treacherous and the weather unpredictable; many pilgrims have lost their lives on the way. Tom drops everything and travels to France to collect his son's ashes and personal effects. Intrigued by the faith of the local police captain who ministers to him after the loss of his son—the captain has walked El Camino three times—and haunted by the last words of his son about the need to start living his life, Tom makes the decision to set out on El Camino in honor of Daniel, carrying his son's ashes with him.

Initially, Tom finds the life of a pilgrim unacceptable: the accommodations are uncomfortable and noisy, the service is not up to his expectations. He behaves like the stereotypical "ugly American," with a bad attitude and unreasonable demands. Tom isn't much interested in making new friends and insists he will go it alone. Only gradually, as Tom delves more deeply into the mystery of El Camino, does he begin to open his heart to other pilgrims along the way. At first, each of Tom's companions on El Camino seems even more spiritually alienated than he. First he meets Joost, a Dutch stoner with a bad marriage, who eats too much and longs for relationship. Joost first claims he is walking El Camino to lose weight for his brother's wedding. Then there is Sarah, a chain-smoker who is the survivor of an abusive relationship and is walking El Camino in pursuit of healing. Lastly, there is Jack, a compulsive talker and travel journalist who is walking El Camino in the hope that it will cure his writer's block. They are not likely companions, but their relationships deepen along the route.

Tom also has brief encounters with other pilgrims who change him as he walks El Camino. His faith is stirred through a chance meeting with a priest, Father Frank, who has brain cancer and a pocket full of rosaries. Later, Tom almost quits the pilgrimage when a gypsy boy steals his backpack, including Daniel's ashes. When Ishmael, the gypsy boy's father, returns the backpack to Tom and they start to talk, he begins to learn valuable lessons in the importance of community and forgiveness in father-son relationships. The two men share a bond based on the challenge of raising their sons. Ishmael also encourages Tom to scatter his son's ashes in the sea at Muxia, a coastal town just past Santiago de Compostela, which is, for Ishmael, an authentic holy place.

Gradually, each encounter along El Camino challenges Tom to open his heart, to experience life again. At the end of the film, we don't know much about each pilgrim's future plans, but we do know that all of them, in some way, have received their heart's desire as they participate in the complex rituals celebrated upon entering the cathedral. A powerful scene toward the end of the film shows all four pilgrims at the Pilgrim's Mass, a daily celebration signifying the end of the pilgrimage. All four characters are visibly moved as they watch the giant incense burner, the *Botafumerio*, managed by a team of monks, swing in a semicircle overhead and set loose clouds of incense throughout the cathedral.

Joost, Sarah, and Jack all change their original plans to continue with Tom to Muxia to scatter Daniel's ashes. Then Tom continues on the way, a transformed person, gradually turning homeward. He has experienced visions of Daniel several times along the road. Over time he begins to see the world through his son's eyes, appreciating Daniel's spiritual vision in a deeper way than he had during his son's lifetime. Tom's return home reconnects him with his family, to the wider human community, to the world, and, ultimately, to his own heart and spirit. He arrives back with a sense of optimism and a need to live out what he has learned along the way—from others and from the blessings of Saint James. In this respect, as many pilgrims find as they begin to return home, the sacred journey continues. "If the journey meant anything, it meant that the last steps into Santiago were the first steps of another journey," writes pilgrim Laura Dennett.[3]

The Way is not merely a pilgrimage film: the actual making of the film was an ancestral pilgrimage for those involved in the production. The film is dedicated to Martin Sheen's father and Emilio Estevez's grandfather, Francisco Estevez, who was born in northern Galicia, the same part of Spain as Santiago de Compostela, and at one time also walked El Camino. Sheen got the idea for the pilgrimage while he was at a family reunion in Ireland for his mother's side of the family. Once there, he decided to look into the possibility of a pilgrimage and flew to Spain with his grandson Taylor, Emilio Estevez's son, and with a family friend. (The friend, Matt Clark, plays Father Frank in the film.) There Sheen and his companions walked a portion of El Camino, talked with pilgrims from all over the world, and attended the daily Pilgrim's Mass at the cathedral. In Burgos, his grandson met the daughter of a local innkeeper, Julia, the woman who would eventually become his wife.

Originally, Emilio Estevez was going to focus the film on the romance between Taylor and Julia, but over five years of research he became consumed with the stories of pilgrims walking El Camino and wrote a script that conveys the transformations that can occur along the way. "Emilio called the film *The Way*, and I am proud that he dedicated it to his grandfather, Francisco Estevez," said Martin Sheen. "What started as a journey inspired by my father ended with a tribute to him. It also changed me, my son, and my grandson forever."[4]

In the Middle Ages, walking El Camino de Santiago was considered just as spiritually beneficial to the faithful as a pilgrimage to Jerusalem or Rome. In the pre-Christian era, the route that led over the Pyrenees and across northern Spain to Cape Finisterre had significance for travelers of many kinds, including Roman and Celtic traders, religious travelers, and childless couples hoping for children, believing that the pilgrimage could improve their chances for conception.

Cape Finisterre is one of the most westerly facing points of Europe and was traditionally associated with the end of the earth, "land's end," also known as the Realm of the Dead. Legend has it that Jesus's disciple James traveled to the Roman province of "Hispania" to convert the people there and that he was eventually buried in Spain. By the ninth century, the legend was well enough established to claim that a local monk had been led to the tomb of Saint James by a star. The place became known as *Compostela*, or *Campus de la Stella*—"Field of Stars." Eventually the legend evolved that the site is located under the Milky Way, which was formed by the dust rising from the feet of pilgrims, and represents El Camino de Santiago in the heavens.

The tomb and the church built at Compostela quickly became a pilgrimage site for travelers from France, Britain, Ireland, and northern Europe, rivaling the pilgrimage to Jerusalem, which was more distant and more dangerous. The great cathedral was completed early in the twelfth century. El Camino, known simply as "The Way," is said to be the inspiration for the first guide for travelers, *The Pilgrim's Guide*, published in 1140. Actually, eleven pilgrimage routes lead to Santiago de Compostela, all of them followed prayerfully.

Traditionally, pilgrims embarking on this journey would gather at assembly points in Paris, Vézelay, Le Puy-en-Velay, or Arles to travel in groups, for safety and companionship. In northern Spain, the routes merged into the Camino Francés through Burgos and León before arriving in Santiago de Compostela. The pilgrim's symbol of Santiago de Compostela is the scallop shell, which symbolizes Saint James's connection with the sea—he was a fisherman before answering Jesus's call to join his band of apostles—and suggests the site's association with an earlier fertility cult of Venus. Later on, the scallop shell took on a more practical association as the scoop used to measure out food to pilgrims. Today pilgrims also carry a passport known as a *credencial*, which allows them to stay in the hostels, or *refugios*, along the way and qualifies them to earn a special certificate, a *compostela*, at the end of the journey. At the great entrance to the cathedral, the Portico da Gloria, there is a statue of Saint James. It is customary for pilgrims to touch the left foot of the statue as a signal that the journey has ended. At the Pilgrim's Mass, each day at noon, the starting point and country of origin of those pilgrims who received their *compostela* are read aloud.

Pilgrimage on El Camino de Santiago began to diminish during the fourteenth and fifteenth centuries due to fear of the bubonic plague, which was then ravaging Europe. When Sir Francis Drake attacked the coast of Spain in 1589, the local archbishop took it upon himself to hide the relics of Saint James for safekeeping. The problem was that he neglected to tell anyone where he hid the relics, so for three hundred years their location was unknown, and the numbers of pilgrims dropped even further. James's relics were found during a cathedral renovation in the nineteenth century and placed once again at the high altar. Later, after the end of World War II, an organization was founded to rekindle interest in El Camino de Santiago. In the 1970s and 1980s local priest Elias Valiña Sampedro wrote a new guidebook for pilgrims and organized the marking of El Camino Francés for pilgrims. He managed to obtain surplus yellow paint from the highway department and had yellow arrows pointing to Compostela painted on trees, rocks, and buildings along the route. The publication of Brazilian author Paul Coelho's book *The Pilgrimage* in 1987, which describes the author's own experiences walking El Camino, contributed to renewed interest among pilgrims. In the same year, the Council of Europe declared El Camino de Santiago a European Cultural Route.

In 2003, British art critic Brian Sewell filmed his walk on El Camino de Santiago for a television series called *The Naked Pilgrimage*. Sewell ended his pilgrimage in the traditional way by walking to the sea, making a bonfire on the beach, and burning the clothing he wore during his pilgrimage. He then walked naked into the water in a manner reminiscent of Christian baptism. The symbolism of the ritual suggests that a pilgrimage is a journey that frees the individual from attachments until they stand "naked before God."[5]

THE NEED TO BELONG

Pastor and scholar Eugene Peterson writes that we "live much of our lives in exile, so to be able to spot the people and places that re-establish our true identity is *so* important."[6] The need to return home is an instinct shared between human beings and other living creatures. Every winter millions of monarch butterflies make the journey from as far away as eastern Canada to the

Santuario de la Mariposa Monarca, or the Monarch Butterfly Reserve, in Michoacan, located about one hundred miles north of Mexico City. Here the butterflies come to spend the winter, hunched together in the cruciform branches of the sacred *oyamel* fir trees. Some of these courageous butterflies travel almost two thousand miles, forming orange and black clouds on the way, and risking their lives to return. Each individual butterfly sets forth on the journey alone, and although they are seemingly delicate creatures, their collective weight bends the trees as they cling there, protected by each other from the cold. When spring arrives, the butterflies make their way north once again.

Scientists have studied this pilgrimage of the monarch butterfly, but little is known about how they actually navigate the route to Mexico each year. They may navigate by solar compass or by magnetic field, and yet the inherited wisdom and power within each of these tiny creatures continues to elude the understanding of humankind. Their sense of purpose and endurance, and their ability to offer mutual support are qualities we humans might do well to emulate. Not only are these butterflies important symbols of the wonders of the natural world, they have become, through-out the ages, important symbols of the cycle of all life. As they grow from egg to caterpillar to pupa and then are finally trans-formed into butterflies, they symbolize the cycle of life, death, and resurrection or rebirth. Their story is an illustration of the importance of the journey home and the importance of a sense of belonging that instills wisdom and resilience.

Dutch priest and spiritual writer Henri Nouwen writes, "Loneliness is one of the most universal sources of human suffer-ing today."[7] When we consider the pilgrim's journey home, it is important to note that home is more than the place we live in. In the spiritual sense, our journey home is about returning to a place of *belonging*. "Knowing is a road," writes Canadian poet Anne Carson.[8] One common definition of spirituality is a deep sense of meaning and purpose with a sense of belonging that promotes integration, acceptance, and wholeness. The major religious traditions of the world—Christian, Jewish, Muslim, Buddhist, Taoist, Confucian to name but a few—all stress the need for human beings to create places where they can thrive, where they feel accepted for who they are and welcomed unconditionally. For those who do not subscribe to religious or spiritual traditions, the need to belong is also a deeply ingrained human value that promotes inner healing and wholeness. Today, modern education, with its primary stress on information and reason, may neglect skills that teach people ways to form human relationships and contribute to their own need for belonging.

Sharon Daloz Parks, a scholar of faith development, studies the lives of people who not only thrive personally, but who also practice a commitment to the common good. One of her findings is that such people typically have two major sources of support in their early lives, *threshold people* and *hospitable spaces*. In childhood and young adulthood, threshold people can be parents or other family members, but are also those outside the family, such as teachers, clergy, and neighbors who contribute positively to the inward journey. Hospitable spaces are those places that provide us with a sense of "home," with support, nurture, and a framework for growth, including family homes, friends' homes, schools, libraries, faith communities, and voluntary organizations. For many sacred travelers, the pilgrimage is another way of encountering threshold people, those companions met along the way who open up new ways of relationship and new learning.

Pilgrimage is also a source of hospitable spaces, both existential and material, the type of spaces that encourage new insights, nurture deeper relationships, and promote personal and spiritual growth. As the Mad Hatter says in *Alice in Wonderland*, "How you get there ... is where you will arrive." It is a helpful insight for pilgrims everywhere. Today our "networks of belonging" take on an increasing variety of forms—not only face-to-face-relationships but also our bonds with people who are geographically dispersed and connected to us by telephone, social networks, e-mail, and Skype, with only occasional direct encounters. Even those individuals who appear to live in solitude are connected to others in ways that help them find meaning, whether it is a shared religious tradition or a commitment to ecology and environmental awareness that awakens them to deep connections with other sentient beings.

Sharon Daloz Parks believes that everyone needs a psychological home that is crafted through connections and interactions between individuals and their primary community. No individual alone is the sole actor in the drama of human development. As Parks says, we all need "tribe." Human beings have formed small tribal groups for most of our history. We need a place or places of dependable connection, where we have a sense of the familiar and a secure sense of belonging.

Parks sees the power of belonging as twofold. First, the security of a sense of belonging allows individuals the freedom to grow and become themselves. Second, a sense of belonging comes with boundaries that can either protect and nourish us or hinder us, limiting our chances to experience the fullness of life. For the pilgrim, the importance of a sense of belonging is also twofold. For some, it can serve as an anchor, which opens them to exploration or growth. Other pilgrims may be at a life stage where their sense of belonging needs to be rethought because it is, in some way, inhibiting their promise in ways that are no longer nourishing or sustainable. "Faith is a patterning, connective, relational activity embodied and shaped not within the individual alone but in the comfort and challenges of the company we keep," writes Parks. "Transformations in the meaning of the self, therefore, may also require transformation of the social world."[9]

Within the realm of spiritual development, a sense of belonging is integral to an individual's ability to feel loved by God. "The heartbeat of our time has everything to do with our individual relationship between freedom and belonging," writes poet David Whyte.[10] From the time of our birth throughout our life span, the basic human and spiritual need to belong never leaves us. Unfortunately, there are many people who did not receive the unconditional love and nurture at an early age that helps instill a secure sense of belonging. So it is far easier to feel that God rejects them than it is to believe that the Divine loves them infinitely. The Bhagavad Gita explains that by growing in spiritual insight, we move from believing *in* God to belonging *to* God. People who belong inhabit more than a physical space. A home is not limited to a building; it is also the spiritual and social center of the people who live there. Home is where we ultimately belong—it is the place where we are welcomed, the place where we find love, and the place where we find healing when we need it. "We are all longing to go home to some place we have never been—a place half-remembered, and half-envisioned we can only catch glimpses of from time to time," writes Starhawk. "Arms to hold us when we falter. A circle of healing. A circle of friends. Someplace where we can be free."[11]

In her memoir *Belonging: A Culture of Place*, writer, cultural critic, educator, and leading African American feminist bell hooks[12] recalls her life's pilgrimage and her decision to return to her Kentucky roots. In her book, bell hooks looks at questions like "What does it mean to call a place home? When can we say that we truly belong?" Throughout her memoir, she follows her life's "repetitive circular journey" through a number of moves and back again and explores questions of place and belonging through a "geography of the heart." The journey begins in bell hooks's rural Kentucky birthplace, where she introduces family and shows the creative ways they created a life of dignity from working the land. She claims membership in several different yet interrelated cultural traditions—Appalachia and the American South, rural life and city life. Her education and her work inspired moves to California, Wisconsin, Connecticut, Ohio, and New York, where she lived "split in my mind and heart." She also traveled to San Francisco, Seattle, Tucson, Charleston, and Santa Fe, thinking at different times of her life that those places might be home. The story of her rural Kentucky home is not a romantic one; despite her strong sense of home and belonging, hooks writes honestly about the difficulties of her family's attempt to earn a living and sustain themselves through sharecropping. At the same time she reveals the psychological strength and dignity of the black farming families of her rural community. The patterns of relationship in her home community gave bell hooks some shelter from the racism and classism of the dominant white culture that surrounded them. In the hills, poor people, both black and white, lived slightly beyond the culture that subjugated blacks and dehumanized poor whites, though not without varying degrees of mutual distrust and fear.

As a child, bell hooks became a voracious reader and excelled in segregated schools, where her mentors were supportive black women teachers. When segregation was abolished, her new school was intended to foster new educational opportunities, but hooks also mourned the loss of the kind of education she received from the black women teachers who understood her own community and life experience. Part of the conventional wisdom in many small rural communities is the reality that the most gifted and promising need to go elsewhere if they are to achieve their potential, thus draining human resources out of the state. For bell hooks, this exodus out of the rural areas had an impact similar to mountaintop removal:

> Returning to Kentucky, making my life in a small town, I knew that this was the end of my journey in search of home.... I am called to use my resources not only to cover and protect damaged green space but to engage in a process of hilltop healing.... I am doing the work of self-healing, of earth healing, of reveling in this piecing together my world in such a way that I can be whole and holy.[13]

Intense suicidal thoughts eventually led bell hooks to psychotherapy as a way to heal. But even when she felt that therapy was
not helping her, bell hooks believed that healing was there to be
found, if only she could connect the past with her present.

> Away from Kentucky my heart was spinning and it
> was only when the spinning stopped that I could see
> clearly and heal. Initially this clarity did not lead me to
> Kentucky.... Since my native place was indeed the site and
> origin of the deep dysfunction that damaged my spirit I
> did not believe I could be safe there. All my longing to
> belong, to find a culture of place, all of the searching I
> did from city to city, looking for that community of like
> minded souls was waiting for me in Kentucky, waiting
> for me to remember and reclaim.[14]

Today bell hooks is distinguished professor in residence at Berea
College in Kentucky, and the journey home has given her time
to spend with her aging parents, as they (as her father says) "go
down the mountain." She believes that in the pilgrimage of life,
if one is to live a *mindful* life, it is as important to choose a place
to die as it is to choose where and how to live. In returning to
Kentucky, to the place where she felt she belonged, bell hooks
did not naively assume that she would be returning to an ideal
world. Quite the contrary, in fact. For hooks, an essential part
of her journey home is to work on the social and environmental
issues that have a profoundly negative impact on the lives of
people there, especially the poor. Yet her journey home gave her
a feeling of belonging that she never had anywhere else, through
unbroken ties to the land, its people, and their manner of speech.
"Coming back to my native place I embrace with true love the
reality that 'Kentucky is my fate'—my sublime home."[15] In this
way, bell hooks's journey home reveals an important aspect of
pilgrimage: sometimes we don't know our true home, or where

we most belong, until we leave there. The pilgrim's journey home is an opportunity to integrate the learning and experiences of the present with the memories and relationships of our past.

HOME AND PILGRIMAGE

"Pilgrims are persons in motion—passing through territories not their own—seeking something we might call completion," writes theologian Richard R. Neibuhr.[16] Key to any pilgrimage experience is the need for the pilgrim eventually to journey home. If the sacred art of pilgrimage is not about escapism, avoiding problems, or forgetting where we come from, we need to return home. The way of the pilgrim is essentially about fostering greater *connection* between our past, our present, and our future.

Writer and Unitarian Universalist minister Sarah York writes about the connections between pilgrimage and the journey home in her book *Pilgrim Heart: The Inner Journey Home*. For York, pilgrimage is essentially about the journey home. "Our external journeys participate in an internal pilgrimage," she writes. "As I imagine it, all travel, inward and outward, is soul travel." York believes that there is a huge difference between those who leave home intending never to return and those who leave but plan to come back. Rather than abandoning their commitments to seek the spiritual life, York argues that pilgrims today are more interested in setting forth receptive to change and growth, with the commitment of returning home more spiritually aware. It is the inward journey of the heart that provides a context for the human longing to feel at home. For some, the yearning to return home may be about a specific place or house, but for others it is more about feeling at home in the universe, in community, in the natural world, or in a physical body:

> Thomas Wolfe was right: you can't go home again. You can't go home again because home is not what it was

and you are not who you were. You can't go home again because it has changed and you have changed. Home, it turns out, is more in time than in space, more in events than in time, more in people than in events, more in our own minds than in people. Home is ours to create and long for, to remember and to dream about.[17]

Sarah York believes it is the experience of "homesickness" that often triggers a spiritual quest. When something happens that disturbs the illusion of order and control that we have created for ourselves, it stirs a deeper longing for a sense of home in "space and time." The inward journey of pilgrimage takes us to those places where we feel a sense of rootedness, even if we find ourselves physically in a strange and faraway place. "The goal of any sacred journey, physical or metaphysical, is to feel more *at home*," writes York. "Our task once we have returned is to imbue our everyday lives with a sense of grounding in our spiritual understandings—in those gifts of holy wisdom that have taught us how to be more at home no matter where we are."[18]

Farmer, writer, and academic Wendell Berry criticizes what he sees as the prevailing notions of home merely as symbols of affluence and social status rather than as a place for dwelling and a symbol of connection. Parallel to the call to pilgrimage is the call to journey home. Just as refusing to leave home can become a barrier to psychological and spiritual growth, so we should question the efficacy of continuous journeying without putting down roots in places that give us a sense of belonging and a home. "And the world cannot be discovered by a journey of miles, no matter how long, but only by a spiritual journey, a journey of one inch, very arduous and humbling and joyful, by which we arrive at the ground at our feet, and learn to be at home," writes Berry.[19]

Popular author Marianne Williamson claims that our homes both reflect who we are and can transform who we are.

To become whole, we need the journey and we need to journey home. What does it say about our relationship with home if we live in societies where there are so many homeless, some literally without shelter, and some with physical homes but rootless lives and spirits? "Does the road wind up-hill all the way? / Yes, to the very end," writes English poet Christina Rosetti. "Will the day's journey take the whole long day? / From morn to night, my friend."[20]

Diarmuid O'Murchu, a Roman Catholic priest and social scientist, writes about the needs of adult spiritual development for the twenty-first century. He notes that adulthood needs to be redefined from the models of the 1960s and 1970s. Not only are people living longer, but we also need to develop more flexibility as to our roles in life if we are going to realize our potential. For many people, developmental models suggesting that identity is fixed have meant it was not until retirement, when they were no longer bombarded by the demands of work, mortgage, and family, that they could step back, enter into more reflective space, and take the risks that involve life changes. Without reflective space, many adults lack the opportunity to probe life's deeper questions and reclaim ancient wisdom, leaving us with a quality of spiritual engagement more appropriate for children.

O'Murchu believes that because of a range of inherited ways of understanding life, many adults live far from themselves and consequently live far from the Divine. Now is the time, he argues, for a spirituality of "homecoming" befitting adults in a mature relationship with their God. "We need to come home to a new way of being, and seeing, and doing. For people of adult faith, *homecoming* is the great spiritual challenge of our time."[21] O'Murchu argues that "homecoming" should be the new spiritual metaphor in response to the spiritual hunger of our century. Well-worn metaphors for the spiritual journey, such as "exile," "alienation," and "estrangement," are no longer empowering images for the adult journey, for "something from deep within us tells us we should be able to feel at home on this earth."[22] Spiritual homecoming is about personal and societal transformation; it is not so much what we do as what we allow to embrace us.

Recently, the International Organization for Migration, an intergovernmental body based in Switzerland, determined that human migration is considered one of the defining global issues both now and in the future. More and more people are living outside their place of birth than at any time in human history. Approximately 192 million people have moved from their place of origin. On a more personal level, to "move house," or change one's place of residence, is considered one of the three most highly stressful life events. People all over the world are on the move, and not always for happy reasons. Ruth Walker points out that prior to the eighteenth century, the word *moved* was more likely to refer to strong emotion, as in *deeply moved*, than to a change of residence. "Evidently people tended to stay put before then. It wasn't so easy in those days to just pack up your treasures in bubble wrap and hit the road."[23]

"Did you know you had a true home?" asks Vietnamese Buddhist monk and teacher Thich Nhat Hanh. "No one can take it away from you. Other people can occupy your country, they can even put you in prison, but they cannot take away your true home and your freedom."[24] Sharon Daloz Parks notes that "home" may be the most powerful word in the English language because it recalls the source of our being and our aspirations for the future. "To be at home is to have a place in the scheme of life—a place where we are comfortable; know that we belong; can be who we are; and can honor, protect, and create what we truly love," writes Parks. "To be at home within one's self, place, community, and the cosmos is to feel whole and connected in a way that yields power and participation."[25]

Diana Eck, professor of comparative religions and Indian studies at Harvard University, has throughout her life found that she has two homes. The first is the home of her birth, Bozeman,

Montana, and the second is Banaras, India, the holy city of her pilgrimages:

> Today these two places, Bozeman and Banaras, both convey the spiritual meaning of the word *home* to me. And these two rivers, the Gallatin and the Ganges, both flow with living waters I would call holy. Worlds apart, they carry currents of life and meaning whose confluence is in me, deep in my own spiritual life. All of us have such rivers deep within us, bearing the waters of joining streams.[26]

Pilgrimage is a transformational experience, which moves the pilgrim from home and back again in order to view the self and the world differently. For pilgrims merely to reach their destination is not enough, unless upon returning home they are compelled to make changes. Powerful encounters with the Divine motivate us to reevaluate our relationships, examine how we spend our time, and reach out in new ways with a heightened sense of purpose. Each individual has her or his own gifts and skills to give back to the world, and an experience of pilgrimage often clarifies this call. Ultimately, spiritual practices are intended to do more than enhance the life of a sole individual. They also empower individuals to become more conscious and contributing members of the human community and of our home planet.

We live in a global era where people often operate in ways disconnected from a sense of home, which is all too evident today in the devaluation of human life and our lack of care for our environment. John Inge, a theologian and bishop in the Church of England, writes, "The skyscrapers, airports, freeways and other stereotypical components of modern landscapes—are they not the sacred symbols of a civilization that has defied reach and derided home?"[27] Both spiritually and psychologically the idea of "home" means more than a place to sleep; it is also a place of belonging, a place where we go and are automatically taken in and given sustenance and love. French mystic and social philosopher Simone Weil writes about the human hunger for a sense of home as a need for roots. "A human being has roots by virtue of [his or her] real, active, and natural participation in the life of a community, which preserves in living shape certain particular treasures of the past and certain particular expectations of the future."[28]

Sharon Daloz Parks writes about the relationship between what she refers to as the "twin metaphors" of *home* and *pilgrimage*. She criticizes the tendency in the West to use the image of "journey" as the controlling metaphor of the spiritual life, without equally stressing what she views as its companion metaphor, "home." Parks argues that the future of our planet is dependent upon reconnecting the metaphors of journey *and* home, detachment *and* connection, pilgrims *and* homemakers. "For the primary task before us, both women and men, is not of becoming a fulfilled *self* (or a faithful nation) but rather to become a faithful *people*, members of a whole human family, dwelling together in our planet home, guests to each other in 'the household of God.'"[29] Similarly, Diana Eck has noted that both Mahatma Gandhi and Martin Luther King Jr. used the image of the household as a way to envision the close kinship between all people. "A household gathers together a large and usually complex extended family with all the diversity and temperament and personality that human beings have," she writes. "There is no household without its arguments, but its foundation is undergirding love and its language the two-way language of dialogue."[30]

Parks believes that the strength of the metaphor "journey," together with a sense of transcendence and reaching beyond the present, is integral to the spiritual life. Yet it is of limited value if human beings do not also honor a sense of the spiritual in what is present, immediate, and ultimate. In other words, it is possible in the exhilaration of the journey to lose touch with the spirit in our midst. Parks suggests that *homemaking* is a primary spiritual activity, where nourishing space is created and where dreams and images for the common life flourish. She notes that it is only in the last two hundred years—a time when images of home became private and domesticated—that images of home and pilgrimage have been linked in the spiritual imagination.

Parks believes that we are at a point in human history when the source of hope for the future of our societies and our planet may depend on our ability to reconnect people with pilgrimage and homemaking as twin metaphors in the public imagination. Rising incidents of homelessness and domestic violence may be associated with how we emphasize the spiritual benefits of the journey but at the same time undervalue the need for people to create and nurture their homes across the life span. Martin Luther King Jr. said, "To ignore evil is to become an accomplice to it."[31] Returning home requires pilgrims not only to respect the marginalized and destitute, but also to work for their empowerment and mutual thriving.

For example, theologian Denise Starkey has found a sense of "spiritual homelessness" among survivors of childhood abuse and has connected it with their continued experience of suffering in adulthood from addiction, violence, homelessness, and post-traumatic stress disorder. Writing from the perspective of home design, Xorin Balbes argues in his work *SoulSpace* that in order to satisfy the yearning of our hearts for the experience of home, we must more carefully tend to the place we live in. When our habitations are a reflection of our spirits, then we can more easily experience the home within. "Where you live and what you live with are an extension of who you are," he writes. "I want you to consider the possibility that your home is an extension and a physical representation of who you are—and who you have been. Your space holds all your unfinished emotional business and baggage; the interior design of your home is a mirror of the interior design of you."[32]

STORIES OF THE JOURNEY HOME

A major theme that emerges throughout pilgrim narratives is the reality of returning home, as well as the impact that reality has on someone who faces the end of one journey and looks toward an unknown future. Some pilgrims anticipate with sadness leaving friends and adventures behind, while others experience anxiety in facing the future, not knowing how their transformed selves will fit into their old life. And there are some who cannot wait to return home to share their experiences with those they love. After the intensity of a pilgrimage experience, the journey home becomes a time of further reflection, integration, and a changing awareness of lessons learned along the way. What returning home means will vary with each individual pilgrim, and yet we know that we all must take up that part of the journey.

One type of sacred journey that speaks to the realities of the journey home is the ancestral pilgrimage.[33] The family holds great mythic power in people's lives, yet at the same time romantic notions about real families are not helpful illusions for personal and spiritual growth. The family home is for some people a sacred space, a dwelling for the soul, and a place of enlightenment. For other people, the family has effectively wounded the soul and has caused serious damage to the lives of its members. Psychologists Connie Zweig and Steve Wolf suggest that the wounds of the family can set us on the path toward greater consciousness. But instead of trying to bury these wounds through feelings of bitterness or revenge, this path requires an effort to be open to the awareness of something much bigger. Then instead of burying our wounds, we can learn to carry them and use them as a means for deepening our empathy and compassion for ourselves and for others. Russian author Leo Tolstoy said that our great duty as humans is to sow the seeds of compassion in each other's hearts. Learning and telling the stories of family can contribute to healing and to reclamation of a positive sense of home.

Those on an ancestral pilgrimage may be exploring their family of origin, some feature of their background hitherto unexplored, or places that have connections with those who came before. For example, it is not uncommon for those who work on their family histories to uncover information about relatives from the past and decide to go on pilgrimage to learn more about them, consequently reshaping their own sense of identity in the process. Many people who were adopted as children decide at some point in their lives to go on pilgrimage to the place of their birth or travel to meet a birth parent or sibling for the first time. In a similar way, some birth parents seek out and meet children given up for adoption as a way to reconnect, in the process healing a part of themselves neglected or suppressed earlier in life. Family members separated for years or generations through conflict or trauma may at some time decide to go on pilgrimage to reconnect with their shared history. "All happy families are alike," Leo Tolstoy wrote in *Anna Karenina*, "and each unhappy family is unhappy in its own way." Tolstoy's insight is that every family carries its own pain and brokenness, and it is from these shadows that some of the deepest truths emerge.

Sometimes the focus of an ancestral pilgrimage might not be our blood relatives but rather people who are not part of our family but have shaped our lives in profound ways, sometimes even more deeply than our family of origin. For some, school reunions are a form of ancestral pilgrimage; for others, reunions of military units or of religious communities constitute pilgrimages. All are significant places we yearn to return to and experience once again. In some cultures, visiting graves or other burial sites is a form of ancestral pilgrimage. What these all have in common is an intimate connection to the ways we experience, as Sharon Daloz Parks notes, the threshold people and the hospitable spaces that shape our lives and influence the way we identify who we are and our life's purpose. As we progress through the pilgrimage of life, we sometimes yearn to return to the people and places that have shaped our pasts to gain new insights into who we are and how we see the world.

Traces of the Trade (2008) is a film based on the ancestral pilgrimage of members of the DeWolf family from Bristol, Rhode Island. Producer Katrina Browne got the idea of making the film while she was at divinity school, where she received a family history written by her grandmother that mentioned the DeWolf family's involvement in the slave trade. The admission triggered something in Browne. Although earlier in her life she had a vague idea that her family may have had a role in the slave trade, she never pushed past the family mythology with which she grew up. Although the family had its roots in Rhode Island, a state historically associated with shipbuilding, the family narrative stressed New England's patriotic and democratic values from the time of the American Revolution. Bristol, Rhode Island, was a major port and center of Atlantic trade. Members of the DeWolf family were the civic and religious leaders of Bristol for generations—businesspeople, political officials, and clergy.

After Katrina Browne received her grandmother's family history, she was motivated to dig deeper into the story and to begin to question the mythology that had grown up not only around the DeWolf family, but also around New England's complicity with slavery. During the course of her research, Browne discovered that not only did the DeWolfs own slaves and profit from the slave trade, but her ancestors were the largest slave-trading family in the history of the United States. From 1769 until 1820, members of the DeWolf family transported an estimated ten thousand enslaved Africans across the Middle Passage, amassing an enormous fortune in the process. One ancestor in particular, James DeWolf, nicknamed "Captain Jim," became a United States senator from Rhode Island and was considered to be the second wealthiest man in the United States.

Browne decided that she needed to uncover more of this history before she could even begin to determine her own next steps. She put together the itinerary for a DeWolf family pilgrimage beginning in Bristol, Rhode Island, at the Episcopal church the family attended for generations. The next stop was Ghana in West Africa, where rum was traded for captured African men, women, and children, and then on to Cuba, where slaves were either taken to family-run plantations or sold at auction. The last stretch of the triangular trade, and the pilgrimage itself, was from Cuba back to Rhode Island, where the sugar and molasses from the family's plantations were turned into rum in family-owned distilleries.

Browne wrote to over two hundred DeWolf descendants about the pilgrimage; some ignored her, and a few were angry that she would dredge up such unpleasant family history. "I want to begin with our family and try to better understand the whole can of worms: privilege, shelteredness, productive feelings of guilt, fear, etc.," Browne wrote in her letter to relatives. "I would like to invite fellow descendants to do the journey with me—literally, as well as existentially," she wrote.[34] Ten family members, including Browne, made the pilgrimage, becoming, as one DeWolf cousin wrote, "the Family of Ten."

The ancestral pilgrimage of the DeWolf family was wrenching and illuminating for all involved as they studied, reflected, shared arduous travel, and met with the descendants of the people their family enslaved long ago. The members of the Family of Ten did not know each other terribly well before their ancestral pilgrimage, but those relationships changed profoundly in the process, some coming to feel as close as siblings rather than distant cousins on a family tree. Both appalled at the actions of their ancestors and yet committed to knowing the full truth, the pilgrims were painfully transformed and believe they will never see the world quite the same way again. Though they traveled to common destinations, characteristically the impact of the experience on individual pilgrims differed in terms of how they would focus their energies when they returned home.

Katrina Browne, a first-time filmmaker, completed *Traces of the Trade* and now works extensively with religious and civic groups, educating people on the issues raised by the film and by fostering dialogue and reconciliation. One member of the group, an Episcopal priest, has worked through his denomination nationally to bring the need for further efforts to combat racism to the fore. Another family member, an attorney, works from a legal perspective on reparations. Thomas Norman DeWolf, a former elected official in the state of Oregon, has written and spoken widely on the need for racial reconciliation:

> In recounting my journey with nine distant cousins, my intent is to stimulate both reflection and serious conversation. We are better than we sometimes imagine, and we are not yet all we are capable of becoming. We can remain mired in the mistrust, avoidance, and the distance from previous generations and pass them on to our descendants—or we can commit ourselves to becoming aware, to listening to each other's stories, to embracing the truth, and recognizing and honoring each other's humanity. In doing so, we can finally break through the scars to clean the living wound properly and begin the healing ... together.[35]

A different example of ancestral pilgrimage is the story of Carolyn Jourdan. Jourdan was a wealthy lawyer on Capitol Hill, with a Mercedes and an expensive condo, when she received the news that her mother had had a heart attack. As Jourdan's mother was the receptionist for her father's medical practice in the Smoky Mountains, the situation was dire. Dr. Jourdan was the only physician available for miles, and he desperately needed her help if his office were to remain open during her mother's illness. Thus began Carolyn Jourdan's ancestral pilgrimage, recounted in her memoir, *Heart in the Right Place*.

What Jourdan describes as her trial and her "journey to the heart of things" begins with her recollection of an image from her childhood. As a child, her father showed her an x-ray of a little girl with a heart literally in the wrong place—the child's heart was located on the right side of her chest instead of the left. When she was a child, she asked questions about it, like "How does the little girl say the Pledge of Allegiance?" She knew that having a heart in the wrong place was not a good thing for the little girl or for people in general. Thirty years later the image still haunted Jourdan, though her questions grew more serious, like "What point was God trying to make with the little girl's life?" "Despite my early fears that my destiny was to spend my entire life as an utterly powerless witness to one medical disaster after another," she admits, "I'd eventually grown up and landed a good job in a city far from the mountains of East Tennessee, neatly sidestepping my role as spectator to any more catastrophes. Or so I thought."[36]

Jourdan's memoir is full of images of the heart, and she shares the stories of all the companions she meets along the way who changed not only her heart, but the whole direction of her life and work. She first left Washington, D.C., certain that she was only going to assist her father for as long as necessary, but as days turned into weeks, the lives and circumstances around her challenged her to look into her own heart in ways that her work as a lawyer did not require. Eventually, Jourdan replaced her Mercedes with an old postal Jeep and started appearing in the office wearing scrubs instead of business suits. These external signs of her journey reflected the experiences of her inner pilgrimage. She writes of that time:

> God, this was a heartbreaking job. I wanted my real life back where I did not have to face tragedy suddenly, intimately, as a likely but unpredictable part of a normal workday. I was afraid to let myself feel the full reality of it

because it would hurt. A lot. So I tried to hold everything
at a safe distance. I was biding my time to get away from
this level of reality altogether.[37]

Ironically, by working as a receptionist in her father's medical practice, she discovered what had eluded her in what many would deem a more responsible job as an attorney for the United States Senate. She learned by watching her father working tirelessly for the poor every day, whether he got paid or not, that if she really wanted to make sure that her heart was in the right place, she could stay and work at his side in Strawberry Plains:

> In Washington, I could seem like a big deal for an entire
> nation full of strangers. Here, I was a lowly friendly face
> to the sick people of a small rural community. I desperately wanted to see myself as somebody who mattered
> in this world. That's what I really wanted. Surely I was
> meant for more important things than working in a little
> country doctor's office. Wasn't I?[38]

A pivotal point in her journey home occurred when her childhood friend Henry, the operator of the heart-lung machine at the local hospital, invited her to witness open-heart surgery. Henry is not only technically proficient in his job, he is mystical about what his work means. Henry sees heart bypass surgery as a "medical sacrament," because it gives the patient an experience of the afterlife, a taste of God, just the way Jesus did after he was held under the water by John the Baptist. It is Henry's devout wish for each patient to be changed by the experience of heart surgery, not only physically, but in the way each of them see the direction of their lives. He hopes the change occurs not because they are afraid of their own mortality, but because in seeing God they have tasted their *immortality*. "You do the best you can for as long as you can and then, no matter what happens, you keep coming back day after day and doing it again," was Henry's explanation of his vocation as a healer.

When Jourdan first saw a human heart, she exclaimed that it doesn't look like much, and Henry replied that many of the most important things in the world don't look like much. "Our whole lives were set up to give us every possible opportunity to do the right thing, to mature into good people.... We had to take what we *were* and what we *had* and do the best we could with them. There were no extra bonus points for visibility or magnitude. I'd always aimed for the big score, but now I understood better," mused Jourdan.[39] Carolyn Jourdan eventually realized, when she returned home to Washington, that the people she had met in East Tennessee were there for her at a critical point in her life; they became the ones who "saved" her.

"In the stormy ocean of life, take refuge in yourself," writes Thich Nhat Hanh.[40] After her mother died, Mary Paterson took up yoga and meditation as a way to come to grips with her devastating grief. Years later, when her father died, Paterson felt that she had lost all connection to her familiar inner home. Her response was to commence a forty-day retreat at Thich Nhat Hanh's Plum Village in the Aquitaine countryside of France. Across many religious traditions, the notion of the forty-day cycle is considered an important period of healing and regeneration. The ancient yogis believed that a forty-day sacred journey advances one on the path toward wisdom. The Buddha sat under the Bodhi Tree for just over forty days, Moses was transformed after forty days on Mount Sinai, Jesus fasted and prayed in the desert for forty days, and Muhammad prayed for forty days in a cave. Within the Christian tradition, the period of prayer and intentional practice known as Lent is forty days before Easter, the Feast of the Resurrection. During her own forty-day retreat, Mary Paterson meditated, walked, gardened, and listened to dharma talks in order to learn "how to take refuge in my wise self, and to find Home."[41]

Ancestral pilgrimages are often a way to process grief brought on by the death of those most significance to our sense of home—parents, siblings, children, friends, those who are the threshold people of our life histories. Through the Buddhist practice of *mindfulness*, Mary Paterson hoped to touch "life deeply in every moment." Her desire "to take refuge in the self" is related to the "mindful awareness" that unites body and mind, generates new insight, and roots one in compassion and wisdom.[42] "We are going home in every moment—we are practically going home in every moment to mother earth, to God, to the ultimate dimension, to our true nature of no birth, no death," writes Thich Nhat Hanh. "That is our true home. We have never left our home."[43]

As is the case of ancestral pilgrimages and forty-day retreats of all kinds, not every day was filled with a new awakening for Mary Paterson. She had to cope with the complaints and the needs of others around her, many of whom were also Americans having a hard time settling into the simple accommodations at Plum Village. Through her meditation and encounters with other retreatants, as well as her experiences of healing, Paterson came to know the nuns in her hamlet better. At one particularly poignant time, she was enveloped by the sweet and melodious voice of one of the nuns, Sister Prune, singing a French lullaby. Paterson did not know the words to the song, but she responded to the boundless music and found herself carried to a realm of peace where she was reunited with her mother. It is said that mantras sung with complete devotion can produce miracles, and Paterson felt as if her mother came to her just as she did when she was a child. Not only did Sister Prune's transcendent voice evoke the healing energies of Mary Paterson's mother, but her voice nourished everyone present. "I will never again think of a lullaby as a song for only a child," writes Paterson. "After all, the five-year-old Mary is somewhere inside of me and she wants to be sung to. It helps soothe the pain."[44]

Toward the end of her retreat experience at Plum Village, Paterson became convinced that mindfulness practice is an essential life skill and that being aware of what is truly in the moment is the only way to gain the kind of insight you need to transform yourself. If you can do that, then you can also transform the pain and the suffering in the world. Compassion and love for all creation comes from the home within each of our wise selves. "I think now of this yearning for a true Home that had launched me on my pilgrimage to Plum Village—the quest for a strong, wise place to dwell, to transcend the pain and loneliness of losing my parents, and to skillfully navigate the turbulent waters of life…. I have never left my Home."[45]

Another type of pilgrimage rooted in images of home is the journey to places of geographical or spiritual significance to the pilgrim. Sociologists Christopher P. Scheitle and Roger Finke of Pennsylvania State University spent five weeks in a rented Dodge Charger, traveling across the country in search of a larger experience of the religious diversity of the United States. For the most part, the two men were not on a pilgrimage linked with their family history or religious traditions. Instead, for these researcher-pilgrims, the experience of "home" that they desired was revealed through visiting temples, synagogues, churches, mosques, and other religious sites in an effort to discover the connections between people of faith. "In the end," Finke said, "it's about how you connect with the supernatural being you believe in."[46]

Weary of the misinformation and negative assumptions between and about different religious groups, Scheitle and Finke hoped not only to provide accurate information, but to make a record of their journey that would encourage others to walk through the open doors into the spiritual homes of some of America's religious communities. The researchers visited a black church in Memphis, a Mormon congregation in Utah, a cowboy church in Texas, Taoist and Buddhist temples in San Francisco, the International Society for Krishna Consciousness in Berkeley, Our Lady of Peace Shrine in Wyoming, and a Hasidic Jewish community in Brooklyn, New York, to name just a few.

As Scheitle and Finke returned to their home in central Pennsylvania, they realized that while they were impressed and even amazed by what they discovered on their journey, some of the most profound learning came from unexpected encounters with people and faith communities along the way. Their journey home, moreover, inspired them to investigate the religious diversity in their own midst in central Pennsylvania. Although Scheitle and Finke returned to their actual homes after their pilgrimage across the American religious landscape, they realized that their journey continues: "We confess that our journey is far from over. For each new discovery, we uncovered a plethora of new questions. For each new experience, we found so many more to explore."[47] The journey home always evokes new meaning and new possibilities.

At the end of *The Wizard of Oz*, when Dorothy realizes that the power to return home has always lived inside her, she leaves the Emerald City by clicking her heels together and repeating the mantra "There's no place like home." And she returns home in an instant—but changed by all she learned on her pilgrimage to Oz and the companions she met along the way. She is still Dorothy, and at the same time she is different from the person who left Kansas in a tornado. The final stage of any pilgrimage, that which closes the sacred circle, is the journey home. Human beings of every era have had a deep yearning for a sense of home, and that is no less true today. We live at a time when our capacity to share sacred spaces and holy places, physically and materially through our religious centers, and psychologically and spiritually through shared prayer and meditation, is critical for the many people who yearn to find a place where they can belong. Experiencing sacred spaces and holy places that evoke a sense of home is critical to deepening spiritual practice and better enables us to open ourselves to more than our limited experience of the world and of the Divine.

Questions for Your Own Exploration

1. Where is "home" for you? What or where is that place where you feel you truly belong?

2. Sharon Daloz Parks writes about the need for all who contribute to the common good to have *threshold people* and *hospitable places.* Who were/are the threshold people in your own life? Where/what were/are the hospitable places?

3. How do you practice homemaking? How do you contribute to shaping the common good in the environments you inhabit (household, workplace, communities, planet)?

CHAPTER 6

PREPARING
TO PRACTICE

*Spiritual practice, by uprooting our personal
mythologies of isolation,
uncovers the radiant, joyful heart within each of us
and manifests this radiance to the world.*
                        —*Sharon Salzberg (b. 1952)*

*We are always in the presence of God. Prayer is
acknowledging that we are in that presence.*
                        —*Desmond Tutu (b. 1931)*

*Meditation and praying change your spirit into
something positive. If it is already positive, it makes
it better.... I feel that chanting for thirty-five years
has opened a door inside me, and that even if I never
chanted again, that door would still be there. I feel
at peace with myself....*
                        —*Tina Turner (b. 1939)*

"Pilgrimage is feet-on-the-ground spirituality," writes Jan Sutch
Pickard of the Iona community.[1] As a spiritual practice, the

sacred art of pilgrimage is an opportunity for pilgrims to cultivate their inner life (or inner voice) in a way that leads to a greater sense of peace and compassion—a sense that pervades all of life. Historical theologian Margaret Miles writes of spiritual practice as "a way to deconstruct the socialization and conditioning inscribed on the body, mind and heart by the world to produce a new organizing center of the self."[2]

The importance of spiritual practice is an essential ingredient in the spiritual traditions of the world, as well as for those who cultivate their inner lives beyond the borders of one particular tradition. A spiritual practice, also referred to as a reflective practice, is a regular ritual that opens our hearts, connects us to the Divine, awakens us to the present moment and the world around us, and reminds us of what is most important. Some spiritual practices are communal activities, such as public worship, which aim to open us to an experience of the Divine and inspire us. Other spiritual practices are those personal rituals we perform each day, such as forms of meditation that give us energy and center us, reinfusing our daily lives with meaning. All forms of spiritual practice, both communal and individual, are based on connections, illuminating our relationships with the self, other people, all creatures, and the wider world. Spiritual practices also connect us to the wise ones of the past and are shaped by us for the future.

BEGINNING SPIRITUAL PRACTICE

Jack Kornfield, one of the leading Buddhist teachers in the United States, writes in *A Path with Heart*, "As one matures in spiritual life, one becomes more comfortable with paradox, and appreciative of life's ambiguities, its many levels and inherent conflicts. One develops a sense of life's irony, metaphor, and humor and a capacity to embrace the whole, with its beauty and outrageousness, in the graciousness of the heart."[3]

One way of doing this is by adopting spiritual practices that sharpen our attention and make us more aware of each moment.

For the purpose behind regular spiritual practice is not to take on duties for God or to make something spiritual "happen." Genuine spiritual practices are not about taking on more tasks, but about receiving spiritual gifts. They are intended to create openings, to make space, to grab our attention in the midst of our harried lives so that the spirit of the Divine, already present, can be made known to us. Psychiatrist Paul Fleischman writes, "The man or woman on the path seeks every moment as the one in which to activate life's highest blessing."[4] Although many of us have been brought up to believe that thinking and doing are separate functions, through spiritual practice the two "ways" are inextricably linked as meaningful action. Regular spiritual practice is so powerful because it makes us more aware of and in awe of every living creature, including ourselves. It helps keep us on the path of our inward journey and supports us to embrace the changes that lead to transformation. Over time, our spiritual practices become woven together and become a way of life.

Two forms of spiritual practice that aid every pilgrim are *letting go* and *gratitude.* The ability to let go of preconceived notions about what should happen or what will happen during a pilgrimage helps a pilgrim remain open to the mystery of what *is* happening in the moment. Part of the beauty of the pilgrimage experience is that what occurs is often beyond what the pilgrim expects or anticipates. It is not uncommon for pilgrims to set forth believing they are motivated to go on a pilgrimage for one set of reasons and then to discover along the way that the journey is about something else entirely.

To be vulnerable to the experiences on the journey and let go of old patterns is crucial if a pilgrim is to be open to the possibility of transformation. Similarly, the practice of gratitude supports the positive energy and flexibility needed for a pilgrim to experience the journey to the fullest. The practice of gratitude moves us to accept responsibility for our own growth and actions, positive and challenging, which are very much a part of the inward journey to the center of the heart. A spirituality of abundance, or an orientation to the practice of gratitude, also helps the pilgrim recognize the small blessings along the way, the subtle nuances of the Divine, as well as experience the mystery and awe that are part of the journey.

The need for healing on a variety of levels—spiritual, physical, emotional, relational, sociological—is one of the primary motivations for pilgrimage, and yet many do not see it as a part of spiritual practice. Healing is positive and potent; it seeks to reconcile those parts of ourselves that prevent us from being whole. Some interpret healing as spiritual energy, the presence of the Divine in a human life, or the reconciling action of God throughout all creation. "Healing occurs when you align with the pure, positive energy that created the planet and that keeps your heart beating and your blood chemistry normal," writes physician Christine Northrup. "Healing occurs when you're in harmony with your life's purpose and those who are meant to accompany your path. Healing occurs when you have a sense of safety and security in your life."[5] As a spiritual practice, healing involves the body, soul, and spirit—it is the process whereby we release what is harmful and begin to cultivate what will strengthen us. "Healing comes from the same root as 'whole' and 'holy,' just as 'cure' comes from the same root as 'care,'" writes spiritual activist Claudia Horwitz. "To be healed, therefore, is to be whole and holy. To care for oneself is to begin to find a cure for the world."[6]

Often times, people who have suffered some form of religious abuse or who have been victimized by religious groups are leery about adopting spiritual practices. Such fears are well founded and still prevalent today. At the same time, it is important to continue to distinguish between spiritual practices that are life-affirming and those that deny life, inculcating fear, mistrust, suspicion, and intolerance. Howard Thurman once wrote, "To state what I mean categorically, the religion of the inner life at its best is life-affirming rather than life-denying, and must forever be involved in the Master's instruction."[7] Generally speaking, the life-affirming spiritual practices Thurman speaks of empower individuals and groups to grow intellectually, become more socially responsible, and be moved to create a more humane world. The signs of life-affirming spiritual practices are love, understanding, compassion, and peace. Moreover, life-affirming spiritual practices will sustain us in times of pain and struggle. Preparation for pilgrimage is an ideal time to evaluate one's own spiritual practice or to seek to develop one. Some will find it valuable to meet with a spiritual director, clergyperson, or guru during the period of preparation before a pilgrimage; others may want to join a group of like-minded seekers.

One of the key issues that arise for many people when considering spiritual practice is the question of time. Many of us never feel that we have enough time to do all we want or need to do. We exert an enormous amount of energy working for the good of our families, friends, businesses, and the planet but have difficulty setting aside time for our own healing and transformation. Monastics often are engaged in spiritual practice up to six hours a day, but that kind of freedom from other pursuits is not available to most people. Perhaps the question should be framed this way: If you think you do not have time for regular spiritual practice, what are you willing to give up or modify to make it happen? Reflect on your patterns and how you use your time over the course of a week. How do you waste time? How might some of that time be claimed for spiritual practice?

From a slightly different perspective, it is also true that spiritual practice can be interwoven into the fabric of your daily life in such a way that a great deal of "extra" time is not required. Is it possible to rework your morning or evening for some minutes of intentional silence? If you commute via public transportation, is it possible to use that time for reading or journal writing? Is it possible for you to integrate intentional spiritual practice into other daily activities, such as walking, exercise, cooking?

For some people, regular spiritual practice begins with preserving time within their schedule for a regular Sabbath, either as silent time or as a time to devote to family or other relationships. Perhaps your Sabbath keeping means a time without answering e-mails or the telephone, or it may be time spent with others sharing a common meal and conversation.

Maintaining regular spiritual practices require discipline, yet at the same time it should grow naturally out of your daily routine in ways that will allow you to keep the commitment. If you find yourself avoiding a particular spiritual practice, try to reflect on and understand what the avoidance is about. Overall, spiritual practice is not intended to be easy, yet we also need to find rituals and ways of being that open our hearts and help us to live most creatively and deeply. Just as pilgrimage by itself is a spiritual practice with many paths, so are many pilgrims supported by a variety of different spiritual practices. Some that may be of help in preparation, throughout the pilgrimage, and upon returning home include the following:

walking meditation	healing
letting go	forgiveness
gratitude	worship
journal writing	yoga, bodywork
photography	storytelling
prayer	intentional silence
poetry	shared meals/cooking
meditation	artistic endeavors— painting, drawing
honoring the body	
rule of life	music, singing, chant
	Sabbath keeping

nature walks

hiking

inspirational reading

reading sacred texts

service

grieving

fasting

celebration

planting/gardening

walking the labyrinth

creating sacred space

living simply

compassion

living abundantly

gratitude

hospitality

peacekeeping

stargazing

homemaking

knitting, crocheting, quilting

compassionate listening

discernment

loving-kindness

visiting sacred sites

This list of spiritual practices is not exhaustive, nor will all of them appeal to every individual pilgrim or group. What matters most is that spiritual practice requires a daily commitment. In other words, it is not the *quantity* of spiritual practices we attempt, but the *quality* of the sustained practice. Wise pilgrims are those who reevaluate their spiritual practice and look for ways to integrate old and new into the journey.

For pilgrims who do not already have a regular spiritual discipline, it is often helpful to include one, such as discernment, into preparation for the journey. As you look at the list of spiritual practices, which ones give you energy? Which first grab your attention? Which speak to your heart? Go to those spiritual practices that seem to answer these questions first as you experiment with integrating them into your life. Keep in mind that none are a quick fix; lasting changes occur only gradually, over time. It is also optimal to maintain consistent spiritual practices, since frequently changing back and forth may be an impediment to emergent understanding.

THE PRACTICE OF PRAYER AND MEDITATION

Integral to the pilgrim's journey to the center of the heart are the related spiritual practices of prayer and meditation, both in themselves and as practices linked to other rituals, such as walking, chanting, and keeping silence. For some pilgrims, the idea of prayer or meditation is second nature, either because they were raised in homes and traditions that fostered growth in spiritual practices from a young age or because they began to practice in adulthood and have that experience to draw upon. For others, spiritual practices such as prayer and meditation may be an idea or a yearning, but they lack the instruction in technique or the help of spiritual companions who can help them build confidence. Still others may be fearful of or antagonistic to prayer and meditation because of negative experiences they have had with organized religion, and preparation for pilgrimage is one way of beginning to look at what regular spiritual practice might mean for them.

The cultivation of the sacred art of silence, or intentional silence, is an important spiritual practice that aids both prayer and meditation. The discipline of keeping silent also supports pilgrimage practice because it encourages the pilgrim to engage in self-awareness and reflection. Even for those taking part in a group pilgrimage, as well as those who connect with companions along the way, setting aside some time for silent contemplation is an important spiritual practice. In our culture full of noise, incessant background music, and constant electronic connection, some detachment from the outside world can quiet our hearts and promote the development of our inner life and authentic voice. Desert spirituality also supports another kind of spiritual practice, that of self-emptying silence, which takes us beyond our egos into a space that is vulnerable, beyond language, and finally into joy. Though the practice of silence is much lauded among the spiritual traditions of the world and is certainly part of monastic pilgrimage and isolated wilderness journeys, many people lack hands-on experience that they can draw upon in meditation and prayer. It takes considerable practice not only to develop a tolerance for silence, but also to learn to begin to "listen" to it as an aid to reflection and a means of enhancing our creativity. Some people cultivating silence find it helpful to maintain a regular practice, such as a particular time of day or particular days during the year. Cultivating silence is not a competitive sport; what matters is not how much time you spend in silence, but the quality of the silence for each individual. Some will find cultivating an hour of silence challenging, while others will find a day of silence—or a year or two, as some practice—bliss.

Although prayer and meditation are integral to diverse religious traditions around the world, there is no single way to do them. It is also true that humans are born with the capacity to be spiritual beings, and some would argue that other creatures are born with that capacity as well. The ability to feel and express love, for instance, is characteristic of the spirit that dwells within us. Yet for some people, for a variety of reasons, this spiritual capacity remains undeveloped or dormant. For them, additional support in how to participate in prayer and meditation is helpful.

Getting the Most from Prayer

Anne Lamott, in *Help. Thanks. Wow. The Three Essential Prayers*, suggests that prayer is communication from the heart to "that which surpasses understanding," or to God, or to the Good, "the force that is beyond our comprehension but that in our pain or supplication or relief we don't really need to define or have proof or any established contact with.... Or let's say it is a cry from the deep within to Life or Love, with capital L's." She began to pray after she hit rock bottom through drug and alcohol abuse, and at that time "Help" became the first, greatest, and hardest prayer—it meant that she had to admit defeat and surrender to a higher power. "Thanks" then became her prayer of relief, when help came along. "Wow" is what Lamott refers to as the prayer of praise and awe—when we are finally rendered speechless, when we discover the beauty of nature, or when something miraculous happens to us. Lamott believes that prayer is ultimately about connecting the Divine with our own very limited experience: "It's sort of like blinking your eyes open.... It's sort of like when ... Dorothy lands in Oz and the movie goes from black and white to color, and it's like having a new pair of glasses, and you say, 'Wow!'"[8]

"Prayer is an invitation to God to intervene in our lives," writes Jewish scholar Abraham Joshua Heschel,[9] and part of the wisdom in Anne Lamott's approach to prayer is that she keeps the invitation simple. People who are new to prayer tend to make it more complicated than necessary. There are some people who are gifted at elaborate extemporaneous prayers, and certainly traditional prayers and well-composed contemporary prayers can be startling in their beauty. At the same time, prayers from the heart are not about literary quality or the skill of an orator, but about authenticity.

An anonymous fourteenth-century mystical text, *The Cloud of Unknowing*, refers to prayer as "the attention of the heart." Through it we shift into another level of consciousness and begin a conversation with a higher being. As a spiritual practice, prayer gives voice to our intentions. Sometimes it is grounded in a particular concern or request, but there is also a desire to bear witness. "How you pray, when you pray, and why you pray is a direct reflection of your understanding of the Divine and the roles that it plays in your life," writes spiritual teacher and holistic practitioner Iyania Vanzant.[10] Prayer as a spiritual practice is a way to listen to the Divine. Reading prayers silently or aloud connects us with our spiritual ancestors and religious traditions.

When people of faith pray, they do so in the belief that God is acting in the universe. But seekers, agnostics, and others who do not necessarily believe in God also pray out of their own beliefs, questions, and needs. While the rituals of prayer may vary, the intent to renew spiritual connection with the holy is consistent. The following practical steps are helpful in terms of experiencing prayer as a spiritual practice:

- Set aside a time to pray each day. Although other opportunities and motivations arise during the course of a day, regular practice through an established prayer time is optimal. It can be any time of the day and does not have to be long in duration. What is important is that you have time set aside, freed from other distractions and preoccupations.

- Choose a location that supports you in prayer. You can pray at any time and in any place. You can pray in silence privately or in a group setting. What is important is to choose locations that evoke the prayers within you. Some people find that holy place or sacred space in the corner of one of the rooms of their home, in a house of worship, or out of doors, in nature. What is important is to select an environment that reminds you of your connection with the Sacred.

- Pray with your body. Some people pray best while walking, some by sitting, some by kneeling, some by dancing. Remember that your whole body is connected to the spiritual practice of prayer.

- Prepare yourself for prayer. It is not always easy to focus with intention when we have a busy day ahead of us or are exhausted after a day of challenging work. That is why religious traditions developed ways to help those who pray prepare for what they are about to practice and to help them focus on their connection with the Sacred. Preparation for prayer may include a few moments of silence or lighting a candle. It may involve washing the hands or face, anointing, facing a particular direction, burning incense or paper, ringing a bell, making the sign of the cross, or genuflecting. Any of these practices can be a means of preparation for prayer.

- Open your prayer. Some people begin their prayers with a particular call to worship or a verse from a sacred text. Prayer may be practiced silently or aloud, with your eyes open or closed. Some find it helpful to open prayer with traditional forms that have been memorized or are read aloud, while others begin prayer as if it were an informal conversation.

- Open your heart. Focus on your inward self and concentrate on your heart, which is the spiritual center. What questions and concerns are in your heart? Cultivate gratitude, and express thanks for life's gifts. Prayer is a two-way communication, so take care to also listen with your heart, and be prepared for a response, even if it is not the response that you expected or wanted.

- Express your intention. People pray with many intentions, including requests for help, healing, guidance, and peace. For some, the reason behind the prayer is best expressed through a question: What are you seeking?

- Lastly, end your prayer. Close the sacred circle. Some end their prayers by saying a certain word, such as *Amen*. Others conclude their prayers through a gesture or change of position.

Getting the Most from Meditation

Author Claudia Horwitz makes the following observation about the relationship between prayer and meditation: "Like meditation, prayer invites us to be still and to focus. But while meditation is a practice of paying attention, prayer is a practice of voicing intention, even if the intention is simply to listen and bear witness."[11] There are many forms of meditation, and it can be practiced either within a religious tradition or independent from it. On the most basic level, meditation teaches us how to be still. It is a form of silent concentration with the goal of focusing and clearing the mind of the many competing distractions of daily life. As a practice, the aim of meditation is to move beyond conditioned "thinking" and into deeper levels of self-awareness. Once the mind is clear it is possible to enter more fully into a state of pure relaxation and focus, thus creating a more positive outlook.

As people mature in their meditation practice, they are able to access an inner calm even in the most challenging circumstances. Theoretically, the more you meditate, the more profound your experiences may become. To reach a more advanced state of meditation, many have found it helpful to study with a teacher who can give advice on useful techniques. For those starting a meditation practice, the following guidelines may be helpful:

- Find a space or create an environment where you can be as free as possible from distractions like ringing telephones, e-mail, music, and television. Some people find it helpful to meditate outdoors, while others find a space within their home. A candle, flowers, incense, or some other pleasing element can enhance the meditation site. Soft music or nature sounds are an asset to meditation for some people, though others find them distracting. Pure silence works well for many people, as Diana Eck writes: "Hunger for God requires the cultivation of silence. Even in the engagement of hunger, crisis, and activity, we need to seek the inner space where we may be sustained and renewed."[12]
- Find time to meditate. Those just starting a meditation practice should try for five to ten minutes. Those more experienced may meditate for twenty to thirty minutes or more. It is possible to meditate any time of the

day, though many practitioners do so first thing in the
morning or before bed. Because you need to be alert to
meditate, some teachers recommend that you be free of
alcohol or non-prescription drugs for at least twenty-four
hours before meditation. Since the digestive system can
also be a distraction to meditation, other recommenda-
tions include waiting two hours after a full meal or an
hour after a caffeinated drink.

- Get comfortable. Find a level sitting position that is
comfortable, and relax your body. Remove any clothing
or jewelry that might be confining. Keeping your back
straight and upright, relax your arms and place your
hands in your lap or on your knees. You do not need
to sit in any particular position; the important thing is
to keep your back straight to help with your breathing.
Take a mental inventory of each part of your body in
order to notice any tension, including the small muscles
in your face, and relax that tension. You should feel comfortable enough to focus, but not so comfortable that you
fall asleep.

- Focus on your breathing. The most challenging part of
the meditation process is clearing your mind of distractions. Close your eyes to enable concentration, and rest
your attention on the flow of your breath, the sensation
of air moving through you. Ideally, you should breathe
in through your nose and out through your mouth.
Take a deep breath and fill your lungs. Relax. The goal
here is to gradually let the distractions of your mind
slip away. Some find it helpful to visualize the breath
as positive energy entering your body. When a distraction pops up, don't try to ignore it or get frustrated—
acknowledge it, visualize it, and then watch it pass
away. As you mature in your practice, fewer distractions
will arise. Continue to focus on your breath until you

feel completely relaxed, at peace. During this phase of the practice, some find repeating a mantra helpful in staying focused.

- Ease yourself back into awareness. If you are just starting a meditation practice, this might be the point for you to begin to slowly ease yourself back into your habitual state of awareness. If you are more experienced, however, you might take your meditation to the next step through visualization. That is, focus on an object until it gradually becomes real to you in your mind. For instance, you could focus on a beautiful stone or flower, a peaceful place, or a warm candle flame. Feel the positive impact of the image. When you breathe in, imagine that you are breathing in the positive image. As you focus on the image, try to remember every detail about it—what do you see, smell, and hear? With each breath, imagine it filling your body. Picture the positive image healing you and healing others who need it.

- End your meditation. As you grow in your meditation practice, you will be able to identify signs that suggest that the session is complete. There is no fixed schedule for meditation practice, but you will learn to notice subtle changes in your focus that suggest the session is at an end. Perhaps you have a significant breakthrough during meditation, with a new insight or idea, and find the session coming to its natural conclusion. Either way, you will want to move slowly out of the meditative state; otherwise you might feel stressed or anxious. Slowly become aware of yourself in your environment and allow your visual image to fade away. Open your eyes and take a few breaths. If your schedule allows it, spend some quiet time after meditation, perhaps with another spiritual practice such as reading or writing in your journal.

Some pilgrims, including those who walk the labyrinth, find the spiritual practice of walking meditation a helpful way to cultivate mindfulness. For the Buddha, the mind and the body were two aspects of the same thing, but most of us experience them as separate. While our body is in motion, our mind is elsewhere. But when we understand the interconnectedness of our mind and body, then we are better able to stay within the present moment. While practicing walking meditation, each time your feet touch the earth allow yourself to be fully present to the here and now. As you take one step, focus on your foot as it presses down on the earth. Then when you have fully arrived, take the next step and so on.

Christine Valters Paintner writes about the practice of walking meditation, or "contemplative walking," in her book *Water, Wind, Earth & Fire*. Contemplative walking is slow and deliberate *mindful* walking. Be aware that each step is a gift, and be open to what unfolds before you. If you find your attention is diverted from the walking, notice the thought but gently turn your attention back to the walking. Paintner calls contemplative walking a process that includes, *noticing*, *wondering*, and *returning*. Notice your surroundings, the path before you, and allow creation to speak to you. Wonder about the things you have noticed, both in your body and in nature. Finally, as you return, reflect on what has happened on the journey and the questions that still linger. When practicing walking meditation, you do not need to cover a long distance or reach a particular destination. Rather, the emphasis is on being in the moment and keeping your awareness on your body and its surroundings.[13]

There are many benefits to regular meditation practice. These include greater resistance to stress-related disorders, more confidence and a more positive outlook, increased productivity, less vulnerability to addiction, growth in wisdom and compassion, and more peace of mind—to name just a few. Furthermore, we can experience some of these gains even when we are only beginning to meditate, before we have been successful at maintaining focus or clearing the mind. When beginning a meditation practice, it is important to be patient with yourself, because it is not something that can be immediately mastered. For pilgrims, regular meditation; sitting or walking; before, after, and during; the pilgrimage may contribute significantly to the depth of the spiritual experience.

SPIRITUAL PRACTICES
IN PREPARING FOR PILGRIMAGE

During the Middle Ages, prospective pilgrims weighed many practical and spiritual considerations before they set forth on their journey. Travel was dangerous in the premodern world—disease and violence were prevalent, and pilgrims set out knowing that they had little control over when or if they would return home. Hence the importance of careful preparation and planning. As we have seen, the nature of these preparations depended on the pilgrims' religious tradition and on the length of the journey they planned. Pilgrims needed to attend to the needs of the body and spirit while on the road, as well as arranging for the support of their families and a means of livelihood during their absence. Some pilgrimage traditions also stressed the need to be debt free or at least not to incur further debt by going on a pilgrimage. Others suggested a range of spiritual practices for pilgrims that were designed to prepare body and spirit for the journey. Enlisting the encouragement of those at home for a pilgrimage, both spiritual and material, has also been a key element throughout the ages. Not only do family, friends, and religious communities send a pilgrim off on a life-altering event, but they also participate in their own way through providing sustenance and by maintaining the home base.

It is important to note here that not everyone is able to travel to one of the major pilgrimage destinations far from home. Staying closer to home does not make a pilgrimage any less valuable as a spiritual practice; a weekend or a weeklong experience, as time permits, is filled with possibilities. Look for those sacred sites and holy places close to home that you have previously overlooked. Perhaps there are sites associated with your family history or vocational interests that have been part of the landscape of your imagination but that you have never seen in person. These, too, hold rich opportunities for pilgrimage and should not be overlooked. As noted throughout this book, the key to pilgrimage is the connection between the inward and outward journey to the center of the heart, not a particular physical destination.

Regardless of the distance to be traveled, those who go on pilgrimage today benefit as much from careful preparation and planning, spiritual practices, and connections with home as did the travelers of the Middle Ages. Although modern travel is in many ways less arduous than in ages past, and while communication throughout the world has been revolutionized, the sacred art of pilgrimage is still demanding. The work of transformation, as a process of deep change, calls for a great deal of physical, mental, and spiritual stamina from the pilgrim. In the following section, you will find information on the practical aspects of planning pilgrimages, as well as some suggestions for spiritual practices to support the journey and considerations on returning home at the end of a pilgrimage.

PRACTICAL ADVICE FOR PLANNING A PILGRIMAGE

- Start planning well in advance of your estimated departure. If your pilgrimage includes long-distance travel, make sure that you create a concrete itinerary, listing all the important details: transportation, tickets, and visas; hotels, inns, and hostels; meal plans; climate; and medical care along the route. If you have specific dietary needs or require special medical care, it is wise to make provisions ahead of time, when you are still in the planning stages. While some pilgrims manage very well without extensive advance planning, keep in mind that as many pilgrimage sites around the world grow increasingly popular, it will be more difficult to arrive without a reservation and still obtain housing. Especially if you are planning a group pilgrimage, make sure you have a reliable travel coordinator, preferably someone who has worked with such groups previously. As you plan, try to anticipate difficulties and develop alternative plans that take into account inclement weather, delays, injuries, accidents, and getting robbed. Setting out realistically prepared will free you to focus on the deeper intent of your journey.

- Do research. One of the most effective ways to prepare for a pilgrimage is to talk to people who have done the same thing. Find out the nitty-gritty details, including what they learned and the mistakes they made. Read everything you can find on the subject.

- Honestly assess your physical stamina and need for comfort. For pilgrimage sites located in areas where rugged travel is necessary or where hiking or climbing is an option, it is important to honestly assess your condition, including your ability to meet the physical challenges. Pilgrimages such as walking El Camino or climbing Mount Fuji are traditions that have existed for centuries, but hiking hundreds of miles in rough terrain and climbing mountains involve a high degree of physical conditioning. Pilgrims who are best prepared to participate in these experiences on foot are likely to be those who have previous experience as hikers and climbers or who train at home in advance. If you have never hiked or climbed before and the training needed isn't an option, it is far better to seek modes of travel that will support you on the journey and allow you to safely reach your destination.

- Pack well and live simply, bringing only what you can carry by yourself comfortably. Work hard at limiting the possessions you bring with you to what you really need. If you pack badly, you may have to shop for what you need along the way, and you may end up having to carry a lot of nonessentials. Durable clothing and comfortable footwear are a must. Take the climate and the time of year into careful consideration. Bring physical necessities, such as medications, and an extra pair of glasses from home.

- Practice moderation. Spiritual masters frequently counsel pilgrims to free themselves from addictive behaviors and foods, including caffeine, nicotine, and alcohol, before and during pilgrimages. What constitutes addiction is highly variable, yet in spiritual terms the intent is to remove dependencies that get in the way of spiritual growth and that interfere with the focus of the pilgrimage. Practically speaking, there is also the reality that high-end coffee establishments, while known throughout the world, are not located adjacent to all pilgrimage destinations. (Though it may be just a matter of time before they do begin to spring up!) For some, the challenge is not food and drink, but the loss of regular access to handheld electronic devices, such as cell phones or tablets. For people addicted in this way, it is advisable to limit exposure to once a day or to forgo using technology entirely—except in emergencies. Some pilgrims today, particularly those who spend much of their personal and professional lives networked, deliberately choose pilgrimage destinations where such access is restricted. Overall, practicing moderation means that pilgrims exercise some detachment from the demands and coping mechanisms of their usual lives in order to be fully present to the unfolding of their inward and outward journey.

- Plan departure rituals. Setting forth on pilgrimage is an auspicious event that should be marked as a special occasion. If you are religious or spiritual, ritual practice might involve prayer and meditation and/or a formal departure ritual with friends and family. Or you might wish to observe your departure by taking enough time to say good-bye to family, friends, or animal companions or plan a dinner before your departure. You might compose poetry, paint, or begin a pilgrimage journal. It is important for you to try to capture the reality that you are about to enter liminal space—something transformative is about to begin!

- After completing your pilgrimage, it is also important to set aside time to reflect on what you learned and to document your experience in some way, whether through a journal, scrapbook, blog, film, website, or any other medium that is comfortable for you. Although it can be hard to resist the tendency to rush back into daily life, even a brief pause for reflection helps the pilgrim to arrive fully home, ready for the next stage of life!

GUIDELINES FOR VISITING HOLY PLACES AND SACRED SPACES

One of the principal activities of many pilgrimages is visiting holy places and sacred spaces. Just as the travel-related aspects of pilgrimage take active preparation, so do arrival at the destination and experiencing distant sites. One helpful resource is the religious etiquette book by Stuart M. Matlins and Arthur Magida, *How to Be a Perfect Stranger.* An important aspect of any pilgrimage is the consideration of the impact of the visit on the sacred sites and the people who live there. Following are a few issues for consideration:

- Most publicly accessible sacred sites have websites now, and these should be consulted for regulations, hours, handicap access, and so on. Note that many sacred sites have limits in terms of the numbers of people they can accommodate, the time of year that visits are possible, and the number of people available to handle your request. Keep in mind that response time in other cultures is not necessarily as instantaneous as in our own.

- Consult the calendar and site schedule to make sure that your visit does not conflict with worship or other events at the pilgrimage site. If you're planning to visit with a group, you should always contact the site in advance and make a scheduled visit. Houses of worship also need to accommodate unexpected events, such as funerals, so confirm your visit a day in advance.

- If you're visiting a sacred site of a tradition other than your own, make sure you know if it is open to visits from members of other traditions. Try to find out under what conditions such a visit is possible and what forms of etiquette should be observed. Remember that you are a guest when visiting holy places and sacred spaces. Do not assume that you have a right to be there, and graciously defer to those who host the site.

- Avoid visiting while worship is in session unless you have consulted with your hosts and you have given them a clear sense of the purpose of the visit. Would you like to observe or participate in worship? Would you rather view the site during downtime?

- Avoid visiting sacred sites during times of silence—unless you intend to treasure the silence as well. In general, it is wise and appropriate to follow the customs and behaviors of adherents when visiting holy places and sacred spaces.

- Make sure that you are aware of which areas are open to the public, which are reserved for members of the faith community, and which are inaccessible during particular occasions, such as festivals, holy days, weddings, or funerals.

- Decide whether you want to visit on your own or if it might be mutually enriching to go with other pilgrims on a group experience.
- Consult a religious etiquette book in advance for advice on dress and codes of conduct for specific sacred sites. Generally, modest dress in muted colors is best for men and women—and no shorts or bare shoulders. In some sacred sites, visitors might be expected to cover their heads or remove their shoes.
- If you have a specific contact person at a particular sacred site, find out how that person would like to be addressed—by you or by your group, if you're traveling with others.
- Check with the site about the use of photography and/or video cameras. Some prohibit photography of any kind during worship; in others, particular areas are off-limits. For instance, some sites allow photography outdoors on the grounds, but not in the sanctuary or temple itself or during worship. Under no circumstances should you violate the rules of your hosts in this regard. And remember that it is inappropriate to film or take photographs of others visiting the site, particularly while they're in prayer or meditation, without their permission.
- Turn off your cell phone or put it on silent mode when you're visiting sacred sites. In general, do not use electronic devices in holy places or sacred spaces. Never talk on the phone, text, or use electronic devices during worship or other solemn occasions.
- Do not smoke, eat, drink, or bring food or drink into sacred sites.
- It is always a good idea to visit sacred sites quietly and respectfully. Be aware of your impact on other visitors as well as members of the community, including those present for prayer or meditation, and take care not to disturb anyone with loud conversations, phone calls, or texting.

- Once inside a sacred site, take time to acclimate yourself and tune into your environment. Before rushing to
  take photographs (if that's allowed), absorb the subtle
  characteristics of the interior. Many sacred spaces have
  areas where you can sit and settle into the site for a few
  moments. As architects say, "listen" to the building or
  the environment. Look at the structure, shapes, contours,
  colors, materials, light, symbols, and ornamentation of
  the space. Experience the site with as many of your senses
  as possible. (Sometimes when we rush to take photographs, we lose out on the experience itself.) Ask yourself,
  "How does this sacred site relate to its religious tradition?
  What makes this site sacred?" Pause long enough to commit the site to memory, not only through how it looks but
  also how it smells, sounds, and feels to the touch. After
  you have experienced the site in a contemplative way,
  then it is appropriate to take pictures (if that's allowed)
  and consult your guidebook.
- If you're visiting with children or youth, be attentive to
  their needs as well as the needs of other pilgrims. Help
  young people appreciate the site, and be aware of when
  they want to go!
- If you are traveling with companion animals, carefully
  research the regulations for them before you depart for
  a site, and make sure that their presence is welcome.
  Different traditions and cultures have different views
  about having animals in sacred sites. This is an area
  where it is best to exercise considerable caution.
- Become a "sustainable pilgrim." That is, be aware of your
  impact on the people and the environment of all sacred
  sites as an integral part of your pilgrimage. Practice gratitude for the privilege of visiting a sacred site, and demon-
  strate your appreciation by honoring those encountered
  at the site, as well as the material environment. Never

damage a sacred site or the natural environment in order to bring home souvenirs; instead, look to take home your memories and objects sanctioned by the site itself. Lastly, ensure the care and protection of sacred sites for future generations by making a financial or other material contribution in proportion to your means.

- After you visit a holy place or sacred space it is important to take time to reflect on what you saw and experienced. This can be accomplished in a variety of ways—journaling, blogging, painting, sketching, voice recording, and meditation are all means whereby the experience can be processed. Once again, try to recollect the experience in terms of as many of your senses as possible. Remember that self-reflective practice is what is important in distinguishing a pilgrimage from another type of visit or travel experience.

- After you have reflected on your own experience, it can be helpful to continue the conversation with others, especially if you are traveling as part of a group or with companions met along the way. Other ways of sharing and discussing your experience include online discussion groups, interactive websites, blogging, and social media sites, such as Facebook. Some pilgrims create digital scrapbooks or form a "meet-up group" with other people interested in sharing their own experiences about visits to particular holy places or sacred spaces.

Pilgrims interested in visiting sacred sites who follow these guidelines will not only minimize potential disappointments and disasters, but will also save themselves anxiety and misunderstanding that could have a negative impact on their experience. Moreover, the practices of "sustainable pilgrimage" contribute to the continuity and preservation of sacred sites, thereby ensuring their availability for future generations of pilgrims.

THE BENEFITS OF GROUP PILGRIMAGES

The growth of interest in pilgrimage throughout many parts of the world has contributed to increasing numbers of organized group pilgrimages, many assembled by local faith communities and organizations. These pilgrimage experiences are a good option for people who do not desire to travel alone, as well as for faith communities and organizations that use them for building relationships or as a source of education or solidarity with another group. Because pilgrimage as a spiritual practice is shared by many of the religions of the world, group pilgrimages are also a common format for interreligious dialogue and education.

In an effort to combat the rise in Holocaust denial that has surfaced around the world in recent years, the Center for Interreligious Understanding in Carlstadt, New Jersey, organized a pilgrimage to two Nazi concentration camps, Dachau and Auschwitz, for prominent Jewish and Muslims leaders from the United States. "The best way to convince someone about the truth of something is to let them see it for themselves and experience it for themselves," said Rabbi Jack Bemporad of the Center for Interreligious Understanding. "I feel that it was important to take Muslim leaders who have a really significant following in the American-Muslim community." Of the eight Muslim leaders who made the pilgrimage, some had worked previously with Jewish groups in interreligious dialogue. One group member was on record as doubting the extent of the Holocaust, though he recanted before the trip. The imams were deeply moved by the pilgrimage, especially after speaking to Holocaust survivors, seeing their tattooed numbers, and seeing the victims' hair, suitcases, and belongings. "Almost everybody was in tears," said Imam Muzammil Siddiqi, of the Islamic Society of Orange County in California, a frequent participant in interreligious events.

Participants in the pilgrimage also agreed that the historical realities of the Holocaust should not be eclipsed by the last sixty years of tensions in the Middle East. "Whatever happened post-Holocaust should not diminish the evil that was the Holocaust.... It was a very moving experience for all of us imams, in particular myself. I had never seen anything like this.... I could not comprehend how much evil could be unleashed." On their return to the United States, the Muslim leaders who participated in the pilgrimage released a statement citing the six million Jewish deaths among the twelve million Holocaust deaths overall and condemning any attempt to deny this historical reality as being contrary to the Islamic code of ethics.

These examples of group interreligious pilgrimages avoided the traps of "spiritual tourism" by emphasizing mutual respect in relationships through the compassionate sharing of stories, dialogue, and listening. The importance of a shared planning process contributed to a deeper spiritual encounter between people of different religious traditions. Furthermore, group pilgrimage experiences that honor the uniqueness of different religious traditions are careful to honor the parameters set by hosts and guests alike. Integral to the interreligious pilgrimages mentioned here is the awareness that the experience must in some way be connected to the participants' home community and evaluated by all who are part of the experience.

Guidelines for Planning Group Pilgrimages

- If the pilgrimage is for a local group, the planning process and orientation should give plenty of opportunity for input into the itinerary. In the case of interreligious pilgrimages or pilgrimages between two or more groups, each group should have the opportunity to participate in the planning process and orientation.
- Group pilgrimages should be conducted only in those areas and under conditions considered acceptable by the hosts and sponsored by those who have extensive experience with the sites and people visited.

- Pilgrimages are best built around a long-term relationship between the communities involved. On-off travel experiences may be exciting but do not usually contribute to relationships between groups of people.
- The pilgrimage should include a component that links the experience to the home community.
- The relational aspect of the pilgrimage should emphasize a mutual and reciprocal relationship, both between members of the group itself and with the host, rather than one group creating an experience for another.
- Group pilgrimages are most effective when they require advance study and, whenever possible, an orientation program that incorporates knowledge of one's own tradition as well as other traditions and cultures.
- Ideally, the design of the group pilgrimage will allow for the host community to be an integral part of the planning process and to determine the parameters of their hospitality.
- For a pilgrimage to move beyond tourism, it is important for individual and group reflection and/or spiritual practices to be a central part of the experience.
- In order to honor the relationships forged through group pilgrimages, it is important for all participants—organizers, group members, hosts—to contribute to the evaluation.
- Practices of "sustainable pilgrimage" that apply to individuals are just as important for groups. In all cases, pilgrimage groups should take seriously the impact of their presence on pilgrimage sites, the people who live there, and the natural environment. Groups should discuss in advance of departure the importance of traveling "lightly" and ways the experience can be positive for members and for the hosts. Pilgrimage groups should always plan to make a financial contribution to hosts and sacred sites and to be mindful of not damaging local environments.

KEEPING A RECORD OF YOUR PILGRIMAGE

A common spiritual practice for many pilgrims is journal writing. Even people who do not consider themselves writers or who are shy about sharing their experiences with readers find it helpful to record the story of their journey. Not only does a journal record the physical aspects of the journey—sights, sounds, smells, events, companions—but it is also an opportunity to recollect the ongoing internal process of the inward journey. For some, this kind of writing is the way they are best able to express their hopes, concerns, visions, dreams, and questions while on a pilgrimage. Many published pilgrim narratives available now and throughout history are, in fact, published journals or edited versions of the same. Similarly, it is not uncommon for pilgrims to document and share their experiences through blogging.

Journal writing allows you to read your own reflections from the past in the future. If you tend to process your reflections while talking aloud, an audio journal made by recording speech during the pilgrimage is another form of reflective practice.

If you have a visual memory, the best record of your pilgrimage may be through the use of images, such as drawing, or through the medium of photography. Thomas Merton considered photography a form of silent contemplation. "Photography is essentially about the play of light and dark, illuminations and shadow, much as the spiritual journey and our life pilgrimages are a practice of paying attention to these elements of our lives and how the holy is revealed in each," writes artist Christine Valters Paintner.[14] By recording images throughout the journey, you are able to reflect on the inward and outward landscapes of your sacred journey.

Journal keeping, whether through writing, blogging, speaking, or creating images, is a form of meditation and a profound way to come to know yourself and the Divine more deeply. The recording of questions, thoughts, prayers, and images is also a means of ongoing reflection. "A journal is a record of experience and growth," wrote Henry David Thoreau.

"Here I cannot afford to be remembering what I said or did, but what I am and aspire to become."[15] Over time, those who practice journal keeping develop a distinctive style and manner of expression. As a future pilgrim, consider journal keeping as a spiritual practice, and keep the following suggestions in mind:

- Write, speak, or create images in your journal (blog) in your own "voice." As a spiritual practice, a journal is not about living up to another's expectations or standards of excellence; rather, it is about faithfully depicting *your* journey. It is your choice whether to show a journal to others at another time or to keep it entirely to yourself.
- For some, it is helpful to begin a journal session with a moment of silence or prayer. Focus on what you are about to begin, and offer thanks for spirit and wisdom that dwell within. Ask for guidance to see the world every day through the eyes of the heart. Be attentive to the spirit of the Divine that dwells within you.
- Typically, journal keeping involves more than recording such events as the miles traveled, food eaten, and the time of day. These external phenomena "frame" the *experiences* that you want to record. Be aware of capturing your feelings, dreams, inspirations, and struggles. Words may be interwoven with quotations, diagrams, pictures, poetry, and other literary and artistic expressions that reflect your feelings.
- Journal keeping as a spiritual practice is about honesty. Like all spiritual practices, it is important to embrace journal keeping with a commitment to authenticity. Record what you believe is the truth and how you feel about it, as far as you can. If you have questions, record those. Practice compassion with yourself and others in journal keeping, while opening your heart to wisdom and understanding.

- Keep your journal, tablet, sketchbook, tape recorder, camera, or whatever means you are using to record your experiences accessible. While on pilgrimage, your mind, heart, and spirit will be engaged all day, and it will be helpful to have your tools handy to take notes or make new entries as they reveal themselves to you.

WALKING THE LABYRINTH

Chapter 4 of this book examines the history of the labyrinth and its connection with the sacred art of pilgrimage in terms of the inward journey to the center of the heart. The resources listed at the end of the book include specific information for those interested in learning more about the labyrinth and finding both indoor and outdoor labyrinths across North America and around the world. Walking the labyrinth is a powerful spiritual practice that cultivates personal awareness and contributes to healing and peace. Because it is in many ways a literal journey to the center of the heart, the experience is both deeply spiritual and personally challenging for many people. For the same reason, it is not uncommon for repressed feelings, sometimes buried for years, to come to the surface while walking a labyrinth.

In this way, those who walk the labyrinth as a regular part of their spiritual practice may also benefit from the support of a counselor or a spiritual director. Certainly spiritual and psychological breakthroughs are not part of every experience, and the insights gained from contemplative walking will vary from time to time. Those who do not have previous experience in walking a labyrinth may benefit from attending a workshop or retreat beforehand or working with a facilitator.

There is no single way to walk a labyrinth. Adults tend to enter the threshold quite seriously and deliberately; children tend to skip and laugh through the path. Some dance the labyrinth. Your particular spiritual practice may be shaped by your own motivations and visions. Here are a few general guidelines for those interested in walking a labyrinth as spiritual practice:

- *Prepare for the experience*. Learn more about the history and uses of the labyrinth; knowledge will deepen the meaning of the experience. Reflect on your purpose and what you hope to gain from walking the labyrinth. Search out and, if possible, visit the labyrinth in your vicinity to see it before you walk, to learn about specific guidelines for its use, and to find out when the path is available. There are both outdoor and indoor labyrinths, and the hours of access are highly variable. In some locations, particular times are reserved for groups, so decide in advance if you prefer to walk as an individual at a time when it is quieter or if you would rather be part of a group. Also, find out if the labyrinth site is accessible to people with disabilities. For those with limited walking ability, there are labyrinths where the path is wide enough to accommodate wheelchairs. There are also hand labyrinths where the path can be "walked" by fingertip or by using a tool. Before you enter a labyrinth, it is a good idea to reflect on your intentions, feelings, and questions about the walk, either silently or through journal keeping.
- *Enter the threshold*. Many labyrinth walkers remove their shoes when they enter the labyrinth, a common custom when entering sacred spaces. Some labyrinths, particularly those made of canvas, require that shoes be removed. Remove your watch, and turn off your cell phone. Many labyrinth walkers acknowledge that they are participating in a spiritual practice by beginning with a nod, bow, the sign of the cross, or some other ritual gesture. You may also say a prayer or recite a mantra or affirmation. Take a few moments as you enter the labyrinth to take a cleansing breath and quiet yourself before the walk begins.

- *Walk the inward path*. On the way toward the center, reflect on things you want to leave behind, and release what is no longer useful in your spiritual journey. Open your heart to the whole of your experience, the positive as well as the challenging. Walk at a measured pace, conscious of your body and your feelings. If you encounter others on the path, respect the silence and allow them to pass you. Observe your own process and set a pace that is comfortable for you. It is important to maintain your focus throughout the walk. Over time, experienced walkers coexist with others on the labyrinth seamlessly by cordially sharing the path but also by remaining focused on their own spiritual work. Don't focus on the center as a destination. Instead, strive to be fully conscious of each step on the inward journey.

- *Step into the center*. Labyrinth designs vary in terms of the amount of room at the center. Some centers are roomy enough to accommodate cushions for those who wish to pray or meditate. Sometimes labyrinth walkers choose to sit, kneel, lie down, or prostrate themselves at the center; some centers are standing room only. When you reach the center, take some time to reflect on the journey. Ask yourself what insights or questions surfaced during the journey. What images came to mind? This part of walking the labyrinth is about being attentive to your sacred center and to the power of the Divine. In many labyrinths, you may remain at the center as long as you wish. Some walkers find journal keeping helpful at that point, hoping to record what they learned during the inward journey. Staying still and present in silence is also an appropriate spiritual practice at the center.

- *Begin the return path*. As you leave the center, you will walk the path that brought you there. Reflect on your experience of the center and what you wish to take back to your daily life. This is about the integration of wisdom. In the same way you took measured steps inward, take the necessary time to walk intentionally outward, savoring every step along the way. Try to resist the temptation to return at a faster pace. As you leave the labyrinth, it is appropriate to once again acknowledge your departure by making a ritual gesture.

• *Reflect on the experience.* Try to plan your time so that you are able to reflect on your experience after you leave the labyrinth. Journal keeping or another spiritual practice that helps you integrate the experience and return positively to your everyday life is often helpful.

For some pilgrims, walking the labyrinth is a once-in-a-lifetime spiritual experience. Others find it helpful to walk the labyrinth as a regular part of spiritual practice or when confronted with the need for healing or dealing with a particular issue or problem. Most who walk the labyrinth agree that it is a powerful spiritual practice for those who want to forge a deeper connection into the center of the heart of the Divine.

RETURNING HOME

The return home is as much a part of the sacred art of pilgrimage as setting forth and the journey along the way. Spiritual practice offers opportunities to make the most of returning home in order to integrate the pilgrimage experience into the rest of your life. The Welsh poet R. S. Thomas writes eloquently about the pilgrim's need to bring something back home: "... a lock of God's hair, stolen from him while he was asleep; a photograph of the garden of the spirit. As has been said, the point of travel is not to *arrive* but to *return home* laden with pollen you shall work up into honey the mind feeds on."[16]

For pilgrims who travel in groups, it is important to leave adequate time at the end of the pilgrimage to have some sort of closure, either through a shared meal or through a storytelling session. Once home, storytelling is an effective way of sharing the experience with families, friends, and coworkers, as is the sharing of artifacts or photographs from the experience. Similarly, upon returning home, you might want in some way to express gratitude by making a contribution to the site or to the site's hosts. You may decide to use returning home as an opportunity to renew or begin crafting a rule of life that reflects what you now consider to be important and to plan how you are going to structure all aspects of your life to reflect these priorities.

Returning home to family, friends, and coworkers is an opportunity for all involved to practice compassion. Pilgrims need to realize that those at home have not had the same experiences and thus may not be as interested in every story they tell about the pilgrimage. Transformational experiences by definition change people, and it is best for those returning and those who have remained at home to greet these changes with patience and understanding as they are integrated into daily life. Those at home should realize that returning pilgrims are still processing their experiences and may not yet know how to express the impact of those experiences. Some of the changes will evolve over time.

Community prayer and rituals of welcome and thanksgiving for returning pilgrims have always been an important part of the return home across traditions and cultures. Some faith communities have formal liturgies for these occasions, and they may also be designed individually and conducted at home as a way to celebrate a pilgrim's return through shared stories, food, music, and other rituals of thanksgiving and companionship. Some pilgrims also create sacred spaces within their home upon their return, either through displays of photographs or artifacts or through home altars and meditation spaces. Sacred spaces in the home connect returned pilgrims with their past journey and allow others in the home to share more significantly in the encounter.

The sacred art of pilgrimage is a journey to the center of the heart of the Divine. Pilgrimage is a spiritual practice that opens the heart and leads us to our deepest desire. Pilgrimage has been a spiritual practice for centuries, a shared human experience, and a path of transformation for many. A metaphor for the path of human life, the journey is open to all. When we walk the path, we join together with one another, with the Divine, and with all the pilgrims across time and space who have gone before us, in a way of life that recognizes the sacredness of all creation, of our neighbors, and of ourselves.

May the stars light your way! May all your sacred travels be filled with countless blessings!

Questions for Your Own Exploration

1. What is your spiritual practice? What are the joys and challenges of the practice for you?

2. Reflect on the list of spiritual practices in this chapter. Are there any practices there or elsewhere in your experience that you feel might contribute to your spiritual growth?

3. As you reflect on the pilgrimage of life, where do you see yourself now? How might you live more joyfully in the present moment?

ACKNOWLEDGMENTS

This book has been a labor of love—an opportunity to reflect on pilgrimages from years past and look forward to the journeys of the future.

I would like to thank Cynthia Shattuck, Nancy Fitzgerald, Emily Wichland, Kaitlin Johnstone and all the editorial staff of SkyLight Paths for their enthusiastic support of the project.

Friend and colleague John Ratti enriched the text with his keen editorial eye and wise counsel as well as his deep experience with books and all things spiritual.

Thanks also to Erik Carter who contributed greatly to the book as a research assistant by finding gems on the journey home and ever searching for additional resources.

A research leave granted by Claremont School of Theology, Claremont Lincoln University, gave me the focused time to complete the manuscript. Financial support was granted through a Conant Fund Grant from the Episcopal Church.

NOTES

CHAPTER 1. JOURNEYS ACROSS
TRADITIONS AND CULTURES

1. Robert C. Sibley, *The Way of the Stars: Journeys on the Camino de Santiago* (Charlottesville: University of Virginia Press, 2012), 3.

2. Averages for religious pilgrimages from Edward C. Sellner, *Pilgrimage: Exploring a Great Spiritual Practice* (Notre Dame, IN: Sorin Books, 2004), 9.

3. Amy Benedict, "Deepen Your Practice: A Neighborhood Pilgrimage," *Spirituality and Health,* January 6, 2012, spiritualityhealth.com/blog/deepen-your-practice-a-neighborhood-pilgrimage/.

4. Victor Turner and Edith Turner, *Image and Pilgrimage in Christian Culture: Anthropological Perspectives* (New York: Columbia University Press, 1995; first published 1978).

5. Edith Turner, *Heart of Lightness: The Life Story of an Anthropologist* (New York: Berghahn Books, 2006), 92.

6. Quoted in Squire Rushnell, *When God Winks at You* (Nashville: Thomas Nelson, 2006), 40.

7. E. Turner, *Heart of Lightness*, 93.

8. V. Turner and E. Turner, *Image and Pilgrimage,* 18.

9. Benjamin of Tudela, "Travels," in M. Komroff, *Contemporaries of Marco Polo* (New York: Dorset House, 1989), 274.

10. Gregory of Nyssa, *On Pilgrimages,* trans. W. Moore and H. A. Wilson, *St. Gregory of Nyssa Resources Online and in Print,* www.elpenor.org.

11. Dennis E. Trout, *Paulinus of Nola: Life, Letters and Poems* (Berkeley: University of California Press, 1996), 96.

12. Egeria, *Egeria: Diary of a Pilgrimage* (Westminster, MD: Newman Press, 1970), 18.

13. Margery Kempe, *The Book of Margery Kempe,* trans. B. Windeatt (New York: Penguin, 1986), 103.

14. Mary C. Earle, *Celtic Christian Christianity* (Woodstock, VT: SkyLight Paths, 2011), 109.

15. Ziauddin Sardar, *Muhammed: All That Matters* (New York: McGraw-Hill, 2012), 130.

16. Paul Gwynne, *World Religions in Practice: A Comparative Introduction* (Malden, MA: Blackwell, 2009), 373.

17. Quoted in Edward C. Sellner, *Pilgrimage* (Notre Dame, IN: Sorin Books, 2004), 96.

18. James Harpur, *Sacred Tracks: 2000 Years of Christian Pilgrimage* (Berkeley: University of California Press, 2002), 180.

19. Stephanie Paulsell, "In Woolf's footsteps," *Christian Centur* (May 16, 2012): 35.

20. John Malkin, "Pilgrimage to India with MC Yogi," *Spirituality and Health* (November–December 2012): 78–85.

21. Jeff Baker, "Pico Iyer Talks about the Dalai Lama, Leonard Cohen and the Virtues of Traveling within Yourself," *The Oregonian* (April 4, 2010), www.oregonlive.com.

22. Sam Mowe, "The Atheist Pilgrim: An Interview with Stephen Bachelor," *Tricycle* (Fall 2012): 103.

23. NPR staff interview, "Leibovitz Takes a 'Pilgrimage' for Artistic Renewal" (November 8, 2001).

24. Annie Leibovitz, *Pilgrimage* (New York: Random House, 2011), see preface.

25. Quoted in "Stay-at-Home Pilgrims Find Salvation Online," IOL News, (January 9, 2001), www.iol.news.za.

26. Harpur, *Sacred Tracks,* 181.

27. Mark W. MacWilliams, "Virtual Pilgrimage to Ireland's Croagh Patrick," in *Religion Online: Finding Faith on the Internet,* ed. Lorne L. Dawson and Douglas E. Cowan (New York: Routledge, 2004), 223–237.

CHAPTER 2. THE WAY OF THE HEART

1. George Mendoza, "Testimonial," www.holychimayo.us/santuario/othertestimonials.html.

2. Russell Contreras, "For Two Centuries, Miracles Sought at New Mexico's El Santuario de Chimayó," *Huffington Post* (November 30, 2011) www.huffingtonpost.com/2013/03/28/el-santuario-de-chimayo.html.

3. See "My New Mexico," www.evanderputten.org.

4. Stephen Prothero, "A Pilgrimage in Chimayó," *Harvard Theological Review* (1991–1992), 17.

5. Augustine of Hippo, *Confessions*, trans. Henry Chadwick (New York: Oxford University Press, 2009), 3.

6. Mary C. Earle, *Marvelously Made: Gratefulness and the Body* (New York: Morehouse, 2012), 30.

7. Christine Valters Paintner, *Lectio Divina—The Sacred Art: Transforming Words & Images into Heart-Centered Prayer* (Woodstock, VT: SkyLight Paths, 2011), 8–9, 158.

8. Howard Thurman, *Meditations of the Heart* (Boston: Beacon Press, 1981), 173.

9. Boris Vysheslavtsev, cited in Jim Forest, *The Road Is Emmaus: Pilgrimage as a Way of Life* (Maryknoll, NY: Orbis Books, 2007), 20.

10. Quoted in Elizabeth Canham, *Heart Whispers* (Nashville: Upper Room, 1999), 65; Joan Chittister, *The Monastery of the Heart* (Katonah, NY: BlueBridge Books, 2011), 145.

11. Shirley du Boulay, *The Road to Canterbury* (Harrisburg: Morehouse, 1995), 9.

12. Quoted in Joan Chittister, *The Monastery of the Heart* (Katorah, NY: Bluebridge, 2011), 145.

13. Quoted in Parker Palmer, *Let Your Life Speak* (San Francisco: Jossey-Bass, 1999), 76.

14. Dag Hammarskjold, *Markings* (New York: Knopf, 1970), 48.

15. Belden C. Lane, *Landscapes of the Sacred* (Baltimore: Johns Hopkins University Press, 2001), 15.

16. Phil Cousineau, *The Art of Pilgrimage* (Berkeley: Conari Press, 1998), 104.

17. J.R.R. Tolkien, *The Hobbit* (New York: Random House, 1996), 4.

18. Paul Coelho, *The Pilgrimage* (San Francisco: Harper San Francisco, 1995), 95.

19. Ibid., 97.

20. Paul Coelho, *The Alchemist* (San Francisco: Harper San Francisco, 1994), 8.

21. Cousineau, *The Art of Pilgrimage,* 13.

22. Robert C. Sibley, *The Way of the Stars* (Charlottesville: University of Virginia Press, 2012), 150–151.

23. Elizabeth Gilbert, *Eat, Pray, Love* (New York: Penguin, 2006), 327–328.

24. Jennifer Lash, *On Pilgrimage* (New York: Bloomsbury, 1991), 226.

25. Eric Weiner, *Man Seeks God: My Flirtations with the Divine* (New York: Twelve, 2011), 235–240.

26. *Way of the Pilgrim,* trans. Helen Bacovcin (New York: Random House, 1978), 9, 24–25.

27. C. S. Lewis, *Pilgrim's Regress* (Grand Rapids, MI: Eerdmans, 1992), 123.

28. Sue Monk Kidd and Ann Kidd Taylor, *Traveling with Pomegranates: A Mother-Daughter Story* (New York: Viking, 2009), 233.

29. Ted Swartz, "Laughter Is Sacred Space," *Huffington Post* (September 20, 2012), www.huffingtonpost.com/ted-swartz/laugterissacred.html.

30. C. G. Jung, *Collected Works,* trans. R.P.C. Hull, ed. H. Read, 20 vols. (Princeton, NJ: Princeton University Press, 1953–1979); vol. 17, 41.

31. Thomas Merton, *Mystics and Zen Masters* (New York: Farrar, Strauss & Giroux, 1988), 92.

32. David Whyte, *Crossing the Unknown Sea* (New York: Riverhead Books, 2002), 5.

33. Quoted in Donald Chinula, *Building King's Beloved Community* (Cleveland: United Church Press, 1997), 29.

34. C. G. Jung, *Collected Works*, vol 17, 331.

35. Lao Tzu, *Tao Te Ching* (Bloomington, IN: Indiana University Press, 2008), 131.

36. Gabriel Marcel, *The Mystery of Being* (London: Horvill Press, 1950), 185.

37. du Boulay, *The Road to Canterbury*, 232.

38. Joseph Campbell, *The Hero with a Thousand Faces* (Novato, CA: New World Library, 2008), 23.

39. Jean Dalby Clift and Wallace B. Clift, *The Archetype of Pilgrimage: Outer Action with Inner Meaning* (Eugene, OR: Wipf & Stock, 1970), 10.

40. Rainer Maria Rilke, *Letter to a Young Poet* (Novato, CA: New World Library, 2000), 35.

41. Clift and Clift, *Archetype of Pilgrimage,* 13.

42. Frederick Buechner, *Listening to Your Life* (New York: HarperCollins, 1992), 186.

43. Parker Palmer, *Let Your Life Speak: Listening to the Voice of Vocation* (San Francisco: Jossey-Bass), 9.

44. Kathleen Norris, *Dakota* (New York: Ticknor & Fields, 1993), 130.

45. Coelho, *The Alchemist,* 131.

46. Chittister, *Monasteries of the Heart*, 16.

47. Ibid., 21.

48. Ibid., 159.

49. Ibid., 218–219.

50. C. G. Jung, *Collected Works,* vol. 12, 17.

51. Cyprian Consiglio, *Prayer in the Cave of the Heart*, 6.

52. Ibid., 102.

53. Kallistos Ware, "The Power of the Name," www.Scribd.com.

54. David Steindl-Rast, *A Listening Heart: The Art of Contemplative Living* (New York: Crossroad, 2012), 9–14.

55. *Thich Nhat Hanh: Essential Writings,* ed. Sister Annabel Laity (Maryknoll, NY: Orbis Books, 2001), 119–121.

56. Pema Chōdrōn, "Lojong: How to Awaken Your Heart," www.shambhalasun.com.

57. Jack Kornfield and C. Trungpa, "The Pure Raw Heart Has the Power to Heal the World," (June 2011) 24, no. 6, www.friendsofsilence.net

58. Hidayat Inayat Khan, "Sufi Wisdom: Religion of the Heart," http://sufiwisdom.com.

59. *A Year with Rumi: Daily Readings* (New York: HarperCollins, 2009), 9.

60. Jalal al-Din Rumi, *The Book of Love,* trans. C. Barks (New York: HarperOne, 2003), 33.

CHAPTER 3. HOLY PLACES, SACRED SPACES

1. Margaret Silf, *Sacred Spaces: Stations on a Celtic Way* (Brewster, MA: Paraclete Press, 2001), 10.

2. Val Webb, *Stepping Out with the Sacred* (New York: Continuum, 2010), 60.

3. Mary C. Earle, *Celtic Christian Spirituality* (Woodstock, VT: SkyLight Paths, 2011), 24.

4. Ibid., 36.

5. Freddy Silva, *Legacy of the Gods: The Origins of Sacred Sites and the Rebirth of Ancient Wisdom* (Charlottesville, VA: Hampton Roads, 2011), 288.

6. Ibid., 12.

7. Christine Valters Paintner, from her website, Abbey of the Arts, www.abbeyofthearts.com.

8. Roger W. Stump, *The Geography of Religion: Faith, Place and Space* (Lanham, MD: Rowman & Littlefield, 2008), 301.

9. Philip Jenkins, "Pilgrims of Our Time," *Christian Century* (May 18, 2010): 45.

10. Michael J. Crosbie, *Architecture for the Gods* (New York: Watson-Guptill, 2000), 9.

11. Ibid., 11.

12. Quoted in Philip Carr-Gomm, *Sacred Places: Sites of Spiritual Pilgrimage From Stonehenge to Santiago de Compostela*, (New York: Metro Books, 2008), 219.

13. Quoted in Carr-Gomm, *Sacred Places*, 2–13.

14. Quoted in Carr-Gomm, *Sacred Places*, 135.

15. Bonnie Bowman Thurston, *Belonging to Borders: A Sojourn in the Celtic Tradition* (Collegeville, MN: Liturgical Press, 2011), 41.

16. Carr-Gomm, *Sacred Places*, 138.

17. Tom Teicholz, "Cynthia Ozick: The Art of Fiction" *The New Paris Review*, no. 95, the parisreview.org/interviews.

18. Harpur, *Sacred Tracks*, 177.

19. Ibid., 178.

20. Holly Ellyatt, "How Religious Pilgrimages Support a Multi-billion Dollar Industry," *CNBC* (December 6, 2012).

21. Jennifer Lash, *On Pilgrimage* (London: Bloomsbury, 1999), 38.

22. Carr-Gomm, *Sacred Places*, 220.

23. Carr-Gomm, *Sacred Places*, 21.

24. Carr-Gomm, *Sacred Places*, 12.

25. Carr-Gomm, *Sacred Places*, 203.

26. Kathryn Glover, "Walking in Faith: Reflections on a First-Time Visit to the Holy Land," *Virginia Seminary Journal* (Fall 2010): 31.

27. David Zucchino, "What Ecotourism Should Be," *UU World* (Fall 2011): 22.

28. Michael Stausberg, *Religion and Tourism: Crossroads, Destinations and Encounters* (New York: Routledge), 78–79.

29. Miroslav Volf, "Reluctant Pilgrim. A Visit to the Jordan," *Christian Century* (November 5, 2009): 13.

30. Kathy Galloway, "Prayers for Pilgrims," *Inspiration Pilgrimage*, http://inspirationpilgrimage.blogspot.com/2007/05/prayers-for-pilgrims.html.

31. Testimony from participants of the Zen Peacemakers Auschwitz Retreat, see www.zenpeacemakers.org.

CHAPTER 4. WALKING THE LABYRINTH

1. Quoted in Di Williams, *Labyrinth* (Glasgow: Wild Goose, 2011), 74.

2. Virginia Westbury, *Labyrinths* (Cambridge, MA: DaCapo Press, 2001), 12.

3. Quoted in Westbury, *Labyrinth,* 11.

4. Quoted in Westbury, *Labyrinth,* 12.

5. Jill Purce, *The Mystic Spiral* (New York: Thames and Hudson, 1974), 19.

6. See "What Is a Labyrinth?," Rainbow-Labyrinths, http://rainborw-labyrinths.co.za.

7. Richard Whitaker, "Eternity Now. A conversation with the great trickster Wavy Gravy," *Parabola*, 36, no. 2 (Summer 2011), 76.

8. Quoted in Carr-Gomm, *Sacred Places*, 81.

9. See "The History," Damanhur, www.thetemples.org.

10. Carr-Gomm, *Sacred Places*, 76.

11. See "The Labyrinth," Damanhur, www.thetemples.org.

12. Carr-Gomm, *Sacred Places*, 78.

13. Quoted in Lauren Artress, *The Sacred Path Companion* (New York: Riverhead Books, 2006), 3.

14. Helen Raphael Sands, *The Healing Labyrinth: Finding Your Path to Inner Peace* (New York: Barron's, 2001), 24.

15. Interview, SKH with Paul Holbrook, October 25, 2012.

16. Quoted in Jim Forest, *The Road to Emmaus* (Maryknoll, NY: Orbis Books, 2007), 6.

17. Joan Chittister, "In Search of the Divine Feminine," *Huffington Post* (November 17, 2011) www.huffingtonpost/joan-chittister-search-divine-feminine.html.

18. Quoted in Helen Raphael Sands, *The Healing Labyrinth* (New York: Gaia Books, 2001), 32.

19. Ibid., 14.

20. Helen Curry, *The Way of the Labyrinth: A Powerful Meditation for Everyday Life* (New York: Penguin Compass, 2000), 77.

21. Quoted in Carr-Gomm, *Sacred Places,* 101.

22. Quoted in Cousineau, *The Art of Pilgrimage*, 149.

23. Sands, *Healing Labyrinth,* 36.

24. Carr-Gomm, *Sacred Places*, 101.

25. "Mingyur Rinpoche enters the path of wandering yogi," www.chronicleproject.com/stories.

26. Thich Nhat Hanh, "Walk Like a Buddha: Arrive in the Here and the Now," *Tricycle* (Summer 2011): 83.

27. Ibid., 85.

28. Ibid., 83.

29. Carolyn Scott Kortge, *The Spirited Walker* (New York: HarperCollins, 1998), xvi.

30. Vienna, quoted in Di Williams, *Labyrinth: Landscape of the Soul* (Glasgow: Wild Goose Publications, 2009), 35.

31. Sands, *The Healing Labyrinth,* 56.

32. T. S. Eliot, "Little Gidding," *Four Quartets* (Orlando: Harcourt, 1943), 240.

33. Lauren Artress, *The Sacred Path Companion: A Guide to Walking the Labyrinth to Heal and Transform* (New York: Riverhead Books, 2006), 29, 42–43.

34. Ibid., 39–41

35. Lauren Artress, *Walking a Sacred Path: Rediscovering the Labyrinth as a Spiritual Practice* (New York: Riverhead Books, 2006), 176.

36. Artress, *Sacred Path Companion,* 175.

CHAPTER 5. THE JOURNEY HOME

1. Katherine Gypson, "Freya Stark's Afghanistan," www.literary-traveler.com (February 25, 2012).

2. Quoted in Judith Fein, "Transformative Travel/Spain," *Spirituality & Health* (November–December 2009): 64.

3. Laura Dennett, *A Hug for the Apostle* (Toronto: Macmillan Canada, 1987), 16.

4. "The Way, Pilgrimage Movie Background," *Tired Road Warrior* (October 22, 2011), http://rogerhansen.wordpress.com.

5. Quoted in Carr-Gomm, *Sacred Places*, 87.

6. Eugene Peterson, *Run with the Horses* (Downers Grove, IL: IVP, 2010), 145–146.

7. Henri Nouwen, *Reaching Out* (New York: Bantam Books, 1975), 9.

8. Anne Carson, "Kinds of Water," *Grand Street* 6 (Summer 1987): 177.

9. Sharon Daloz Parks, *Big Questions, Worthy Dreams: Mentoring Young Adults in Their Search for Meaning, Purpose and Faith* (San Francisco: Jossey-Bass, 2000), 89–90.

10. Whyte, *Crossing the Unknown Sea*, 235.

11. "Starhawk" quoted in "Gaiam Life," http:// blog.gaiam.com.

12. bell hooks is the pen name of Gloria Watkins. The name is taken from her grandmother and is intentionally spelled in the lowercase to distinguish the author and to emphasize the content of the works, rather than the identity of the author.

13. bell hooks, *Belonging: A Culture of Place* (New York: Routledge, 2009), 68–69.

14. Ibid., 18, 21.

15. Ibid., 24.

16. Quoted in Edward C. Sellner, *Pilgrimage*, 27.

17. Sarah York, *Pilgrim Heart: The Inner Journey Home* (San Francisco: Jossey-Bass, 2001), 22.

18. Ibid., 172.

19. Wendell Berry, "A Spiritual Journey," www.panhala.net.

20. Quoted in Clyde Nichols, *Lift Up Your Eyes* (Bloomington, IN: Author House, 2011), 100.

21. Diarmuid O'Murchu, *Adult Faith: Growing in Wisdom and Understanding* (Maryknoll, NY: Orbis Books, 2010), 103–104.

22. Ibid., 107.

23. Ruth Walker, "Deeply Moved by Moving," *Christian Science Monitor Weekly* (June 18, 2012): 47.

24. Thich Nhat Hanh, *Essential Writings* (Maryknoll, NY: Orbis, 2011), 122.

25. Parks, *Big Questions, Worthy Dreams,* 34.

26. Diana L. Eck, *Encountering God: A Spiritual Journey from Bozeman to Banaras* (Boston: Beacon Press, 2003), 1–2.

27. John Inge, *A Christian Theology of Place* (Burlington, VT: Ashgate, 2003), 17.

28. Quoted in Inge, *A Christian Theology of Place,* 137.

29. Sharon Daloz Parks, "Home and Pilgrimage: Companion Metaphors for Personal and Social Transformation," *Soundings* 72 (1989): 315.

30. Eck, *Encountering God,* 228.

31. Martin Luther King Jr., *Where Do We Go From Here?* (Boston: Beacon Press, 1968), 91.

32. Xorin Balbes, *SoulSpace: Transform Your Home, Transform Your Life* (Novato, CA: New World Library, 2011), 3.

33. I first learned of the term *ancestral pilgrimage* from Christine Valters Paintner, Abbey of the Arts, www.abbeyofthearts.com.

34. Katrina Browne, quoted in Thomas Norman DeWolf, *Inheriting the Trade: A Northern Family Confronts Its Legacy in the Largest Slave-Trading Dynasty in U.S. History* (Boston: Beacon Press, 2008), 7.

35. DeWolf, *Inheriting the Trade,* 250–251.

36. Carolyn Jourdan, *Heart in the Right Place: A Memoir* (Chapel Hill, NC: Algonquin Books, 2008), 2.

37. Ibid., 124.

38. Ibid., 128.

39. Ibid., 297.

40. Quoted in Mary Paterson, *The Monks and Me: How 40 Days at Thich Nhat Hanh's French Monastery Guided Me Home* (Charlottesville, VA: Hampton Roads, 2012), xv.

41. Paterson, *Monks and Me,* xvii.

42. Ibid., xvi.

43. Thich Nhat Hanh, *Essential Writings,* ed. Sister Annabel Laity (Maryknoll, NY: Orbis Books, 2001), 122–123.

44. Paterson, *Monks and Me,* 80.

45. Ibid., 231.

46. David Briggs, "'Places of Faith' Tells What Really Goes on in America's Temples, Mosques and Churches," *Huffington Post* (January 21, 2012): www.huffingtonpost.com/david-briggs/inside-edition-places-of-faith.html.

47. Christopher P. Scheitle and Roger Finke, *Places of Faith: A Road Trip across America's Religious Landscape* (New York: Oxford University Press, 2012), 237.

CHAPTER 6. PREPARING TO PRACTICE

1. Jan Sutch Pickard quoted in www.inspirationpilgrimage.com.

2. Margaret R. Miles, "Can Religion Serve the Common Good in the 20th Century?," *Stanford Report* (June 16, 1999).

3. Jack Kornfield, *A Path with Heart: A Guide through the Perils and Promises of Spiritual Life* (New York: Bantam Books, 1993), 309.

4. Paul Fleishman, *Cultivating Inner Peace* (Onalaska, WA: Pari Yatti, 2003), 24.

5. Christine Northrup, "Heal Your Life," www.healyourlife.com.

6. Claudia Horwitz, *The Spiritual Activist: Practices to Transform Your Life, Your Work, and Your World* (New York: Penguin Compass, 2012), 59.

7. Howard Thurman, *Essential Writings* (Maryknoll, NY: Orbis Books, 2006), 18.

8. Anne Lamott, *Help. Thanks. Wow. The Three Essential Prayers* (New York: Pilgrim Group, 2012). Quotations from interviews with the author: "Anne Lamott Distills Prayer into 'Help, Thanks, Wow,'" NPR Books (November 19, 2012).

9. Abraham Joshua Heschel and Ruth Goodhill, *The Wisdom of Heschel* (New York: Scribners, 1970), 207.

10. Iyania Vanzant, *Every Day I Pray* (New York: Simon & Schuster, 2001), 15.

11. Horowitz, *The Spiritual Activist*, 59.

12. Eck, *Encountering God*, 154.

13. Christine Valters Paintner, *Water, Wind, Earth & Fire* (Notre Dame, IN: Sorin Books, 2010), 120.

14. From the author's website, www.abbeyofthehearts.com.

15. Henry David Thoreau, "The Journal of Henry David Thoreau," *New York Review of Books* (2009): 362.

16. R. S. Thomas, "Somewhere," *Collected Poems, 1945–1990* (London: J.M. Dent, 1993), 293.

SUGGESTIONS FOR FURTHER READING

Artress, Lauren. *The Sacred Path Companion: A Guide to Walking the Labyrinth to Heal and Transform*. New York: Riverhead Books, 2006.

―――. *Walking a Sacred Path: Rediscovering the Labyrinth as a Spiritual Practice*. New York: Riverhead Books, 2006.

Carr-Gomm, Philip. *Sacred Places: Sites of Spiritual Pilgrimage from Stonehenge to Santiago de Compostela*. New York: Metro Books, 2008.

Chittister, Joan. *The Monastery of the Heart: An Invitation to a Meaningful Life*. Katonah, NY: BlueBridge, 2011.

Clift, Jean Dalby & Wallace B. Clift. *The Archetype of Pilgrimage: Outer Action with Inner Meaning*. Eugene, OR: Wipf & Stock, 2004.

Codd, Kevin A. *The Field of Stars: A Pilgrim's Journey to Santiago de Compostela*. Grand Rapids, MI: Eerdmans, 2008.

Coelho, Paul. *The Alchemist*. HarperCollins, 1991.

―――. *The Pilgrimage*. New York: HarperCollins, 1991.

Coleman, David & Chris Polhill. *Pilgrimage: A Liturgy for Setting Out on a Pilgrimage and a Prayer for the Journey*. Glasgow: Wild Goose Publications, n.d. (Download), www.ionabooks.com.

Consiglio, Cyprian. *Prayer in the Cave of the Heart: The Universal Call to Contemplation*. Collegeville, MN: Liturgical Press, 2010.

Cousineau, Paul. *The Art of Pilgrimage: The Seeker's Guide to Making Travel Sacred*. Newburyport, MA: Conari Press, 1998.

Earle, Mary C. *Celtic Christian Spirituality: Essential Writings—Annotated & Explained*. Woodstock, VT: SkyLight Paths, 2011.

Eck, Diana. *India: A Sacred Geography*. New York: Harmony Books, 2012

Forest, Jim. *The Road to Emmaus: Pilgrimage as a Way of Life*. Maryknoll, NY: Orbis Books, 2007.

Foster, Charles. *The Sacred Journey*. Nashville: Thomas Nelson, 2010.

George, Christian. *Sacred Travels: Recovering the Ancient Practice of Pilgrimage*. Downers Grove, IL: IVP Books, 2006.

Harnden, Philip. *Journeys of Simplicity: Traveling Light with Thomas Merton, Bashō, Edward Abbey, Annie Dillard & Others*. Woodstock, VT: SkyLight Paths, 2007.

Harpur, James. *Sacred Tracks: 2000 Years of Christian Pilgrimage*. Berkeley, CA: University of California Press, 2002.

Harvey, Andrew. *A Walk with Four Spiritual Guides: Krishna, Buddha, Jesus & Ramakrishna*. Woodstock, VT: SkyLight Paths, 2007.

Hermkens, Anna-Karina, Willy Jensen and Catrien Notermans. *Moved by Mary: The Power of Pilgrimage in the Modern World*. Burlington, VT: Ashgate, 2009.

Hind, Rebecca. *Sacred Journeys: Rituals, Routes and Pilgrimages to Spiritual Fulfillment*. London: Carlton Books Ltd., 2009.

———. *Sacred Places: Sites of Spirituality & Faith*. London: Carlton Books Ltd., 2012.

Hunt, James B. *Restless Fires: John Muir's Thousand-Mile Walk to the Gulf in 1867–68*. Macon, GA: Mercer University Press, 2012.

Jones, Tony. *The Sacred Way: Spiritual Practices for Everyday Life*. Grand Rapids, MI: Zondervan, 2015.

Jourdan, Carolyn. *Heart in the Right Place*. Chapel Hill, NC: Algonquin Books, 2008.

King, Chris. *Pathways for Pilgrims: Discovering the Spirituality of the Iona Community in 28 Days*. Glasgow: Wild Goose Publications, 2012.

Laity, Sister Anabel, ed. *Thich Nhat Hanh: Essential Writings*. Maryknoll, NY: Orbis Books, 2001.

Leibovitz, Annie. *Pilgrimage*. New York: Random House, 2010.

Lewis-Kraus, Gideon. *A Sense of Direction: Pilgrimage for the Restless and Hopeful*. New York: Riverhead, 2012.

Markides, Kyriacos C. *Inner River: A Pilgrimage to the Heart of Christian Spirituality*. Colorado Springs, CO: Image Books, 2012.

Paintner, Christine Valters. *The Artist's Rule: Nurturing Your Creative Soul with Monastic Wisdom—A Twelve-Week Journey*. Notre Dame, IN: Sorin Books, 2011.

Palmer, Parker. *Let Your Life Speak: Listening to the Voice of Vocation*. San Francisco: Jossey-Bass, 2000.

Parks, Sharon Daloz. *Big Questions, Worthy Dreams: Mentoring Young Adults in Their Search for Meaning, Purpose and Faith*. San Francisco: Jossey-Bass, 2000.

Paterson, Mary. *The Monks and Me: How 40 Days at Thich Nhat Hanh's French Monastery Guided Me Home*. Newburyport, MA: Hampton Roads, 2012.

Porter, Venetia. *Hajj: Journey to the Heart of Islam.* Cambridge, MA: Harvard University Press, 2012.

Schaper, Donna and Carole Ann Camp. *Labyrinths From the Outside In,* 2nd Ed: *Walking to Spiritual Insight—A Beginners Guide.* Woodstock, VT: SkyLight Paths, 2013.

Scheitle, Christopher P. and Roger Finke. *Places of Faith: A Road Trip across America's Religious Landscape.* New York: Oxford University Press, 2012.

Scott, Robert. *Miracle Cures: Saints, Pilgrimage and the Healing Power of Belief.* Berkeley, CA: University of California Press, 2010.

Sibley, Robert C. *The Way of the Stars: Journeys on the Camino de Santiago.* Charlottesville, VA: University of Virginia Press, 2012.

Stausberg, Michael. *Religion and Tourism: Crossroads, Destinations and Encounters.* New York: Routledge, 2011.

Steindl-Rast, David. *Essential Writings.* Clare Hallward, ed. Maryknoll, NY: Orbis Books, 2010.

Thoreau, Henry David. *Walden.* New York: Empire Books, 2012.

Turner, Victor and Edith L. B. Turner. *Image and Pilgrimage in Christian Culture.* New York: Columbia University Press, 1978. Reprinted ed: Columbia Classics in Religion, 2011.

The Way of a Pilgrim and the Pilgrim Continues His Way. Helen Bacovcin, trans. Colorado Springs, CO: Image Books, 1982.

Webb, Val. *Stepping Out with the Sacred: Human Attempts to Engage the Divine.* New York: Continuum, 2010.

Webb-Mitchell, Brett. *School of the Pilgrim: An Alternative Path to Christian Growth.* Louisville, KY: Westminster John Knox, 2007.

Weiner, Eric. *Man Seeks God: My Flirtations with the Divine.* New York: Twelve, 2011.

Welch, Sally. *Making a Pilgrimage.* London: Lion, 2009.

Westwood, Jennifer. *On Pilgrimage: Sacred Journeys around the World.* Mahwah, NJ: Paulist Press, 2003.

Whalen, Brett Edward. *Pilgrimage in the Middle Ages: A Reader.* Toronto: University of Toronto, 2011.

Whyte, David. *Crossing the Unknown Sea: Work as a Pilgrimage of Identity.* New York: Riverhead, 2001.

York, Sarah. *Pilgrim Heart: The Inner Journey Home.* San Francisco: Jossey-Bass, 2001.

Inspiration

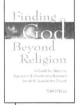

Finding God Beyond Religion: A Guide for Skeptics, Agnostics & Unorthodox Believers Inside & Outside the Church

By Tom Stella; Foreword by The Rev. Canon Marianne Wells Borg

Reinterprets traditional religious teachings central to the Christian faith for people who have outgrown the beliefs and devotional practices that once made sense to them.

6 x 9, 160 pp, Quality PB, 978-1-59473-485-4 **$16.99**

How Did I Get to Be 70 When I'm 35 Inside?: Spiritual Surprises of Later Life   *By Linda Douty*

Encourages you to focus on the inner changes of aging to help you greet your later years as the grand adventure they can be.   6 x 9, 208 pp, Quality PB, 978-1-59473-297-3 **$16.99**

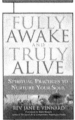

Fully Awake and Truly Alive: Spiritual Practices to Nurture Your Soul

By Rev. Jane E. Vennard; Foreword by Rami Shapiro

Illustrates the joys and frustrations of spiritual practice, offers insights from various religious traditions and provides exercises and meditations to help us become more fully alive.

6 x 9, 208 pp, Quality PB, 978-1-59473-473-1 **$16.99**

Saving Civility: 52 Ways to Tame Rude, Crude & Attitude for a Polite Planet

By Sara Hacala

Provides fifty-two practical ways you can reverse the course of incivility and make the world a more enriching, pleasant place to live.

6 x 9, 240 pp, Quality PB 978-1-59473-314-7 **$16.99**

Spiritually Healthy Divorce: Navigating Disruption with Insight & Hope

By Carolyne Call

A spiritual map to help you move through the twists and turns of divorce.

6 x 9, 224 pp, Quality PB, 978-1-59473-288-1 **$16.99**

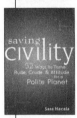

Who Is My God? 2nd Edition

An Innovative Guide to Finding Your Spiritual Identity

By the Editors at SkyLight Paths

Provides the Spiritual Identity Self-Test™ to uncover the components of your unique spirituality.   6 x 9, 160 pp, Quality PB, 978-1-59473-014-6 **$15.99**

Journeys of Simplicity
Traveling Light with Thomas Merton, Bashō,
Edward Abbey, Annie Dillard & Others
By Philip Harnden

Invites you to consider a more graceful way of traveling through life.
PB includes journal pages to help you get started on
your own spiritual journey.

5 x 7¼, 144 pp, Quality PB, 978-1-59473-181-5 **$12.99**
5 x 7¼, 128 pp, HC, 978-1-893361-76-8 **$16.95**

Or phone, mail or e-mail to: SKY LIGHT PATHS Publishing
An imprint of Turner Publishing Company
4507 Charlotte Avenue • Suite 100 • Nashville, Tennessee 37209
Tel: (615) 255-2665 • www.skylightpaths.com

Prices subject to change.

Children's Spirituality

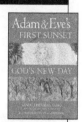

Adam & Eve's First Sunset: God's New Day
By Sandy Eisenberg Sasso; Full-color illus. by Joani Keller Rothenberg 9 x 12, 32 pp, Full-color illus.,
HC, 978-1-58023-177-0 **$17.95*** *For ages 4 & up*

Because Nothing Looks Like God
By Lawrence Kushner and Karen Kushner; Full-color illus. by Dawn W. Majewski
Invites parents and children to explore the questions we all have about God.
11 x 8½, 32 pp, Full-color illus., HC, 978-1-58023-092-6 **$17.99*** *For ages 4 & up*

Also available: **Teacher's Guide** 8½ x 11, 22 pp, PB, 978-1-58023-140-4 **$6.95**

But God Remembered: Stories of Women from Creation to the
Promised Land *By Sandy Eisenberg Sasso; Full-color illus. by Bethanne Andersen*
A fascinating collection of four different stories of women only briefly mentioned in biblical tradition and religious texts.
9 x 12, 32 pp, Full-color illus., Quality PB, 978-1-58023-372-9 **$8.99*** *For ages 8 & up*

Cain & Abel: Finding the Fruits of Peace
By Sandy Eisenberg Sasso; Full-color illus. by Joani Keller Rothenberg
A sensitive recasting of the ancient tale shows we have the power to deal with anger in positive ways. "Editor's Choice." —American Library Association's *Booklist*
Full-color illus., 978-1-58023-123-7 Digital List Price: **$16.95*** *For ages 5 & up Available as an e-book only. For Kindle, nook, iPad and Kobo. Not available directly from SkyLight Paths.*

Does God Hear My Prayer?
By August Gold; Full-color photos by Diane Hardy Waller
Introduces preschoolers and young readers to prayer and how it helps them express their own emotions.
10 x 8½, 32 pp, Full-color photo illus., Quality PB, 978-1-59473-102-0 **$8.99** *For ages 3–6*

The 11th Commandment: Wisdom from Our Children *By the Children of America*
"If there were an Eleventh Commandment, what would it be?" Children of many religious denominations across America answer this question—in their own drawings and words. "A rare book of spiritual celebration for all people, of all ages, for all time." —*Bookviews* 8 x 10, 48 pp, Full-color illus., HC, 978-1-879045-46-0 **$16.95*** *For all ages*

For Heaven's Sake *By Sandy Eisenberg Sasso; Full-color illus. by Kathryn Kunz Finney*
Heaven is often found where you least expect it.
9 x 12, 32 pp, Full-color illus., HC, 978-1-58023-054-4 **$16.95*** *For ages 4 & up*

God in Between *By Sandy Eisenberg Sasso; Full-color illus. by Sally Sweetland*
A magical, mythical tale that teaches that God can be found where we are.
9 x 12, 32 pp, Full-color illus., HC, 978-1-879045-86-6 **$16.95*** *For ages 4 & up*

God's Paintbrush: Special 10th Anniversary Edition
By Sandy Eisenberg Sasso; Full-color illus. by Annette Compton
Invites children of all faiths and backgrounds to encounter God through moments in their own lives. 11 x 8½, 32 pp, Full-color illus., HC, 978-1-58023-195-4 **$17.95*** *For ages 4 & up*

Also available: **God's Paintbrush Teacher's Guide**
8½ x 11, 32 pp, PB, 978-1-879045-57-6 **$8.95**

God's Paintbrush Celebration Kit: A Spiritual Activity Kit for Teachers and
Students of All Faiths, All Backgrounds 9½ x 12, 40 Full-color Activity Sheets & Teacher Folder w/ complete instructions, HC, 978-1-58023-050-6 **$21.95**
Additional activity sheets available:
8-Student Activity Sheet Pack (40 sheets/5 sessions), 978-1-58023-058-2 **$19.95**
Single-Student Activity Sheet Pack (5 sessions), 978-1-58023-059-9 **$3.95**

I Am God's Paintbrush (A Board Book)
By Sandy Eisenberg Sasso; Full-color illus. by Annette Compton
5 x 5, 24 pp, Full-color illus., Board Book, 978-1-59473-265-2 **$7.99** *For ages 0–4*

* A book from Jewish Lights, SkyLight Paths' sister imprint

Sacred Texts—SkyLight Illuminations Series

Offers today's spiritual seeker an enjoyable entry into the great classic texts of the world's spiritual traditions. Each classic is presented in an accessible translation, with facing pages of guided commentary from experts, giving you the keys you need to understand the history, context and meaning of the text.

CHRISTIANITY

Celtic Christian Spirituality: Essential Writings—Annotated & Explained
Annotation by Mary C. Earle; Foreword by John Philip Newell
Explores how the writings of this lively tradition embody the gospel.
5½ x 8½, 176 pp, Quality PB, 978-1-59473-302-4 **$16.99**

Desert Fathers and Mothers: Early Christian Wisdom Sayings—
Annotated & Explained *Annotation by Christine Valters Paintner, PhD*
Opens up wisdom of the desert fathers and mothers for readers with no previous knowledge of Western monasticism and early Christianity.
5½ x 8½, 192 pp, Quality PB, 978-1-59473-373-4 **$16.99**

The End of Days: Essential Selections from Apocalyptic Texts—
Annotated & Explained *Annotation by Robert G. Clouse, PhD*
Helps you understand the complex Christian visions of the end of the world.
5½ x 8½, 224 pp, Quality PB, 978-1-59473-170-9 **$16.99**

The Hidden Gospel of Matthew: Annotated & Explained
Translation & Annotation by Ron Miller
Discover the words and events that have the strongest connection to the historical Jesus.
5½ x 8½, 272 pp, Quality PB, 978-1-59473-038-2 **$16.99**

The Imitation of Christ: Selections Annotated & Explained
Annotation by Paul Wesley Chilcote, PhD; By Thomas à Kempis; Adapted from John Wesley's
The Christian's Pattern
Let Jesus's example of holiness, humility and purity of heart be a companion on your own spiritual journey.
5½ x 8½, 224 pp, Quality PB, 978-1-59473-434-2 **$16.99**

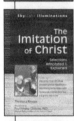

The Infancy Gospels of Jesus: Apocryphal Tales from the Childhoods of Mary and Jesus—Annotated & Explained
Translation & Annotation by Stevan Davies; Foreword by A. Edward Siecienski, PhD
A startling presentation of the early lives of Mary, Jesus and other biblical figures that will amuse and surprise you.
5½ x 8½, 176 pp, Quality PB, 978-1-59473-258-4 **$16.99**

John & Charles Wesley: Selections from Their Writings and Hymns—
Annotated & Explained
Annotation by Paul W. Chilcote, PhD
A unique presentation of the writings of these two inspiring brothers brings together some of the most essential material from their large corpus of work.
5½ x 8½, 288 pp, Quality PB, 978-1-59473-309-3 **$16.99**

The Lost Sayings of Jesus: Teachings from Ancient Christian, Jewish, Gnostic and Islamic Sources—Annotated & Explained
Translation & Annotation by Andrew Phillip Smith; Foreword by Stephan A. Hoeller
This collection of more than three hundred sayings depicts Jesus as a Wisdom teacher who speaks to people of all faiths as a mystic and spiritual master.
5½ x 8½, 240 pp, Quality PB, 978-1-59473-172-3 **$16.99**

Philokalia: The Eastern Christian Spiritual Texts—Selections
Annotated & Explained *Annotation by Allyne Smith; Translation by G. E. H. Palmer,
Phillip Sherrard and Bishop Kallistos Ware*
The first approachable introduction to the wisdom of the Philokalia, the classic text of Eastern Christian spirituality.
5½ x 8½, 240 pp, Quality PB, 978-1-59473-103-7 **$16.99**

Sacred Texts—continued

CHRISTIANITY—continued

The Sacred Writings of Paul: Selections Annotated & Explained
Translation & Annotation by Ron Miller
Leads you into the exciting immediacy of Paul's teachings.
5½ x 8½, 224 pp, Quality PB, 978-1-59473-213-3 **$16.99**

Saint Augustine of Hippo: Selections from *Confessions* and Other
Essential Writings—Annotated & Explained
Annotation by Joseph T. Kelley, PhD; Translation by the Augustinian Heritage Institute
Provides insight into the mind and heart of this foundational Christian figure.
5½ x 8½, 272 pp, Quality PB, 978-1-59473-282-9 **$16.99**

Saint Ignatius Loyola—The Spiritual Writings: Selections
Annotated & Explained *Annotation by Mark Mossa, SJ*
Draws from contemporary translations of original texts focusing on the practical
mysticism of Ignatius of Loyola.
5½ x 8½, 288 pp, Quality PB, 978-1-59473-301-7 **$16.99**

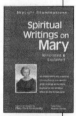

Sex Texts from the Bible: Selections Annotated & Explained
Translation & Annotation by Teresa J. Hornsby; Foreword by Amy-Jill Levine
Demystifies the Bible's ideas on gender roles, marriage, sexual orientation, virginity,
lust and sexual pleasure.
5½ x 8½, 208 pp, Quality PB, 978-1-59473-217-1 **$16.99**

Spiritual Writings on Mary: Annotated & Explained
Annotation by Mary Ford-Grabowsky; Foreword by Andrew Harvey
Examines the role of Mary, the mother of Jesus, as a source of inspiration in history and in life today.
5½ x 8½, 288 pp, Quality PB, 978-1-59473-001-6 **$16.99**

The Way of a Pilgrim: The Jesus Prayer Journey—Annotated &
Explained
Translation & Annotation by Gleb Pokrovsky; Foreword by Andrew Harvey
A classic of Russian Orthodox spirituality.
5½ x 8½, 160 pp, Illus., Quality PB, 978-1-893361-31-7 **$14.95**

GNOSTICISM

Gnostic Writings on the Soul: Annotated & Explained
Translation & Annotation by Andrew Phillip Smith; Foreword by Stephan A. Hoeller
Reveals the inspiring ways your soul can remember and return to its unique,
divine purpose.
5½ x 8½, 144 pp, Quality PB, 978-1-59473-220-1 **$16.99**

The Gospel of Philip: Annotated & Explained
Translation & Annotation by Andrew Phillip Smith; Foreword by Stevan Davies
Reveals otherwise unrecorded sayings of Jesus and fragments of Gnostic mythology.
5½ x 8½, 160 pp, Quality PB, 978-1-59473-111-2 **$16.99**

The Gospel of Thomas: Annotated & Explained
Translation & Annotation by Stevan Davies; Foreword by Andrew Harvey
Sheds new light on the origins of Christianity and portrays Jesus as a wisdom-loving sage.
5½ x 8½, 192 pp, Quality PB, 978-1-893361-45-4 **$16.99**

The Secret Book of John: The Gnostic Gospel—Annotated & Explained
Translation & Annotation by Stevan Davies
The most significant and influential text of the ancient Gnostic religion.
5½ x 8½, 208 pp, Quality PB, 978-1-59473-082-5 **$16.99**

Sacred Texts—continued

JUDAISM

The Book of Job: Annotated & Explained
Translation and Annotation by Donald Kraus; Foreword by Dr. Marc Brettler
Clarifies for today's readers what Job is, how to overcome difficulties in the text, and what it may mean for us.
5½ x 8½, 256 pp, Quality PB, 978-1-59473-389-5 **$16.99**

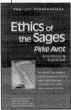

The Divine Feminine in Biblical Wisdom Literature
Selections Annotated & Explained
Translation & Annotation by Rabbi Rami Shapiro; Foreword by Rev. Cynthia Bourgeault, PhD
Uses the Hebrew Bible and Wisdom literature to explain Sophia's way of wisdom and illustrate Her creative energy.
5½ x 8½, 240 pp, Quality PB, 978-1-59473-109-9 **$16.99**

Ecclesiastes: Annotated & Explained
Translation & Annotation by Rabbi Rami Shapiro; Foreword by Rev. Barbara Cawthorne Crafton
A timeless teaching on living well amid uncertainty and insecurity.
5½ x 8½, 160 pp, Quality PB, 978-1-59473-287-4 **$16.99**

Ethics of the Sages: *Pirke Avot*—Annotated & Explained
Translation & Annotation by Rabbi Rami Shapiro
Clarifies the ethical teachings of the early Rabbis.
5½ x 8½, 192 pp, Quality PB, 978-1-59473-207-2 **$16.99**

Hasidic Tales: Annotated & Explained
Translation & Annotation by Rabbi Rami Shapiro; Foreword by Andrew Harvey
Introduces the legendary tales of the impassioned Hasidic rabbis, presenting them as stories rather than as parables.
5½ x 8½, 240 pp, Quality PB, 978-1-893361-86-7 **$16.95**

The Hebrew Prophets: Selections Annotated & Explained
Translation & Annotation by Rabbi Rami Shapiro;
Foreword by Rabbi Zalman M. Schachter-Shalomi
5½ x 8½, 224 pp, Quality PB, 978-1-59473-037-5 **$16.99**

Maimonides—Essential Teachings on Jewish Faith & Ethics
The Book of Knowledge & the Thirteen Principles of Faith—Annotated & Explained
Translation and Annotation by Rabbi Marc D. Angel, PhD
Opens up for us Maimonides's views on the nature of God, providence, prophecy, free will, human nature, repentance and more.
5½ x 8½, 224 pp, Quality PB, 978-1-59473-311-6 **$18.99**

Proverbs: Annotated & Explained
Translation and Annotation by Rabbi Rami Shapiro
Demonstrates how these complex poetic forms are actually straightforward instructions to live simply, without rationalizations and excuses.
5½ x 8½, 288 pp, Quality PB, 978-1-59473-310-9 $16.99

Tanya, the Masterpiece of Hasidic Wisdom
Selections Annotated & Explained
Translation & Annotation by Rabbi Rami Shapiro; Foreword by Rabbi Zalman M. Schachter-Shalomi
Clarifies one of the most powerful and potentially transformative books of Jewish wisdom.
5½ x 8½, 240 pp, Quality PB, 978-1-59473-275-1 **$16.99**

Zohar: Annotated & Explained
Translation & Annotation by Daniel C. Matt; Foreword by Andrew Harvey
The canonical text of Jewish mystical tradition.
5½ x 8½, 176 pp, Quality PB, 978-1-893361-51-5 **$16.99**

Sacred Texts—continued

ISLAM

Ghazali on the Principles of Islamic Spirituality
Selections from *The Forty Foundations of Religion*—Annotated & Explained
Translation & Annotation by Aaron Spevack, PhD
Makes the core message of this influential spiritual master relevant to anyone seeking a balanced understanding of Islam.
5½ x 8½, 338 pp, Quality PB, 978-1-59473-284-3 **$18.99**

The Qur'an and Sayings of Prophet Muhammad
Selections Annotated & Explained
Annotation by Sohaib N. Sultan; Translation by Yusuf Ali, Revised by Sohaib N. Sultan; Foreword by Jane I. Smith
Presents the foundational wisdom of Islam in an easy-to-use format.
5½ x 8½, 256 pp, Quality PB, 978-1-59473-222-5 **$16.99**

Rumi and Islam: Selections from His Stories, Poems, and Discourses—
Annotated & Explained *Translation & Annotation by Ibrahim Gamard*
Focuses on Rumi's place within the Sufi tradition of Islam, providing insight into the mystical side of the religion.
5½ x 8½, 240 pp, Quality PB, 978-1-59473-002-3 **$15.99**

EASTERN RELIGIONS

The Art of War—Spirituality for Conflict: Annotated & Explained
By Sun Tzu; Annotation by Thomas Huynh; Translation by Thomas Huynh and the Editors at Sonshi.com; Foreword by Marc Benioff; Preface by Thomas Cleary
Highlights principles that encourage a perceptive and spiritual approach to conflict.
5½ x 8½, 256 pp, Quality PB, 978-1-59473-244-7 **$16.99**

Bhagavad Gita: Annotated & Explained
Translation by Shri Purohit Swami; Annotation by Kendra Crossen Burroughs; Foreword by Andrew Harvey
Presents the classic text's teachings—with no previous knowledge of Hinduism required.
5½ x 8½, 192 pp, Quality PB, 978-1-893361-28-7 **$16.95**

Chuang-tzu: The Tao of Perfect Happiness—Selections Annotated & Explained
Translation & Annotation by Livia Kohn, PhD
Presents Taoism's central message of reverence for the "Way" of the natural world.
5½ x 8½, 240 pp, Quality PB, 978-1-59473-296-6 **$16.99**

Confucius, the *Analects*: The Path of the Sage—Selections Annotated
& Explained *Annotation by Rodney L. Taylor, PhD; Translation by James Legge, Revised by Rodney L. Taylor, PhD* Explores the ethical and spiritual meaning behind the Confucian way of learning and self-cultivation.
5½ x 8½, 192 pp, Quality PB, 978-1-59473-306-2 **$16.99**

Dhammapada: Annotated & Explained
Translation by Max Müller, revised by Jack Maguire; Annotation by Jack Maguire; Foreword by Andrew Harvey Contains all of Buddhism's key teachings, plus commentary that explains all the names, terms and references.
5½ x 8½, 160 pp, b/w photos, Quality PB, 978-1-893361-42-3 **$14.95**

Selections from the Gospel of Sri Ramakrishna: Annotated & Explained
Translation by Swami Nikhilananda; Annotation by Kendra Crossen Burroughs; Foreword by Andrew Harvey Introduces the fascinating world of the Indian mystic and the universal appeal of his message.
5½ x 8½, 240 pp, b/w photos, Quality PB, 978-1-893361-46-1 **$16.95**

Tao Te Ching: Annotated & Explained
Translation & Annotation by Derek Lin; Foreword by Lama Surya Das
Introduces an Eastern classic in an accessible, poetic and completely original way.
5½ x 8½, 208 pp, Quality PB, 978-1-59473-204-1 **$16.99**

Sacred Texts—continued

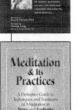

MORMONISM

The Book of Mormon: Selections Annotated & Explained
Annotation by Jana Riess; Foreword by Phyllis Tickle Explores the sacred epic that is cherished by more than twelve million members of the LDS church as the keystone of their faith. 5½ x 8½ , 272 pp, Quality PB, 978-1-59473-076-4 **$16.99**

NATIVE AMERICAN

Native American Stories of the Sacred: Annotated & Explained
Retold & Annotated by Evan T. Pritchard These teaching tales contain elegantly simple illustrations of time-honored truths. 5½ x 8½, 272 pp, Quality PB, 978-1-59473-112-9 **$16.99**

STOICISM

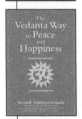

The Meditations of Marcus Aurelius: Selections Annotated & Explained *Annotation by Russell McNeil, PhD; Translation by George Long, revised by Russell McNeil, PhD* Ancient Stoic wisdom that speaks vibrantly today about life, business, government and spirit. 5½ x 8½, 288 pp, Quality PB, 978-1-59473-236-2 **$16.99**

Hinduism / Vedanta

The Four Yogas: A Guide to the Spiritual Paths of Action, Devotion, Meditation and Knowledge *By Swami Adiswarananda*
6 x 9, 320 pp, Quality PB, 978-1-59473-223-2 **$19.99**

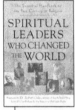

Meditation & Its Practices: A Definitive Guide to Techniques and Traditions of Meditation in Yoga and Vedanta *By Swami Adiswarananda* 6 x 9, 504 pp, Quality PB, 978-1-59473-105-1 **$24.99**

The Spiritual Quest and the Way of Yoga: The Goal, the Journey and the Milestones *By Swami Adiswarananda* 6 x 9, 288 pp, HC, 978-1-59473-113-6 **$29.99**

Sri Ramakrishna, the Face of Silence
By Swami Nikhilananda and Dhan Gopal Mukerji; Edited with an Introduction by Swami Adiswarananda; Foreword by Dhan Gopal Mukerji II 6 x 9, 352 pp, Quality PB, 978-1-59473-233-1 **$21.99**

Sri Sarada Devi, The Holy Mother: Her Teachings and Conversations
Translated with Notes by Swami Nikhilananda; Edited with an Introduction by Swami Adiswarananda 6 x 9, 288 pp, HC, 978-1-59473-070-2 **$29.99**

The Vedanta Way to Peace and Happiness *By Swami Adiswarananda*
6 x 9, 240 pp, Quality PB, 978-1-59473-180-8 **$18.99**

Vivekananda, World Teacher: His Teachings on the Spiritual Unity of Humankind
Edited and with an Introduction by Swami Adiswarananda
6 x 9, 272 pp, Quality PB, 978-1-59473-210-2 **$21.99**

Sikhism

The First Sikh Spiritual Master: Timeless Wisdom from the Life and Teachings of Guru Nanak *By Harish Dhillon* 6 x 9, 192 pp, Quality PB, 978-1-59473-209-6 **$16.99**

Spiritual Biography

Spiritual Leaders Who Changed the World
The Essential Handbook to the Past Century of Religion
Edited by Ira Rifkin and the Editors at SkyLight Paths; Foreword by Dr. Robert Coles
An invaluable reference to the most important spiritual leaders of the past 100 years.
6 x 9, 304 pp, b/w photos, Quality PB, 978-1-59473-241-6 **$18.99**

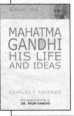

Mahatma Gandhi: His Life and Ideas *By Charles F. Andrews; Foreword by Dr. Arun Gandhi* Examines the religious ideas and political dynamics that influenced the birth of the peaceful resistance movement. 6 x 9, 336 pp, b/w photos, Quality PB, 978-1-893361-89-8 **$18.95**

Bede Griffiths: An Introduction to His Interspiritual Thought
By Wayne Teasdale The first study of his contemplative experience and thought, exploring the intersection of Hinduism and Christianity.
6 x 9, 288 pp, Quality PB, 978-1-893361-77-5 **$18.95**

Spirituality of the Seasons

Autumn: A Spiritual Biography of the Season
Edited by Gary Schmidt and Susan M. Felch; Illus. by Mary Azarian
Rejoice in autumn as a time of preparation and reflection. Includes Wendell Berry, David James Duncan, Robert Frost, A. Bartlett Giamatti, E. B. White, P. D. James, Julian of Norwich, Garret Keizer, Tracy Kidder, Anne Lamott, May Sarton.
6 x 9, 320 pp, b/w illus., Quality PB, 978-1-59473-118-1 **$18.99**

Spring: A Spiritual Biography of the Season
Edited by Gary Schmidt and Susan M. Felch; Illus. by Mary Azarian
Explore the gentle unfurling of spring and reflect on how nature celebrates rebirth and renewal. Includes Jane Kenyon, Lucy Larcom, Harry Thurston, Nathaniel Hawthorne, Noel Perrin, Annie Dillard, Martha Ballard, Barbara Kingsolver, Dorothy Wordsworth, Donald Hall, David Brill, Lionel Basney, Isak Dinesen, Paul Laurence Dunbar. 6 x 9, 352 pp, b/w illus., Quality PB, 978-1-59473-246-1 **$18.99**

Summer: A Spiritual Biography of the Season
Edited by Gary Schmidt and Susan M. Felch; Illus. by Barry Moser
"A sumptuous banquet.... These selections lift up an exquisite wholeness found within an everyday sophistication." — ★ *Publishers Weekly* starred review
Includes Anne Lamott, Luci Shaw, Ray Bradbury, Richard Selzer, Thomas Lynch, Walt Whitman, Carl Sandburg, Sherman Alexie, Madeleine L'Engle, Jamaica Kincaid.
6 x 9, 304 pp, b/w illus., Quality PB, 978-1-59473-183-9 **$18.99**

Winter: A Spiritual Biography of the Season
Edited by Gary Schmidt and Susan M. Felch; Illus. by Barry Moser
"This outstanding anthology features top-flight nature and spirituality writers on the fierce, inexorable season of winter.... Remarkably lively and warm, despite the icy subject." — ★ *Publishers Weekly* starred review
Includes Will Campbell, Rachel Carson, Annie Dillard, Donald Hall, Ron Hansen, Jane Kenyon, Jamaica Kincaid, Barry Lopez, Kathleen Norris, John Updike, E. B. White.
6 x 9, 288 pp, b/w illus., Deluxe PB w/ flaps, 978-1-893361-92-8 **$18.95**

Spirituality / Animal Companions

Blessing the Animals: Prayers and Ceremonies to Celebrate God's Creatures, Wild and Tame *Edited and with Introductions by Lynn L. Caruso*
5¼ x 7¼, 256 pp, Quality PB, 978-1-59473-253-9 **$15.99**; HC, 978-1-59473-145-7 **$19.99**

Remembering My Pet: A Kid's Own Spiritual Workbook for When a Pet Dies
By Nechama Liss-Levinson, PhD, and Rev. Molly Phinney Baskette, MDiv; Foreword by Lynn L. Caruso
8 x 10, 48 pp, 2-color text, HC, 978-1-59473-221-8 **$16.99**

What Animals Can Teach Us about Spirituality: Inspiring Lessons from Wild and Tame Creatures *By Diana L. Guerrero* 6 x 9, 176 pp, Quality PB, 978-1-893361-84-3 **$16.95**

Spirituality—A Week Inside

Making a Heart for God: A Week Inside a Catholic Monastery
By Dianne Aprile; Foreword by Brother Patrick Hart, OCSO
6 x 9, 224 pp, b/w photos, Quality PB, 978-1-893361-49-2 **$16.95**

Waking Up: A Week Inside a Zen Monastery
By Jack Maguire; Foreword by John Daido Loori, Roshi
6 x 9, 224 pp, b/w photos, Quality PB, 978-1-893361-55-3 **$16.95**

Spirituality & Crafts

Beading—The Creative Spirit: Finding Your Sacred Center through the Art of Beadwork *By Rev. Wendy Ellsworth*
Invites you on a spiritual pilgrimage into the kaleidoscope world of glass and color. 7 x 9, 240 pp, 8-page color insert, 40+ b/w photos and 40 diagrams, Quality PB, 978-1-59473-267-6 **$18.99**

Contemplative Crochet: A Hands-On Guide for Interlocking Faith and Craft *By Cindy Crandall-Frazier; Foreword by Linda Skolnik*
Illuminates the spiritual lessons you can learn through crocheting.
7 x 9, 208 pp, b/w photos, Quality PB, 978-1-59473-238-6 **$16.99**

The Knitting Way: A Guide to Spiritual Self-Discovery
By Linda Skolnik and Janice MacDaniels Examines how you can explore and strengthen your spiritual life through knitting.
7 x 9, 240 pp, b/w photos, Quality PB, 978-1-59473-079-5 **$16.99**

The Painting Path: Embodying Spiritual Discovery through Yoga, Brush and Color *By Linda Novick; Foreword by Richard Segalman*
Explores the divine connection you can experience through art.
7 x 9, 208 pp, 8-page color insert, plus b/w photos, Quality PB, 978-1-59473-226-3 **$18.99**

The Quilting Path: A Guide to Spiritual Discovery through Fabric, Thread and Kabbalah *By Louise Silk*
Explores how to cultivate personal growth through quilt making.
7 x 9, 192 pp, b/w photos and illus., Quality PB, 978-1-59473-206-5 **$16.99**

The Scrapbooking Journey: A Hands-On Guide to Spiritual Discovery
By Cory Richardson-Lauve; Foreword by Stacy Julian Reveals how this craft can become a practice used to deepen and shape your life.
7 x 9, 176 pp, 8-page color insert, plus b/w photos, Quality PB, 978-1-59473-216-4 **$18.99**

The Soulwork of Clay: A Hands-On Approach to Spirituality
By Marjory Zoet Bankson; Photos by Peter Bankson
Takes you through the seven-step process of making clay into a pot, drawing parallels at each stage to the process of spiritual growth.
7 x 9, 192 pp, b/w photos, Quality PB, 978-1-59473-249-2 **$16.99**

Kabbalah / Enneagram
(Books from Jewish Lights Publishing, SkyLight Paths' sister imprint)

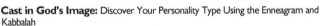

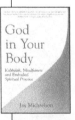

Cast in God's Image: Discover Your Personality Type Using the Enneagram and Kabbalah
By Rabbi Howard A. Addison, PhD 7 x 9, 176 pp, Quality PB, 978-1-58023-124-4 **$16.95**

Ehyeh: A Kabbalah for Tomorrow *By Rabbi Arthur Green, PhD*
6 x 9, 224 pp, Quality PB, 978-1-58023-213-5 **$18.99**

The Enneagram and Kabbalah, 2nd Edition: Reading Your Soul
By Rabbi Howard A. Addison, PhD 6 x 9, 192 pp, Quality PB, 978-1-58023-229-6 **$16.99**

The Gift of Kabbalah: Discovering the Secrets of Heaven, Renewing Your Life on Earth
By Tamar Frankiel, PhD 6 x 9, 256 pp, Quality PB, 978-1-58023-141-1 **$16.95**

God in Your Body: Kabbalah, Mindfulness and Embodied Spiritual Practice
By Jay Michaelson 6 x 9, 272 pp, Quality PB, 978-1-58023-304-0 **$18.99**

Jewish Mysticism and the Spiritual Life: Classical Texts, Contemporary Reflections
Edited by Dr. Lawrence Fine, Dr. Eitan Fishbane and Rabbi Or N. Rose
6 x 9, 256 pp, HC, 978-1-58023-434-4 **$24.99**

Kabbalah: A Brief Introduction for Christians
By Tamar Frankiel, PhD 5½ x 8½, 208 pp, Quality PB, 978-1-58023-303-3 **$16.99**

Zohar: Annotated & Explained *Translation & Annotation by Daniel C. Matt; Foreword by Andrew Harvey* 5½ x 8½, 176 pp, Quality PB, 978-1-893361-51-5 **$15.99**

Spiritual Poetry—The Mystic Poets

Experience these mystic poets as you never have before. Each beautiful, compact book includes a brief introduction to the poet's time and place, a summary of the major themes of the poet's mysticism and religious tradition, essential selections from the poet's most important works, and an appreciative preface by a contemporary spiritual writer.

Hafiz
The Mystic Poets
Translated and with Notes by Gertrude Bell
Preface by Ibrahim Gamard

Hafiz is known throughout the world as Persia's greatest poet, with sales of his poems in Iran today only surpassed by those of the Qur'an itself. His probing and joyful verse speaks to people from all backgrounds who long to taste and feel divine love and experience harmony with all living things.
5 x 7¼, 144 pp, HC, 978-1-59473-009-2 **$16.99**

Hopkins
The Mystic Poets
Preface by Rev. Thomas Ryan, CSP

Gerard Manley Hopkins, Christian mystical poet, is beloved for his use of fresh language and startling metaphors to describe the world around him. Although his verse is lovely, beneath the surface lies a searching soul, wrestling with and yearning for God.
5 x 7¼, 112 pp, HC, 978-1-59473-010-8 **$16.99**

Tagore
The Mystic Poets
Preface by Swami Adiswarananda

Rabindranath Tagore is often considered the Shakespeare of modern India. A great mystic, Tagore was the teacher of W. B. Yeats and Robert Frost, the close friend of Albert Einstein and Mahatma Gandhi, and the winner of the Nobel Prize for Literature. This beautiful sampling of Tagore's two most important works, *The Gardener* and *Gitanjali*, offers a glimpse into his spiritual vision that has inspired people around the world.
5 x 7¼, 144 pp, HC, 978-1-59473-008-5 **$16.99**

Whitman
The Mystic Poets
Preface by Gary David Comstock

Walt Whitman was the most innovative and influential poet of the nineteenth century. This beautiful sampling of Whitman's most important poetry from *Leaves of Grass,* and selections from his prose writings, offers a glimpse into the spiritual side of his most radical themes—love for country, love for others and love of self.
5 x 7¼, 192 pp, HC, 978-1-59473-041-2 **$16.99**

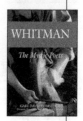

Women's Interest

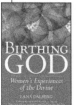

Birthing God: Women's Experiences of the Divine
By Lana Dalberg; Foreword by Kathe Schaaf
Powerful narratives of suffering, love and hope that inspire both personal and collective transformation.   6 x 9, 304 pp, Quality PB, 978-1-59473-480-9 **$18.99**

On the Chocolate Trail: A Delicious Adventure Connecting Jews, Religions, History, Travel, Rituals and Recipes to the Magic of Cacao
By Rabbi Deborah R. Prinz
Take a delectable journey through the religious history of chocolate—a real treat!
6 x 9, 272 pp, 20+ b/w photographs, Quality PB, 978-1-58023-487-0 **$18.99***

Women, Spirituality and Transformative Leadership
Where Grace Meets Power
Edited by Kathe Schaaf, Kay Lindahl, Kathleen S. Hurty, PhD, and Reverend Guo Cheen
A dynamic conversation on the power of women's spiritual leadership and its emerging patterns of transformation.   6 x 9, 288 pp, HC, 978-1-59473-313-0 **$24.99**

Spiritually Healthy Divorce: Navigating Disruption with Insight & Hope
By Carolyne Call   A spiritual map to help you move through the twists and turns of divorce.   6 x 9, 224 pp, Quality PB, 978-1-59473-288-1 **$16.99**

New Feminist Christianity: Many Voices, Many Views
Edited by Mary E. Hunt and Diann L. Neu
Insights from ministers and theologians, activists and leaders, artists and liturgists who are shaping the future. Taken together, their voices offer a starting point for building new models of religious life and worship.
6 x 9, 384 pp, Quality PB, 978-1-59473-435-9 **$19.99**; HC, 978-1-59473-285-0 **$24.99**

Bread, Body, Spirit: Finding the Sacred in Food
Edited and with Introductions by Alice Peck   6 x 9, 224 pp, Quality PB, 978-1-59473-242-3 **$19.99**

Dance—The Sacred Art: The Joy of Movement as a Spiritual Practice
By Cynthia Winton-Henry   5½ x 8½, 224 pp, Quality PB, 978-1-59473-268-3 **$16.99**

Daughters of the Desert: Stories of Remarkable Women from Christian, Jewish and Muslim Traditions
By Claire Rudolf Murphy, Meghan Nuttall Sayres, Mary Cronk Farrell, Sarah Conover and Betsy Wharton
5½ x 8½, 192 pp, Illus., Quality PB, 978-1-59473-106-8 **$14.99** Inc. reader's discussion guide

The Divine Feminine in Biblical Wisdom Literature
Selections Annotated & Explained
Translation & Annotation by Rabbi Rami Shapiro; Foreword by Rev. Cynthia Bourgeault, PhD
5½ x 8½, 240 pp, Quality PB, 978-1-59473-109-9 **$16.99**

Divining the Body: Reclaim the Holiness of Your Physical Self
By Jan Phillips   8 x 8, 256 pp, Quality PB, 978-1-59473-080-1 **$18.99**

Honoring Motherhood: Prayers, Ceremonies & Blessings
Edited and with Introductions by Lynn L. Caruso
5 x 7¼, 272 pp, Quality PB, 978-1-58473-384-0 **$9.99**; HC, 978-1-59473-239-3 **$19.99**

Next to Godliness: Finding the Sacred in Housekeeping
Edited by Alice Peck   6 x 9, 224 pp, Quality PB, 978-1-59473-214-0 **$19.99**

ReVisions: Seeing Torah through a Feminist Lens
By Rabbi Elyse Goldstein   5½ x 8½, 224 pp, Quality PB, 978-1-58023-117-6 **$16.95***

The Triumph of Eve & Other Subversive Bible Tales
By Matt Biers-Ariel   5½ x 8½, 192 pp, Quality PB, 978-1-59473-176-1 **$14.99**

White Fire: A Portrait of Women Spiritual Leaders in America
By Malka Drucker; Photos by Gay Block   7 x 10, 320 pp, b/w photos, HC, 978-1-893361-64-5 **$24.95**

Woman Spirit Awakening in Nature: Growing Into the Fullness of Who You Are
By Nancy Barrett Chickerneo, PhD; Foreword by Eileen Fisher
8 x 8, 224 pp, b/w illus., Quality PB, 978-1-59473-250-8 **$16.99**

Women of Color Pray: Voices of Strength, Faith, Healing, Hope and Courage
Edited and with Introductions by Christal M. Jackson
5 x 7¼, 208 pp, Quality PB, 978-1-59473-077-1 **$15.99**

* A book from Jewish Lights, SkyLight Paths' sister imprint

Prayer / Meditation

Men Pray: Voices of Strength, Faith, Healing, Hope and Courage
Created by the Editors at SkyLight Paths
Celebrates the rich variety of ways men around the world have called out to the
Divine—with words of joy, praise, gratitude, wonder, petition and even anger—
from the ancient world up to our own day.
5 x 7¼, 192 pp, HC, 978-1-59473-395-6 **$16.99**

Honest to God Prayer: Spirituality as Awareness, Empowerment,
Relinquishment and Paradox
By Kent Ira Groff
For those turned off by shopworn religious language, offers innovative ways to
pray based on both Native American traditions and Ignatian spirituality.
6 x 9, 192 pp, Quality PB, 978-1-59473-433-5 **$16.99**

Sacred Attention: A Spiritual Practice for Finding God in the Moment
By Margaret D. McGee
Framed on the Christian liturgical year, this inspiring guide explores ways to
develop a practice of attention as a means of talking—and listening—to God.
6 x 9, 144 pp, Quality PB, 978-1-59473-291-1 **$16.99**

Women of Color Pray: Voices of Strength, Faith, Healing, Hope and Courage
Edited and with Introductions by Christal M. Jackson
Through these prayers, poetry, lyrics, meditations and affirmations, you will
share in the strong and undeniable connection women of color share with God.
5 x 7¼, 208 pp, Quality PB, 978-1-59473-077-1 **$15.99**

Living into Hope: A Call to Spiritual Action for Such a Time as This
By Rev. Dr. Joan Brown Campbell; Foreword by Karen Armstrong
6 x 9, 208 pp, HC, 978-1-59473-283-6 **$21.99**

Praying with Our Hands: 21 Practices of Embodied Prayer from the World's
Spiritual Traditions *By Jon M. Sweeney; Photos by Jennifer J. Wilson; Foreword by Mother Tessa
Bielecki; Afterword by Taitetsu Unno, PhD*
8 x 8, 96 pp, 22 duotone photos, Quality PB, 978-1-893361-16-4 **$16.95**

Secrets of Prayer: A Multifaith Guide to Creating Personal Prayer in Your Life
By Nancy Corcoran, CSJ
6 x 9, 160 pp, Quality PB, 978-1-59473-215-7 **$16.99**

Three Gates to Meditation Practice: A Personal Journey into Sufism, Buddhism,
and Judaism *By David A. Cooper* 5½ x 8½, 240 pp, Quality PB, 978-1-893361-22-5 **$16.95**

Prayer / M. Basil Pennington, OCSO

Finding Grace at the Center, 3rd Edition: The Beginning of
Centering Prayer *With Thomas Keating, OCSO, and Thomas E. Clarke, SJ; Foreword by Rev.
Cynthia Bourgeault, PhD* A practical guide to a simple and beautiful form of medita-
tive prayer. 5 x 7¼,128 pp, Quality PB, 978-1-59473-182-2 **$12.99**

The Monks of Mount Athos: A Western Monk's Extraordinary
Spiritual Journey on Eastern Holy Ground *Foreword by Archimandrite Dionysios*
Explores the landscape, monastic communities and food of Athos.
6 x 9, 352 pp, Quality PB, 978-1-893361-78-2 **$18.95**

Psalms: A Spiritual Commentary *Illus. by Phillip Ratner*
Reflections on some of the most beloved passages from the Bible's most widely
read book. 6 x 9, 176 pp, 24 full-page b/w illus., Quality PB, 978-1-59473-234-8 **$16.99**

The Song of Songs: A Spiritual Commentary *Illus. by Phillip Ratner*
Explore the Bible's most challenging mystical text.
6 x 9, 160 pp, 14 full-page b/w illus., Quality PB, 978-1-59473-235-5 **$16.99**
HC, 978-1-59473-004-7 **$19.99**

Spirituality

The Passionate Jesus: What We Can Learn from Jesus about Love, Fear, Grief, Joy and Living Authentically
By The Rev. Peter Wallace
Reveals Jesus as a passionate figure who was involved, present, connected, honest and direct with others and encourages you to build personal authenticity in every area of your own life.
6 x 9, 208 pp, Quality PB, 978-1-59473-393-2 **$18.99**

Gathering at God's Table: The Meaning of Mission in the Feast of Faith
By Katharine Jefferts Schori
A profound reminder of our role in the larger frame of God's dream for a restored and reconciled world. 6 x 9, 256 pp, HC, 978-1-59473-316-1 **$21.99**

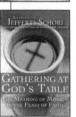

The Heartbeat of God: Finding the Sacred in the Middle of Everything
By Katharine Jefferts Schori; Foreword by Joan Chittister, OSB
Explores our connections to other people, to other nations and with the environment through the lens of faith. 6 x 9, 240 pp, HC, 978-1-59473-292-8 **$21.99**

A Dangerous Dozen: Twelve Christians Who Threatened the Status Quo but Taught Us to Live Like Jesus
By the Rev. Canon C. K. Robertson, PhD; Foreword by Archbishop Desmond Tutu
Profiles twelve visionary men and women who challenged society and showed the world a different way of living. 6 x 9, 208 pp, Quality PB, 978-1-59473-298-0 **$16.99**

Decision Making & Spiritual Discernment: The Sacred Art of Finding Your Way *By Nancy L. Bieber*
Presents three essential aspects of Spirit-led decision making: willingness, attentiveness and responsiveness. 5½ x 8½, 208 pp, Quality PB, 978-1-59473-289-8 **$16.99**

Laugh Your Way to Grace: Reclaiming the Spiritual Power of Humor
By Rev. Susan Sparks A powerful, humorous case for laughter as a spiritual, healing path. 6 x 9, 176 pp, Quality PB, 978-1-59473-280-5 **$16.99**

Bread, Body, Spirit: Finding the Sacred in Food
Edited and with Introductions by Alice Peck 6 x 9, 224 pp, Quality PB, 978-1-59473-242-3 **$19.99**

Claiming Earth as Common Ground: The Ecological Crisis through the Lens of Faith
By Andrea Cohen-Kiener; Foreword by Rev. Sally Bingham
6 x 9, 192 pp, Quality PB, 978-1-59473-261-4 **$16.99**

Creating a Spiritual Retirement: A Guide to the Unseen Possibilities in Our Lives
By Molly Srode 6 x 9, 208 pp, b/w photos, Quality PB, 978-1-59473-050-4 **$14.99**

Creative Aging: Rethinking Retirement and Non-Retirement in a Changing World
By Marjory Zoet Bankson 6 x 9, 160 pp, Quality PB, 978-1-59473-281-2 **$16.99**

Keeping Spiritual Balance as We Grow Older: More than 65 Creative Ways to Use Purpose, Prayer, and the Power of Spirit to Build a Meaningful Retirement
By Molly and Bernie Srode 8 x 8, 224 pp, Quality PB, 978-1-59473-042-9 **$16.99**

Hearing the Call across Traditions: Readings on Faith and Service
Edited by Adam Davis; Foreword by Eboo Patel 6 x 9, 352 pp, Quality PB, 978-1-59473-303-1 **$18.99**

Honoring Motherhood: Prayers, Ceremonies & Blessings
Edited and with Introductions by Lynn L. Caruso
5 x 7¼, 272 pp, Quality PB, 978-1-58473-384-0 **$9.99**; HC, 978-1-59473-239-3 **$19.99**

The Losses of Our Lives: The Sacred Gifts of Renewal in Everyday Loss
By Dr. Nancy Copeland-Payton 6 x 9, 192 pp, HC, 978-1-59473-271-3 **$19.99**

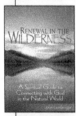

Renewal in the Wilderness: A Spiritual Guide to Connecting with God in the Natural World *By John Lionberger* 6 x 9, 176 pp, b/w photos, Quality PB, 978-1-59473-219-5 **$16.99**

Soul Fire: Accessing Your Creativity
By Thomas Ryan, CSP 6 x 9, 160 pp, Quality PB, 978-1-59473-243-0 **$16.99**

A Spirituality for Brokenness: Discovering Your Deepest Self in Difficult Times
By Terry Taylor 6 x 9, 176 pp, Quality PB, 978-1-59473-229-4 **$16.99**

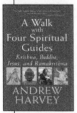

A Walk with Four Spiritual Guides: Krishna, Buddha, Jesus, and Ramakrishna
By Andrew Harvey 5½ x 8½, 192 pp, b/w photos & illus., Quality PB, 978-1-59473-138-9 **$15.99**

Spiritual Practice

Fly-Fishing—The Sacred Art: Casting a Fly as a Spiritual Practice
By Rabbi Eric Eisenkramer and Rev. Michael Attas, MD; Foreword by Chris Wood, CEO, Trout Unlimited; Preface by Lori Simon, executive director, Casting for Recovery
Shares what fly-fishing can teach you about reflection, awe and wonder; the benefits of solitude; the blessing of community and the search for the Divine.
5½ x 8½, 160 pp, Quality PB, 978-1-59473-299-7 **$16.99**

Lectio Divina—The Sacred Art: Transforming Words & Images into Heart-Centered Prayer *By Christine Valters Paintner, PhD*
Expands the practice of sacred reading beyond scriptural texts and makes it accessible in contemporary life. 5½ x 8½, 240 pp, Quality PB, 978-1-59473-300-0 **$16.99**

Writing—The Sacred Art: Beyond the Page to Spiritual Practice
By Rami Shapiro and Aaron Shapiro
Push your writing through the trite and the boring to something fresh, something transformative. Includes over fifty unique, practical exercises.
5½ x 8½, 192 pp, Quality PB, 978-1-59473-372-7 **$16.99**

Conversation—The Sacred Art: Practicing Presence in an Age of Distraction
By Diane M. Millis, PhD; Foreword by Rev. Tilden Edwards, PhD
Cultivate the potential for deeper connection in every conversation.
5½ x 8½, 192 pp, Quality PB, 978-1-59473-474-8 **$16.99**

Pilgrimage—The Sacred Art: Journey to the Center of the Heart
By Dr. Sheryl A. Kujawa-Holbrook
Explore the many dimensions of the experience of pilgrimage—the yearning heart, the painful setbacks, the encounter with the Divine and, ultimately, the changed orientation to the world. 5½ x 8½, 240 pp, Quality PB, 978-1-59473-472-4 **$16.99**

Dance—The Sacred Art: The Joy of Movement as a Spiritual Practice
By Cynthia Winton-Henry 5½ x 8½, 224 pp, Quality PB, 978-1-59473-268-3 **$16.99**

Giving—The Sacred Art: Creating a Lifestyle of Generosity
By Lauren Tyler Wright 5½ x 8½, 208 pp, Quality PB, 978-1-59473-224-9 **$16.99**

Haiku—The Sacred Art: A Spiritual Practice in Three Lines
By Margaret D. McGee 5½ x 8½, 192 pp, Quality PB, 978-1-59473-269-0 **$16.99**

Hospitality—The Sacred Art: Discovering the Hidden Spiritual Power of Invitation and Welcome *By Rev. Nanette Sawyer; Foreword by Rev. Dirk Ficca*
5½ x 8½, 208 pp, Quality PB, 978-1-59473-228-7 **$16.99**

Labyrinths from the Outside In, 2nd Edition: Walking to Spiritual Insight—A Beginner's Guide *By Rev. Dr. Donna Schaper and Rev. Dr. Carole Ann Camp*
6 x 9, 208 pp, b/w illus. and photos, Quality PB, 978-1-59473-486-1 **$16.99**

Practicing the Sacred Art of Listening: A Guide to Enrich Your Relationships and Kindle Your Spiritual Life *By Kay Lindahl* 8 x 8, 176 pp, Quality PB, 978-1-893361-85-0 **$16.95**

Recovery—The Sacred Art: The Twelve Steps as Spiritual Practice *by Rami Shapiro; Foreword by Joan Borysenko, PhD* 5½ x 8½, 240 pp, Quality PB, 978-1-59473-259-1 **$16.99**

Running—The Sacred Art: Preparing to Practice *By Dr. Warren A. Kay; Foreword by Kristin Armstrong* 5½ x 8½, 160 pp, Quality PB, 978-1-59473-227-0 **$16.99**

The Sacred Art of Chant: Preparing to Practice
By Ana Hernández 5½ x 8½, 192 pp, Quality PB, 978-1-59473-036-8 **$16.99**

The Sacred Art of Fasting: Preparing to Practice
By Thomas Ryan, CSP 5½ x 8½, 192 pp, Quality PB, 978-1-59473-078-8 **$15.99**

The Sacred Art of Forgiveness: Forgiving Ourselves and Others through God's Grace *By Marcia Ford* 8 x 8, 176 pp, Quality PB, 978-1-59473-175-4 **$18.99**

The Sacred Art of Listening: Forty Reflections for Cultivating a Spiritual Practice
By Kay Lindahl; Illus. by Amy Schnapper 8 x 8, 160 pp, b/w illus., Quality PB, 978-1-893361-44-7 **$16.99**

The Sacred Art of Lovingkindness: Preparing to Practice
By Rabbi Rami Shapiro; Foreword by Marcia Ford 5½ x 8½, 176 pp, Quality PB, 978-1-59473-151-8 **$16.99**

Thanking & Blessing—The Sacred Art: Spiritual Vitality through Gratefulness
By Jay Marshall, PhD; Foreword by Philip Gulley 5½ x 8½, 176 pp, Quality PB, 978-1-59473-231-5 **$16.99**

About SKYLIGHT PATHS Publishing

SkyLight Paths Publishing is creating a place where people of different spiritual traditions come together for challenge and inspiration, a place where we can help each other understand the mystery that lies at the heart of our existence.

Through spirituality, our religious beliefs are increasingly becoming a part of our lives—rather than *apart* from our lives. While many of us may be more interested than ever in spiritual growth, we may be less firmly planted in traditional religion. Yet, we do want to deepen our relationship to the sacred, to learn from our own as well as from other faith traditions, and to practice in new ways.

SkyLight Paths sees both believers and seekers as a community that increasingly transcends traditional boundaries of religion and denomination—people wanting to learn from each other, *walking together, finding the way.*

For your information and convenience, at the back of this book we have provided a list of other SkyLight Paths books you might find interesting and useful. They cover the following subjects:

Buddhism / Zen	Global Spiritual	Monasticism
Catholicism	Perspectives	Mysticism
Children's Books	Gnosticism	Poetry
Christianity	Hinduism /	Prayer
Comparative	Vedanta	Religious Etiquette
Religion	Inspiration	Retirement
Current Events	Islam / Sufism	Spiritual Biography
Earth-Based	Judaism	Spiritual Direction
Spirituality	Kabbalah	Spirituality
Enneagram	Meditation	Women's Interest
	Midrash Fiction	Worship

Or phone, mail or e-mail to: SKYLIGHT PATHS Publishing
An imprint of Turner Publishing Company
4507 Charlotte Avenue • Suite 100 • Nashville, Tennessee 37209
Tel: (615) 255-2665 • www.skylightpaths.com
Prices subject to change.

Printed in the USA
CPSIA information can be obtained
at www.ICGtesting.com
JSHW022324140824
68134JS00019B/1274

9 781594 734724